THE ☙ TIMES
COMPACT
HISTORY
OF THE
WORLD

THE TIMES

COMPACT

HISTORY

OF THE

WORLD

Edited by Geoffrey Parker

TIMES BOOKS

London

Times Books, London
77-85 Fulham Palace Road,
Hammersmith, London W6 8JB

First published by Times Books (as *The Times
Compact Atlas of World History*) 1995
Second edition 1997
Third edition 2001

Printed and bound in Italy by Rotolito
Lombarda S.p.A.

British Library Cataloguing in Publication Data
A catalogue record for this book is available
from the British Library

ISBN 0 0071 0927 X

EDITOR

GEOFFREY PARKER
*Andreas Dorpalen
Distinguished Professor
of History
The Ohio State University*

Editorial Consultants
Chris Scarre
*McDonald Institute
University of Cambridge*

Richard Overy
*Professor of Modern History
King's College
University of London*

Editorial Direction
Philip Parker

Cartographic Direction and Design
Martin Brown

Cartographers
Cosmographics, Watford
Bartholomew Mapping Services,
Glasgow

Designer
Colin Brown

Place-names Consultant, Index
Pat Geelan

Contents

PART TWO

The World Fragmented

PART THREE

The Rise of
the West

PART FOUR

The Modern World

Introduction

This volume, like *The Times History of the World*, first published in 1978 and now in its fifth edition (and available in 16 languages), attempts to cover the whole story of humankind from its origins, when our ancestors first emerged from the tropical forests of Africa, to the complex, highly articulated world in which we now live.

It differs, however, from the original *History of the World* in three important ways. First, as its name makes clear, it presents the data in a more compact form. Although it includes 80 spreads each contains fewer, simpler maps and (proportionately) more text. Second, every map has been reviewed in order to highlight the salient trends and facts it features. Third, the topics selected for treatment include far more material from the modern period: 24 spreads concentrate on the period since 1914 and no fewer than 17 of them cover the world since 1945.

Nevertheless, although the present volume incorporates new material and differs in other important ways from its predecessor, it rests upon the same principles. Above all, it tries to break away from a concentration on Europe and to offer instead a view of history that is world-wide in conception and presentation and which does justice, without prejudice or favour, to the achievements of all peoples, in all ages and in all quarters of the globe. It thus remains true to the vision of Geoffrey Barraclough, who planned and edited the *History*.

'When we say this is an atlas of world history, we mean that it is not simply a series of national histories loosely strung together. In other words, it is concerned less with particular events in the history of particular countries than with broad movements – for example the spread of the great world religions spanning whole continents... In singling out topics for inclusion we have adhered to the principle of selecting what was important then rather than what seems important now'

The essence of history, as Geoffrey Barraclough realized, is change and movement over time; and the historian's principal mission is therefore to discern the static from the dynamic, the aberration from the trend, and the contingent from the constant. So instead of presenting a series of individual snapshots, *The Times Compact History of the World* emphasizes change, expansion and contraction. It aims to convey a sense of the past as a continuing process and thus to provide a fresh perspective on today's world which will meet the requirements and interests of present-day readers in all parts of the globe.

This revised edition incorporates several new features. First, all the later spreads – both maps and text – have been updated to cover events since the original edition went to press and four new spreads have been added. Second, many other maps have been revised provided with physical bases. Third – a totally new feature – over 80 images and more tables have been included. Finally, errors brought to our attention by readers have been corrected.

GEOFFREY PARKER
December 2000

ONE

The Ancient World

About 6000 years ago, in a few areas of particularly intensive agriculture, the dispersed villages of Neolithic peoples gave way to more complex societies. These were the first civilizations, and their emergence marks the start of a new phase of world history. They arose, apparently independently, in four widely dispersed areas (the early civilizations of America emerged considerably later): the lower Tigris and Euphrates valleys; the valley of the Nile; the Indus valley around Harappa and Mohenjo-Daro; and the Yellow River around An-yang. The characteristic feature of them all was the city, which now became an increasingly dominant social form, gradually encroaching on the surrounding countryside, until today urban civilization has become the criterion of social progress. But the city possessed other important connotations: a complex division of labour; literacy and a literate class (usually the priesthood); monumental public buildings; political and religious hierarchies; a kingship descended from the gods.

Statue of the pharaoh Ramesses II
Great Temple of Abu Simbel, c. 1257 BC

Human origins

The earliest known hominine fossils come from the Afar region of Ethiopia and are 4.5 million years old. Between three and four million years ago, skeletal and fossilized footprints of *Australopithecus afarensis* indicate a serviceable if not fully bipedal gait, hands still partly adapted for specialized tree climbing and a brain approximately one-third the size of ours. This species is the probable ancestor both of the robustly built Australopithecines ('southern apes'), all with large teeth and herbivorous diets, and of our genus *Homo* ('man'). These closely related but nonetheless distinct species not only lived at the same time but side by side in the same habitats.

About three million years ago, *Homo* began to undergo important evolutionary trends, acquiring a larger brain and full bipedalism. As larger brains need better diets to sustain them, the increase in

12

brain size must have been accompanied by a move towards an energy-rich diet including animal proteins. And indeed the earliest-known stone tools, found in Gona, Ethiopia, suggest that 2.5 million years ago meat was a central part of hominines' diet. The sharpened stones were used to cut flesh and pound marrow-rich bones from carcasses either scavenged or hunted and then defended against other carnivores. Burnt bones found in southern Africa indicate that by 1.5 million years ago hominines had learned to cook their food, a development which would have aided digestion by breaking down animal proteins before eating.

This pattern of development was the basis for the colonization by *Homo erectus* of areas outside sub-Saharan Africa around 1.8 million years ago. Then, a million years ago *Homo heidelbergensis* migrated into North Africa and the Near East, reaching northern Europe about 500,000 years ago. Both *erectus* and *heidelbergensis* probably shared a common African ancestor,

A hand-axe from Olduvai Gorge, Tanzania. Handaxes, which are more efficient butchery tools than stone flakes, began to appear around 1.5 million years ago. This probably coincided with an increase in active hunting – as opposed to scavenging – for meat.

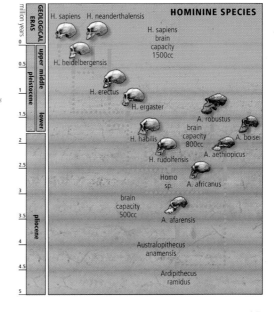

Homo ergaster, best known from the Nariokotome skeleton. All three had brains of about 1,000 cubic centimetres and an adaptable stone technology: the weight and careful shaping of the edges of their distinctive handaxes, whether pointed or oval, made them effective butchery tools.

Stone technology in itself did not play a part in the evolutionary pressures that led to larger brains. The importance of *Homo*'s larger brain had less to do with the food quest than with allowing hominines to remember, to manipulate, to support and to organize others in more complex ways. This in turn allowed them to colonize harsher barrier habitats such as the Sahara at the margins of their homelands from where they could spread into more temperate areas beyond.

From about 500,000 years ago, this early burst of colonization came to a halt. There followed a period during which, through many dispersals of populations and much intermingling of genes, regional populations such as the Neanderthals developed, living side by side with other groups. But from 100,000 years ago, a second major dispersal began when anatomically modern people – *Homo sapiens sapiens* – emigrated from sub-Saharan Africa. By 50,000 years ago, Australia had been reached by boat; 33,000 years ago, the western Pacific islands were colonized; 15,000 years ago, the Americas were reached. Major expansion into the Arctic began about 4500 years as the continental ice sheets retreated. Finally, 2000 years ago, humans began to settle the deep Pacific islands from where they reached New Zealand around 1200 years ago, 1000 years before the island's discovery by Captain Cook.

2 Hominine development

The spread of modern humans

DNA studies have revealed that the first anatomically modern humans (*Homo sapiens sapiens*) arose in Africa between 200,000 and 140,000 years ago. The earliest modern-looking human skulls yet found are about 130,000 years old and come from the Omo basin in Ethiopia and Klasies River Mouth in southern Africa. Around 100,000 years ago, these early populations began to migrate northwards out of Africa.

Archaeological and genetic evidence then point to a further rapid expansion of modern human populations and settlements about 50,000 years ago. There is evidence of lighter, multi-component weapons and of textiles and baskets. Camp sites became more orderly and included cold-weather dwellings and underground food stores. Trading networks also expanded dramatically and raw materials, particularly stone, which had previously been traded over distances of less than 50 miles, were now traded over many hundreds of miles.

Human colonisation of the Old World took place against the background of the Ice Ages. There have been eight Ice Ages in the last 800,000 years, alternating with warmer periods of about 10,000 years known as interglacials. During the Ice Ages, ice sheets advanced across the frozen wastes of the northern hemisphere and temperatures fell by up to 15 degrees centigrade. With so much of the earth's water locked into the ice sheets, sea levels fell,

opening up land bridges, but half the area between the tropics became desert as rainfall diminished. Animals withdrew to warmer latitudes during cold phases and humans, too, must have migrated with these changing climates, although they could also adapt to the cold through the mastery of fire, the invention of clothing, and new social and communication skills.

For many thousands of years, *Homo sapiens sapiens* shared the world with *Homo erectus* in East Asia and with Neanderthals in Europe and West Asia, both groups in many ways as sophisticated and successful in their mastery of their environments as *Homo sapiens sapiens*. The similarities between these contemporary hominine species are in most respects more striking than the differences. Nonetheless, the greater social sophistication of *Homo sapiens sapiens* proved decisive in allowing them to colonize a much wider range of habitats than any previous hominine.

By 12,000 years ago, the last Ice Age was drawing to a close. As temperatures rose, vegetation spread and animals re-colonized the cold northern wastes. With them went hunters and gatherers. Meanwhile, in South-West Asia, people had begun to move beyond their existing resources and to investigate new ways of producing food and manipulating plants and animals in the first experiments in farming.

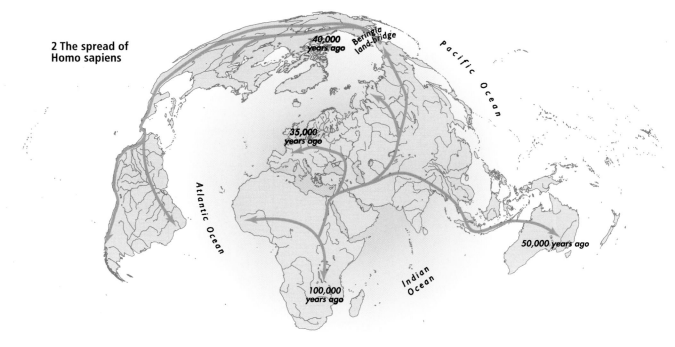

2 The spread of Homo sapiens

maximum extent of ice caps
grassland scrub
mammoth steppe
temperate desert
savannah
loess
tropical deserts
ancient coastline
tropical forest refuges
modern coastline
forest steppe
cave art site
other sites

Kanto Plain
Sokchang-Ni
ngia land-bridge
SIBERIA
Zhoukoudian Upper Cave
Arctic Ocean
Salawusu
Tongliang
Malta
Buret
Shlenka
Shestakovo
Anyi
SUNDA
Sokchang-Ni
Kanto Plain
Pacific Ocean
Laharia-Dih
A
S
I
SUNDA
SAHUL
Pushkari
Kostienki
Amvrosievka
INDIA
Nawamoyn
Krakow Spadzista
Puritjarra
EUROPE
WEST ASIA
AUSTRALIA
Grotta dei Fanciulli
Lascaux
Kastritsa
Koonalda
Lake Mungo
Murray
Altamíra
Paglicci
Kebara Cave
Wadi Al-Hammeh
Kutikina
eva Morin
Wadi Jilat
Parpalló
Tamar Hat
Haua Fteah
Indian Ocean
Taforalt
Wadi Kubbaniya
Nile
Sahara
AFRICA
Omo
Ishango
Nasera
Depression Cave
Sehonghong
Klasies River Mouth
Boomplaas
Nelson Bay Cave

A bison from the caves at Altamíra, near Santander in northern Spain. This 14,000-year-old masterpiece comes from the painted ceiling of a chamber covered with depictions of animals. The painters used more than one colour and exploited the natural contours of the ceiling to give a number of the creatures three-dimensional form. It remains among the most potent and vivid images created by the artists of the late Ice Age in Europe.

The origins of agriculture

The period 10,000 to 4000 BC witnessed three critical developments: the origins of settled life; the first farming; and the first cities. The origin of agriculture is often termed the 'Neolithic revolution', but archaeology reveals only gradual changes in techniques of food acquisition over thousands of years until present-day climatic conditions began to prevail, around 8000 BC.

Until then, humankind consisted of bands of hunters and gatherers who, although more numerous than ever before, pursued a lifestyle that differed little from that of their predecessors. In China and west Asia, however, new lifestyles began to develop, based on cultivation rather than collecting plant foods. Within the next 2,000 years substantial villages appeared in certain regions; and 5,000 years later there were towns and cities.

This decisive quickening in the pace of human development stemmed largely from the beginning of agriculture: the deliberate alteration of natural systems to promote the abundance of an exploited species or set of species. Many parts of the globe, especially those between latitude 10° South and 50° North, have contributed to the present-day repertory of domesticated plants and animals (map 1). Among the earliest and most important centres of cereal cultivation were South-West Asia, where the wild ancestors of wheat and barley grew; China and South-East Asia, where millet and rice thrived; and Mesoamerica, which developed maize as a staple crop. In Africa, people in the lands south of the Sahara and in the high grasslands of North-East Africa domesticated a wide variety of native plant species. Generally, cereal cultivation characterized temperate regions while root or tree crop cultivation – potatoes, yams, bananas – predominated in tropical zones.

At the same time, useful local animal species were domesticated to provide meat, milk, hides or wool, and (except in the Americas, which lacked suitable animals) an important source of power for ploughing and other agricultural tasks. On the steppe-lands of central Eurasia, animal-keeping prevailed over plant cultivation, and the domestication of the horse facilitated a specialized life-style based on nomadic herding.

The exact origins of agriculture remain unknown, but once chosen, farming developed a momentum of its own: there was no easy turning back, and the very success of the new lifestyle induced other fundamental changes. The ensuing increase in food resources made possible a spectacular growth of human population between 8000 and 4000 BC. It also required cooperative effort, particularly after the introduction of

MESOAMERICA

Cereals	Pulses
Maize	Common bean
Teosinte	Runner bean
	Tepary bean

Fruits	Other Crops
Avocado	Chilli pepper
Tomato	Squashes

NORTHERN SOUTH AMERICA

Pulses	Root Crops
Common bean	Manioc
Lima bean	Potato
	Sweet Potato
	Yam

Fruits	Other Crops
Guava	Cashew
Pineapple	Chili pepper
Soursop	Cocoa
Sweetsop	Peanut
	Quinoa
	Squashes

African rock art painting
From around 9000 BC to 3000 BC the climate in the Sahara was much more favourable than today. Rock art paintings depict a great variety of plants and animals such as elephant, lion and buffalo as well as, from about 6000 BC, domesticated cattle.

irrigation led to the establishment of settled organized societies, at first in villages and later in towns
and cities, and the development of new technologies,
social systems and ideologies.

The transformation from hunting and gathering
to agriculture, from a migratory to a sedentary life,
was a decisive event in world history. Hunters and
gatherers survived but, as farming spread, they
retreated to the marginal world environments
where agriculture could not secure a foothold (map
2). Both absolutely and relatively, their numbers
declined until today their representatives survive
only in hot deserts (the Kalahari and central
Australia), in the dense rain forests of the Amazon
basin, central Africa and South-East Asia, and in the
frozen Arctic. Even there, traditional lifestyles –
followed by mankind for millennia – now face the
threat of extinction.

2 The decline of hunting and gathering

world distribution of hunter-gathering peoples

15,000 BC
world population: 10 million
% hunters: 100

AD 1500
world population: 350 million
% hunters: 1.0

1960
world population: 3 billion
% hunters: 0.001

1 The origins of domestic plants and animals to 4000 BC

the origins of domestic plants and animals to 4000 BC

Pacific
Ocean

NORTH
AMERICA

Atlantic
Ocean

Reindeer

SOUTH
WESTERN
STEPPES

CENTRAL
ASIA

CHINA

Pig

Horse

Bactrian Camel

Yak

Chicken

Cattle

Pig

Cattle

Sheep

INDUS

Water Buffalo

Goat

SOUTHWEST
ASIA

SOUTHEAST
ASIA

Pig

Ass

Zebu

SAHARA

Dromedary

NORTHERN TROPICAL AFRICA

CHINA AND SOUTHEAST ASIA

Cereals	Pulses	Root Crops
Asian rice	Mung bean	Taro
Common millet	Soybean	Yams
Foxtail millet		

Fruits	Other Crops
Apricot	Aubergine
Banana	Coconut
Citrus fruits	Sago palm
Mango	Tea
Peach	

SOUTHWEST AND CENTRAL ASIA

Cereals	Pulses	Root Crops
Barley	Broad bean	Carrot
Oats	Chickpea	Parsnip
Rye	Grasspea	Radish
Wheats	Lentil	
	Pea	

Fruits	Other Crops
Apple	Garlic
Date	Onion
Fig	Safflower
Grape	
Olive	
Pear	

NORTHERN TROPICAL AFRICA

Cereals	Pulses	Root Crops
African rice	Cowpea	Yams
Finger millet	Pigeon pea	
Pearl millet		
Sorghum		

Fruits	Other Crops
Tamarind	Coffee
Watermelon	Oil palm
	Sesame

The first farmers of Asia

The first economies to be based on the husbandry of animal and plant staples came into being in South-West Asia. In the upland areas around the Zagros and Taurus mountains, and in Palestine, moister conditions led to the spread of large-seeded grasses – the ancestors of modern wheat and barley – which early hunters quickly appreciated for their nutrition and ease of storage. By 10,000 BC small villages of circular stone-walled huts developed, whose inhabitants lived from both the hunting and herding of gazelle and the harvesting of wild wheat. About 9000 BC, in northern Syria, some communities began to cultivate cereals outside their natural habitat while sheep were domesticated in Mesopotamia. By 7000 BC wheat and barley cultivation was established, as was the herding of goats, from Anatolia to the Zagros mountains, and this agricultural revolution spread shortly afterwards to Greece.

In the 7th and 6th millennia BC, developed Neolithic villages appeared over much of the landscape. Their economies depended on domesticated plants and animals, and on technological developments. Excavations at Çatal Hüyük, 32 acres in area, revealed extensive evidence of wealth (obsidian and semi-processed stones) and house fittings bore elaborate ornaments (including wall paintings and the plastered skulls of wild cattle). Much of the lowland area, however, remained too dry for cultivation. Only the development of irrigation – by spreading water from the rivers that drained from the mountains – allowed settlements to extend to the Mesopotamian plain in the 6th and 5th millennia. Sedentary farming began in South Asia on the Kachi Plain of Pakistan around 7000 BC. The early settlers cultivated barley and wheat, domesticated sheep, cattle and goats, and buried their dead with elaborate grave goods. From 6000 BC onwards, mud-brick storehouses divided into small compartments served as the focal point for food, tools and trade goods.

Plants and animals were independently domesticated in many other parts of the world. In northern China the cultivation of millet, another cereal, began on the great loess plain around the Yellow River and its tributaries around 7000 BC. It remained the staple crop of the region for many centuries. Further south the principal cereal was rice, first cultivated in the Yangtze valley before 6000 BC (map 2). Villages acquired defensive walls, from 8000 BC in the Near East (the first fortified community being Jericho) and from around 3500 BC in China.

Terracotta figurine
Characteristic products of the earliest farming villages are small terracotta figurines of women, with emphasis on their sexual characteristics. This small cult statuette, only 6.5 inches high, came from Çatal Hüyük in south-central Turkey.

In addition, the ox-drawn plough began to be adapted throughout much of Eurasia, enlisting animal traction to increase the efficiency of farming.

The greater size and permanence of farming settlements stemmed from three major factors: firstly, the exceptional productivity of the principal cultivated species could feed large concentrations of people all year round – something hunting and gathering can never do; secondly, plant foods could survive storage over many months, allowing the community to stay in one place and live off the previous harvest while a new crop grows and ripens. Finally, farmers need to live near their fields, both to protect them against human and animal predators and to minimize the travel and transport involved in preparing the ground, in weeding, and in harvesting.

Hunters and gatherers keep their possessions to a minimum, since they must carry everything around; but sedentary communities can produce and accumulate a wide range of items, both utilitarian and for ritual and pleasure – pottery and tools, ornaments and display items. Village farming communities became larger and more differentiated, with specialist craftspeople producing fine ceramics and metalwork. As complexity increased, new forms of social organisation developed, leading around 3000 BC to the first cities.

2 Early Chinese agriculture

- area of loess soil
- redeposited loess
- early millet cultivation
- ---- approximate northern limit of wild rice distribution
- early wet rice cultivation

Chinese settlement
- ▲ 6000–5000 BC
- ■ 6000–4000 BC
- ● 5000–2500 BC

1 The ancient Near East, 12,000–3100 BC

- natural habitat of wild emmer
- natural habitat of wild einkorn and emmer
- southern limit of rain-fed agriculture (300mm average annual rainfall)

ancient sites:
- ● epipalaeolithic, 12,000–9000 BC
- ▲ pre-pottery Neolithic, 9000–6500 BC
- ● pottery Neolithic, 6500–5500 BC
- ○ Chalcolithic
  'Ubaid period, 5500–4200 BC
  Uruk period, 4200–3100 BC
- ▢ multi-period Neolithic-Chalcolithic sites

3500–1500 BC
The rise of civilization

The first civilizations arose in the alluvial basins of four major rivers which drain from the mountain fringes where agriculture began: the Tigris and Euphrates in Mesopotamia, the Nile in Egypt, the Indus in India, and the Yellow River in China. Each proved capable of supplying the high, regular yields needed to support large urban populations. Cities of thousands, and then tens of thousands, evolved. In Mesopotamia, cities already existed by 3500 BC. Egypt adopted urban civilization in about 3200 BC and the Harappan civilization arose in the Indus plain from about 2500 BC. Civilization in north China appears to have developed, again wholly or largely independently, around 1800 BC.

These societies shared many common features: the development of cities; writing; large public buildings; and the political apparatus of a state. The large agricultural surpluses produced by irrigation – some Mesopotamian communities harvested 60, 70 or even 80 grains for each grain sown – made it possible to employ a significant segment of society in activities other than farming, such as manufacture and trade. This in turn led to the emergence of a ruling class which accumulated wealth through the exploitation of labour and the imposition of taxes. In Mesopotamia the ruler was also the chief priest and the temple centre provided a vital element of the political system, its monumental structure

1 The rise of civilization

- fertile land
- centres of urban civilization
- areas of pastoral nomadism

forming a visual reminder to all citizens of the power that governed their daily life. The centralized control found in these societies fostered a special legal system, a standing army, a permanent bureaucracy, and the division of society into distinct classes. The state also supported scribes, who were usually trained and employed within the temples and palaces. The earliest writing was used as a means of keeping track of commodities, wages and taxes; but it soon served other purposes: to preserve religious traditions, which thereby became sacred books; to register social customs, which thereby became codes of law; and to record myths, which thereby developed into history and literature.

Since, apart from agricultural produce, the alluvial plains lacked most other natural resources, an extensive trading activity exchanged luxury goods and raw materials from other areas with the textiles and other manufactured goods of the cities and thus helped to develop other trading centres in a great arc from the eastern Mediterranean to the Indus valley and in China. The cities therefore exercised an influence out of all proportion to their comparatively small geographical extent. True, not all areas were affected: Australia, Africa, Europe and large parts of Asia had no cities; the first civilizations of the Americas did not emerge until about 1500 BC (and, when they did, owed nothing to ideas introduced from outside). Nevertheless the growth of the first urban centres, with their technology, literacy, and class divisions began a new phase in the development of human society.

The Royal standard of Ur from the largest of the royal tombs at Ur. It has panels on each side depicting the activities of the king in peace and war. The war side shows helmeted infantry, four-wheeled battle wagons pulled by asses or onagers, and prisoners being presented to the king.

c e a n

Ob

Yenisey

NOMADS

Atlai Mts

L.Baikal

L.Balkhash

MONGOLIA
hunting fishing and gathering replaced by mounted nomadic pastoralism from the west

Amur

AMUR VALLEY
sedentary village communities supported by salmon fishing and millet farming

G o b i   D e s e r t

Takla
Maka

Kaocheng

Singtai
Lo-yang
Erh-li-t'ou

Anyang
Chengchow

T I B E T

Yellow
Sea

C H I N A

Rupar
Alamgirpur

Panlungchen

ibangan

Brahmaputra

Ganges

GANGETIC PLAIN
colonization of flood plain by rice-farming villages

Wucheng

I N D I A

DECCAN
temporary hunting camps and cattle-herding pens replaced by farming villages

B a y
o f
B e n g a l

90

INDO CHINA
rice farming villages with domestic animals and bronze tool technology

South
China Sea

30

West Asia and Egypt

The earliest of all known civilizations, Sumer, rested upon some 12 city-states in southern Mesopotamia, the largest of them covering about 100 hectares, defended by a wall, and housing perhaps 30,000 people. At first, pre-eminence passed from one city to another, but towards the end of the 3rd millennium powerful leaders established hegemony over ever-wider areas. The first was Sargon (c. 2296-2240 BC), who created a new political centre at Agade (also known as Akkad) before conquering the cities of southern Mesopotamia and claiming authority as far west as Byblos. Sargon's grandson Naram-Sin (2213-2176 BC) enlarged the empire further, but within a generation it disappeared as subject cities asserted their independence. The rise of Agade had long-lasting effects on the region, with Akkadian (whose variants included Babylonian and Assyrian) replacing Sumerian as the main language of Mesopotamia.

Around 2000 BC, a new empire arose around Ur, its hegemony stretching from the Persian Gulf to Nineveh, but Ur also fell after about a century, and a kaleidoscope of shifting alliances brought new cities to prominence, most notably Mari and Babylon on the Euphrates. Under its powerful king Hammurabi (1728-1686 BC), Babylon created another empire that covered the whole of southern Mesopotamia; but, once more, it did not long survive the death of its founder (map 1).

Even before Sargon unified Mesopotamia, Egypt came under the sway of a single ruler. The harnessing of the Nile's annual floods to irrigate the fields on its banks made possible a civilization that lasted for over 25 centuries. Around 3000 BC an Upper Egyptian ruler conquered the Nile delta and established a new capital at Memphis, which for almost 2000 years served as the administrative centre for a densely

1 Early empires of Mesopotamia
- early Sumerian settlement
- empire of Agade, c.2296–2105 BC
- III Ur empire, c.2047–1940 BC
- empire of Hammurabi, c.1728–1686 BC

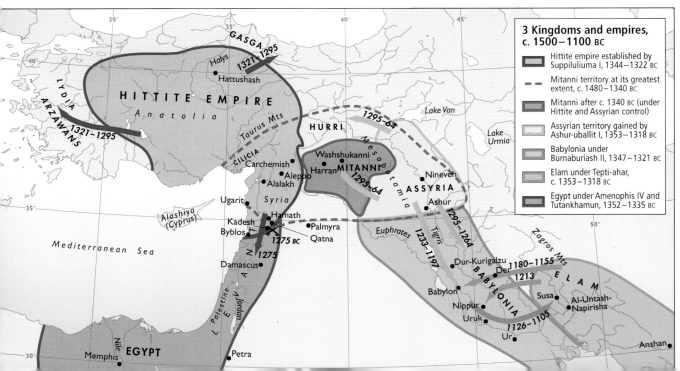

3 Kingdoms and empires, c. 1500–1100 BC
- Hittite empire established by Suppiluliuma I, 1344–1322 BC
- Mitanni territory at its greatest extent, c. 1480–1340 BC
- Mitanni after c. 1340 BC (under Hittite and Assyrian control)
- Assyrian territory gained by Ashur-uballit I, 1353–1318 BC
- Babylonia under Burnaburiash II, 1347–1321 BC
- Elam under Tepti-ahar, c. 1353–1318 BC
- Egypt under Amenophis IV and Tutankhamun, 1352–1335 BC

populated region of some 15,000 square miles running from the first cataract at Aswan to the Mediterranean coast (map 2). At about the same time, writing in hieroglyphic script commenced. During the 'Old Kingdom' period (2685-2180 BC) the rulers of Egypt built a series of massive pyramid-tombs along the desert edge opposite Memphis which emphasised their power and prestige. Then, after a century of invasion and anarchy, the Egyptian state entered a second period of cultural achievement under the able rulers of the Middle Kingdom (2040-1783 BC); and another era of expansion under the XVIIIth and XIXth dynasties (1570-1200 BC). At home they undertook vast building projects, like the rock-cut temple at Abu Simbel created by Ramesses II (1290-1224 BC); abroad they advanced through Palestine into Syria and created an empire that extended almost to the Euphrates.

The continuity of Ancient Egyptian language, religion and culture stood in marked contrast to developments in Mesopotamia. The two civilizations also differed in other respects. First, because of the annual Nile flood, Egypt did not depend to the same extent on irrigation canals and dams; second, although it possessed some cities, they lacked the geographical concentration found in southern Mesopotamia, so that Egypt was more a territorial unit than an agglomeration of city-states. Third, and most important, Egypt rarely suffered foreign invasion. Admittedly the Hyksos, an Asiatic people, overran most of the country in the 18th century BC, but a new native dynasty expelled them c.1570 BC and then pursued the invaders northwards to the upper Euphrates. Egypt's Asiatic empire lasted until about 1200 BC when the 'Sea Peoples', marauders from the Aegean and Asia Minor, attacked all the major powers of the East Mediterranean and initiated a 'Dark Age', concerning which very few historical sources survive, until about 900 BC and the emergence of Assyria.

Babylon and Assyria weathered the storm of the 12th and 11th centuries with greatly reduced territory, and the 10th century saw the beginnings of an Assyrian recovery. In the following century Ashurnasirpal II (883-859 BC) sent his armies north and west and used the wealth they gained to build a spectacular new palace at Nimrud. Even greater gains were made by Tiglath-pileser III (744-727 BC) and Sargon II (721-705 BC) who annexed Babylonia and conquered the Phoenician cities on the Mediterranean coast. Egyptian weakness allowed Esarhaddon (680-669 BC) and Ashurbanipal (668-627 BC) to capture Memphis and Thebes, although the Assyrians did not attempt to formalize their control over Egypt.

To the Old Testament prophets, the Assyrians appeared invincible; yet their control over Babylonia was never secure: the Babylonian king Nabopolassar (626-605 BC) rebelled and, aided by the Medes, sacked the major Assyrian cities including Ashur and Nineveh. The Babylonians then inherited the Assyrian empire, but they too had to fight to keep it. In 605 BC the Egyptians attempted to annex Syria, but were defeated at Carchemish and Hamath. Nebuchadnezzar (604-562 BC) consolidated Babylonian rule, but his successors were unable to maintain their gains and Babylon fell to the Persians in 539 BC.

2 Old Kingdom Egypt, c.2685–2180 BC

- town or city, c.3250–2000 BC
- royal tomb, c.3250–2650 BC
- pyramid, c.2650–2000 BC
- fertile land

A Limestone stela, now in the Louvre, of Naram-Sin of Agade (2213-2176 BC) depicting his victory over the Lullubu of the Zagros mountains. Naram-Sin led many successful campaigns in his reign, leaving rock-reliefs commemorating his achievements near Diyarbakir in Turkey and in the Zagros.

The Americas

The Americas were colonized from Asia late in the last Ice Age, when lowered sea levels turned the Bering Strait into dry land. The subsequent melting of the ice cut off the continent from Eurasia (page 14). It is one of the remarkable facts of human history that despite their geographical separation, development in Old and New Worlds followed much the same path: the adoption of agriculture; the creation of cities and empires; the invention of writing. These two geographical zones continued on parallel paths until the New World was invaded by Europeans after 1492 (page 86). The New World civilizations were highly inventive in their own right, and in some ways in advance of their western counterparts. They produced – quite independent of the Old World – magnificent art, remarkable mathematical and astronomical skills, and monumental architecture.

The inhabitants of Mesoamerica and the central Andes began to experiment with plant cultivation around 7000 BC and farming soon allowed a rapid increase in population. By 800 BC the Olmec on the Gulf of Mexico, the Zapotec at Monte Albán, and the people of Chavín in Peru had developed complex societies with populations that numbered tens of thousands, boasting a hierarchy of social classes, an efficient civil service, a professional priesthood, and specialists in all kinds of tasks, from manufacturing to commerce and government.

Around and between these civilizations, other communities remained at the chiefdom level. Maize, beans and squash cultivation spread from Mexico to north America, and their arrival initiated a period of rapid development. In Ohio and Illinois, between 300 BC and AD 550, Hopewell chiefs built elaborate burial mounds and maintained trade contacts from Florida to the Rockies. Most American chiefdoms were agricultural, based on plant cultivation, but along the north-west coast rich fishing grounds and an abundance of whales and seals supported large villages and a complex ceremonial life by hunting, fishing and gathering alone. Towards the extremities of the continent, however, harsh conditions precluded farming, settlement remained sparse, and nomadic lifestyles persisted (map 1).

The sudden rise of Teotihuacán about AD 100 eclipsed earlier developments in Mesoamerica. Laid out in a precise grid plan and covering 8 square miles (20 km²), its population grew eventually to some 200,000. The nature of the city's economy remains uncertain but the centre, with two mighty pyramids, was planned for rites that included human sacrifice. Whether or not in association with trade, the Teotihuacanos' influence spread widely. They colonized some neighbouring districts and possibly sponsored new towns further afield.

At the same time, the powerful lowland kingdoms of the Maya flourished. Their capitals were

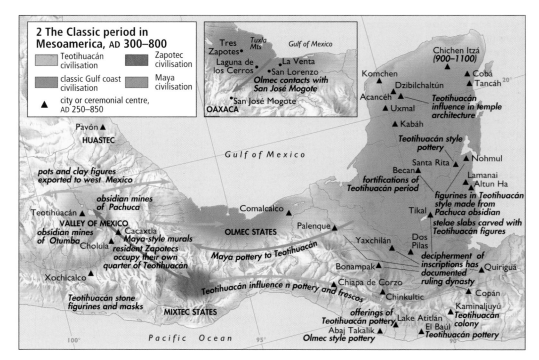

2 The Classic period in Mesoamerica, AD 300–800

- Teotihuacán civilisation
- classic Gulf coast civilisation
- ▲ city or ceremonial centre, AD 250–850
- Zapotec civilisation
- Maya civilisation

pyramid-studded ceremonial centres with extensive suburbs. Voluminous inscriptions in a distinctive hieroglyphic script reveal a sophisticated concern with astronomy and astrology: their experts calculated the exact length of the solar year and the lunar month, and predicted eclipses. However, whether on account of the chronic wars that their carved stones also recorded, or of popular discontent, or of environmental degradation by excessive population – or of all three factors – most of the towns were abandoned between 790 and about 860. Many districts revived in what is known as the 'Post-Classic' period, but the Maya never regained their grandeur (map 2).

A separate group of interrelated civilizations grew up in the central Andes, supported by spectacular irrigation systems in the lowlands and by ingenious terraced fields in the highlands. The Andean peoples developed sophisticated skills in working gold, silver and copper, and used these metals for tools as well as for jewellery. The coast of the central Andes is best known for the graphic pottery of the Moche, dating from AD 100 to 600, which reveals much about the daily life and religion of his makers.

Although its vast distances and harsh topography made this region difficult to unify, the centuries between AD 600 and 1000 saw the rise of a truly imperial power based on Huari in the Peruvian Andes. Many elements of Huari religion and art originated at Tiahuanaco, further south, but were quickly adopted by Huari and then spread by force to many parts of the coast and highlands. For a short time Huari was the capital of a state embracing most of Peru, but around AD 800 the city was sacked and abandoned for ever. The fragile unity soon collapsed and not until the Inca conquests of the 15th and 16th centuries would the central Andes be reunified under a single government (page 72).

The king of Yaxchilán (on the left above) prepares for battle against another Maya kingdom in AD 724. The hieroglyphs above the figures record that one of his wives (on the right above) helped him prepare.

1 Peoples of the Americas, 300 BC to AD 1300

- farming peoples
- chiefdoms
- civilized states
- hunters and gatherers
- site first occupied before AD 600
- site mainly occupied after AD 600

Prehistoric Africa and Australasia

Both Australia and Sub-Saharan Africa have been largely isolated from the rest of the Old World for the last 10,000 years, the former by sea, the latter by desert. Although the inhabitants of North Africa began the transition from hunting and gathering to farming around 8000 BC, the desiccation of the Sahara after about 4000 BC cut off Africa south of the Equator for centuries.

In Australia, the aborigines mostly remained hunters and gatherers adapted to living in a large range of environments from tropical forest to harsh desert. They enjoyed a rich symbolic life, as evidenced by the marking of their sacred places with rock art from at least 25,000 years ago. The colonization of the Melanesian islands occurred considerably later, when settlers from New Guinea, associated with the distinctive Lapita pottery, reached Fiji around 1300 BC and then made their way into Polynesia via Tonga and Samoa, reaching the Marquesas islands in about 150 BC (map 1). From there they spread north to Hawaii (c. AD 400)

and south-west via the Cook islands to New Zealand between AD 750 and 1300. When the Europeans arrived in the 18th century, at least 750,000 aborigines inhabited Australia and up to 150,000 Maoris lived in New Zealand

The geographical isolation of southern Africa was never complete. In the east settlers spread down the Rift Valley from Ethiopia during the first millennium BC, while trans-Saharan trade increased in importance after the introduction of the camel from Asia, around 100 BC. Iron came into use in parts of sub-Saharan Africa after 750 BC. Aided by the new technology, Bantu-speaking farmers and cattle-herders began to colonize southern Africa in the early centuries AD. By the 13th century powerful Bantu chiefdoms had emerged, such as that centred on Great Zimbabwe, and on cattle-raising communities. These engaged in long-distance trade, long before the Portuguese arrived off both the south-east and south-west coasts of the continent at the close of the 15th century

Rock art became common in Australia 25,000 years ago. This more recent painting shows the two 'Lightning Brothers', ancestral spirits of the Wardaman Aboriginal people from northwestern Australia.

Mediterranean Sea

Atlantic Ocean

PHOENICIA

ARABIA

Red Sea

1 Initial settlement of Polynesia and island Micronesia

rock art styles:
- paranamittee engravings
- complex figurative
- simple figurative

the Lapita potters:
— Lapita pottery area
• sites with Lapita pottery
— other contemporary Melanesian pottery traditions
→ settlement of Eastern Polynesia, 150 BC–AD 1000

Hawaiian Islands c. AD 400

Fanning Island

Line Islands

Marquesas Islands c. 150 BC

(Tuvalu, Ellice Islands)

Tokelau Islands

Samoa

Fiji
Tonga
POLYNESIA
Cook Islands
Tahiti — to Easter I. c. AD 400
to Pitcairn I. c. AD 1000

Kermadec Is. c. AD 950

North Island
NEW ZEALAND
South Island
c. AD 750

South Pacific Ocean

2 Africa: the Stone Age to the Iron Age

▲ fishing harpoon site
▩ area of Saharan rock painting, c. 6000–1000 BC
▨ areas of rock painting in southern and eastern Africa
– – approximate extent of cattle herders, 6000–500 BC

● site of cattle domestication
▲ early agricultural site
▽ sites of southern African Stone Age herders
– – approximate extent of iron-using farmers, AD 200–1100
● important metal workers' sites
→ possible arrival of iron technology
○ Greek colonies
● Phoenician or Punic colonies

*Map labels:*
Utica, Carthage, Capeletti, Mogador, Atlas Mountains, Leptis (Homs), Cyrene, Naucratis, Sais, Merimde 4200 BC, Memphis, Fayum 4300 BC, EGYPT, Thebes, Greek colonies from 700 BC

Zemmour, Sahara, Meniet 6000–5000 BC, Adrar Tiouiyne, Uan Muhaggiag, Immidir, Adrar Bous, Hoggar Massif, Tassili Massif, Arlit, Tibesti Massif, Jebel Uweinat, Nubia, Napata, Nuri, KINGDOM OF MEROE 900 BC–AD 400, Meroe 500 BC, Adulis, KUSH, Kadero, Shaheinab 3200 BC, Aksum, KINGDOM OF AKSUM AD 100–1000, Jebel Moya

Tichitt, Adrar, KINGDOM OF GHANA 1st millennium AD, iron, Karkarchinkat, Air, Ennedi, 2000 BC, 3000 BC, Gao, Jenne-jeno proto-urban settlement by 1st century AD, Niger, Ntereso 1400 BC, Daima, Iron-working widespread north of equatorial forest by c. 500 BC, Sudanic Belt, Ethiopian Highlands

Kintampo, 1500 BC, Taruga, Nok, Ife, Atwetwebooso, Igbo Ukwu shrines AD 800–900, Gulf of Guinea, 500 BC iron and cattle, Ileret

Batalimo, possible spread of cultivation to lower Congo 1st millennium BC, Congo forests penetrated by pottery-using peoples late in 1st millennium BC, Funa River 270 BC, east African 'pastoral neolithic' sites, Lake Victoria, Urewe, Elmenteita, Crescent Is., Manda & Shanga, Kwale, Katuruka 5th century BC, Narosura, Sandawe, ports involved in overseas trade by AD 800

Congo, iron and cattle, Great Rift Valley, Lake Tanganyika, late 1st millennium AD cemetery, Sanga, Kalambo, Kalambo, Kwilu, Kilwa, Lake Nyasa

iron and cattle, Lubusi, Kamnama, Nkope, Salumano, Kapwirimbwe AD 200, Kalundu, Zambezi, Ziwa, Gokomere, Great Zimbabwe, Mabveni, Malapati, AD 800, AD 1100, Broederstroom, Lydenburg, Silver Leaves, Phalaborwa, Madagascar, Austronesian settlement

Namib Desert, Kalahari Desert, Snake Rock, Falls Rock, Mirabib, Equus, Witkrans, Limerock, Dikbosch, Blackburn, Doornfontein, Blinkklipkop, Tortoise Cave, Eland's Bay, Diepkloof, Steenberg, Kasteelberg, Nelson Bay, Hawston, Die Kelders, Byneskranskop, domestic sheep herded by 1st century BC

South and South East Asia

The first great Indian civilization emerged in the Indus valley in the 3rd millennium with complex urban societies At Harappa and Mohenjo-Daro, which developed a pictographic writing system (as yet not definitively deciphered) and traded as far afield as Mesopotamia (map 1). Around 1500 BC, for reasons that remain obscure, the major Indus valley cities suddenly collapsed

When the picture becomes clear once again the population of northern India had been transformed, with a Hindu religion, a Sanskrit literature, a caste system and (by about 800 BC) iron working, which enabled the spread of farming communities eastward into the rich plain of the Ganges. By 600 BC at least 16 political units had grown up along the Ganges, the subcontinent's new centre of gravity. By 400 BC war had reduced the states to four, and no doubt the resulting social tensions helped to spread new ethical and religious systems, for in the 6th century Gautama (Buddha), founder of Asia's most pervasive religion, was born in one of these states (see

page 34), while in another Mahavira formulated the teaching of Jainism.

A further turning point came in 320 BC when Chandragupta Maurya seized the state of Magadha on the lower Ganges, and occupied large parts of central India, and in 305 BC annexed the province of Trans-Indus from the successors of Alexander the Great (see page 32). Chandragupta's grandson Ashoka (273-232 BC) expanded this Mauryan empire southwards, bringing the greater part of the sub-continent under his rule and inscribing edicts on pillars and rock-faces all over India as a permanent reminder of his power (map 2). Ashoka's death introduced a troubled period, punctuated by invasions of both Greeks and nomads who founded states in the north-west, such as the Kushan empire, where Hellenistic and Indian influences mingled. Further south, the Satavahanas of the Deccan ruled a state that straddled the peninsula by AD 150. Then, in the 4th century, the Gupta dynasty, created an empire which by AD 400 extended from the Indus to the bay

**1 The Indus civilizations of
Harappa and Mohenjo-Daro,
c. 2500–1750 BC**

○ pre-Harappan settlements

● principal sites of Harappan civilization

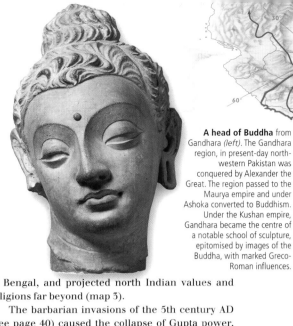

A head of Buddha from Gandhara *(left)*. The Gandhara region, in present-day north-western Pakistan was conquered by Alexander the Great. The region passed to the Maurya empire and under Ashoka converted to Buddhism. Under the Kushan empire, Gandhara became the centre of a notable school of sculpture, epitomised by images of the Buddha, with marked Greco-Roman influences.

of Bengal, and projected north Indian values and religions far beyond (map 3).

The barbarian invasions of the 5th century AD (see page 40) caused the collapse of Gupta power, but it was precisely during this period that Hindu and Buddhist influences began to spread to South-East Asia. The cultivation of rice in this area, beginning as early as 3000 BC, allowed the development of prosperous farming villages. Bronze came into use after about 1000 BC, reflected in distinctive bronze Dong Son drums, and iron followed after about 500 BC (map 4). By AD 300 trading links with India had burgeoned, and Buddhist images appeared by AD 500, notably in Burma, Cambodia, and Java. By AD 700 the construction of Hindu temples in the same three areas had begun.

2 The formation of the Mauryan empire

→ Alexander the Great's eastern campaign, c. 329–325 BC

— Mauryan empire under Chandragupta, c. 297 BC

— Mauryan empire under Ashoka, c. 260 BC

■ ancestral home of the Mauryas

● site of Ashokan inscriptions

● site of Mauryan-age Buddhist stupa

ANGA regions   *CODAS* dynasties
(place names in brackets are Prakrit forms)

3 The Gupta-Vakataka imperial formation,
AD 300–550

■ Gupta core area
■ Vakataka core area
— maximum extent of Gupta empire
— limit of areas at some time under Vakataka rule

4 Prehistoric sites in Southeast Asia

● Neolithic/Bronze Age settlements
● Dong Son drums
● Early Iron Age and urn burial sites

Early Europe

Farming spread from West Asia to Europe about 6500 BC, beginning with the Balkans. Agriculture in these regions involved wheat and barley, sheep and goats, just as in western Asia; but as farming spread beyond into more temperate zones, major adjustments became necessary. New, more robust types of cereal developed, and cattle and pigs became the dominant livestock. By about 5500 BC agricultural communities had developed along the Danube valley, and their descendants spread northwest from there until they reached the Paris basin around 4750 BC. After a brief pause, the final phase saw the spread of farming to the northern fringes of Europe, including Scandinavia and the British Isles, where existing hunter-gatherer communities adopted it by about 4000 BC (map 1).

There has been much debate about whether the spread of agriculture was due to the expansion of colonizing populations from the southeast or to the adoption of the new way of life by existing foragers. Current evidence from archaeology and the analysis of the DNA of modern populations suggests that there was a colonizing element, probably associated with the expansion through the Balkans and the loess lands of central Europe, but that in most of Europe the dominant process was the adoption of agriculture and its material attributes by existing populations, perhaps in part because of the prestige of the new way of life.

Meanwhile, beginning in the Balkans, copper-working spread after c. 4500 BC and by 2500 BC it had become common to alloy the copper with tin to produce bronze. The need for these two raw materials stimulated the development of extensive trade networks, which also conveyed other materials, such as amber from the Baltic. Amber is found as far afield as Mycenae in southern Greece, where graves filled with sumptuous funerary offerings of gold and jewellery appeared from 1600 BC.

Mycenae was not the earliest European state: that honour belongs to the island of Crete where from about 2000 BC 'Minoan' culture, based on palaces decorated with colourful frescoes and equipped with sanitary and drainage systems, developed. Bureaucracy and trade flourished, and a script known as Linear A developed around 1600 BC. Two centuries later, however, the Mycenaeans (named after the fortress of Mycenae in the eastern Peloponnese) took control of Crete and became the principal military and economic power in the

Aegean (see map 2). They adapted the Minoan culture, including its script which they modified (to a form known as Linear B, an early version of Greek) and used to administer their own lands. Mycenaean Greece was divided among a number of independent leaders, each of whom ruled a small kingdom, in much the same way as Greece in the Classical period was divided into city-states (see page 32). The legend of the Trojan War, recorded centuries later in Homer's *Iliad*, is thought to recall a Mycenaean campaign of c. 1250 BC against the city of Troy, strategically situated at the entrance to the Dardanelles, and controlling access to the trade of the Black Sea. But this success, if indeed it occurred, must have been the final fling of the Mycenean warlords because by 1200 BC their palaces lay in ruins, overthrown perhaps by rebellion or by outside attack, and a 'Dark Age' which left very few records ensued all over Greece for the next four centuries.

Snake handler from Knossos
This faience statuette, dating from c.1700 BC, possibly represents a household goddess. Little is known about Minoan divinities, but most appear to be female.

1 The spread of agricultural settlement

→ main routes of agrarian expansion

dates of agricultural settlement
(based on tree-ring corrected radiocarbon dating)

- by 7000 BC
- 7000–6000 BC
- 6000–5000 BC
- 5000–3000 BC
- 3000–2000 BC

bowl cultures early farming groups

• Hembury site of excavated farming village

SPAIN modern state names

The Greek world

TIMELINE

c. 750 BC
First Greek colonizing expeditions

7th-6th centuries BC
Emergence of tyrants in many Greek states

500 BC
Reforms of Cleisthenes establish Athenian democracy

478-404 BC
Athens dominates Aegean through Delian League

431-404 BC
The Peloponnesian War

447 BC
Parthenon begun in Athens

399 BC
Socrates tried and executed at Athens

338 BC
Battle of Chaeronea: Philip II of Macedon gains control of Greece

336-323 BC
Alexander the Great of Macedon conquers the former Persian empire

The Greek heartland is an area of islands and plains divided by mountains. After the collapse of the Mycenaean palace system, the *polis* or city-state emerged and soon became the dominant form of political organization in the Mediterranean world.

The 8th century BC was a period of great transformations in Greece. It saw the appearance of the first monumental public buildings, changes in burial practices and new artistic styles. At the same time, literacy re-emerged, with a new alphabet. Though contact with the wider world had not totally disappeared in previous centuries, it now increased dramatically, above all on the island of Euboea, perhaps as the result of Phoenician exploration and settlement.

From the middle of the century, following in the wake of the Phoenicians, groups of Greeks created settlements around the Mediterranean, first in Italy and Sicily, but by the middle of the 6th century also in north Africa and, to the east, along the Black Sea coast. These included many cities that have remained famous to the present, such as Marseilles and Naples (see map 1). In the central Mediterranean, the Greeks came into conflict with the Carthaginians, who for many centuries disputed control of Sicily with them.

In Asia Minor, however, the Greeks came up against the Persian empire, which first sought to annex the city-states of the Aegean coast and in 490 and 480-479 BC invaded Greece itself. The Persians met with defeat and the next 50 years marked the great age of Greek culture: the tragic drama of Aeschylus, Sophocles and Euripedes; the comedy of Aristophanes; the histories of Herodotus and Thucydides; the splendour of the Parthenon; the sculptures of Phidias. Athens also built up a formidable fleet and used it to create an Aegean empire which the cities of the Peloponnese, led by Sparta, saw as a threat. In 431 BC, Sparta declared war on

The Acropolis (*below*). Acting as the defensive strong point for Athens since the Mycenaean period, the acropolis was also an important religious sanctuary. Its most famous temple was the Parthenon, begun in 447 BC.

3 The campaigns of Alexander

→ Alexander, 334–23 BC → Nearchus, 325–24 BC

2 The Peloponnesian War, 431–404 BC

Legend:
- Athens and members of the Delian League
- ally of Athens
- Sparta and allies
- neutral states
- allies of Athens in Magna Graecia
- allies of Sparta in Magna Graecia
- Athenian campaigns
- Spartan campaigns
- ✕ Athenian victory
- ✕ Spartan victory

Map labels (Peloponnesian War):
Rome, LATIUM, Cumae, Neapolis, Tarentum, MAGNA GRAECIA, Gulf of Tarentum, Tyrrhenian Sea, Adriatic Sea, Epidamnus, MACEDONIA, THRACE, Byzantium, Amphipolis 422, Stagira, Thasos, Lemnos, Aegospotami 405, Lampsacus, Cyzicus 410, Abydos, PERSIAN EMPIRE, Spartalos 429, Cynossema 411, Aegean Sea, Sardes, Lesbos, Arginusae Islands 406, Decelea taken by Sparta 413, Chios, IONIA, Notium 407, Ephesus, Samos, Delium 424, Chaeronea, EUBOEA, Thebes, ATTICA, Athens, Corinth, Piraeus, Elis, Mantinea 418, Argos, Pylos, Sparta, Sphacteria 425, Melos taken by Athens 416, Cythera (taken by Athens 424), Rhodes, CRETE, Mediterranean Sea, Segesta, Himera, Messana, Lipara, Locri, Rhegium, Ionian Sea, Sicily, Selinus, Catana, Gela, Syracuse 413, Camarina

Athens. The Peloponnesian war lasted 27 years and, despite victories on both sides, Athens fatally overstrained her resources with a disastrous expedition against Syracuse in Sicily (415-13 BC) and was finally defeated in 404 BC. Her empire fragmented (map 2).

The 4th century saw more jockeying for power, as Persia sought to intervene in Greek affairs, until the well-trained Macedonian army of King Philip II (359-336 BC) first subdued the city-states and then united them under his leadership for an attack on Persia. Philip's remarkable son Alexander (336-323 BC) invaded Asia Minor with an army of 35,000 men, both Greeks and Macedonians, in 334 BC; moved on

to annex Egypt (332 BC) and the Persian empire (331 BC); and campaigned successfully in India and Central Asia (map 3). Alexander's death in 323 BC and the ensuing struggles between his leading generals created three major powers: Macedon, Egypt, and the Seleucid kingdom of western Asia.

Although politically the empire of Alexander the Great proved ephemeral, in other respects its consequences endured. Alexander and his successors founded some 70 cities, not merely as military strongholds but as cultural centres, and thus Greek culture and language spread throughout the entire region, as far as the borders of India.

1 Greek colonization in the Mediterranean world, 750–550 BC

Legend:
- Greek heartland in 750 BC
- Greek parent community
- Greek oracular shrine
- Phoenician or Punic settlement
- Etruscan city
- 8th-century Greek colony
- 7th-century Greek colony
- 6th-century Greek colony
- Philistine city

Map labels (Greek colonization):
Bay of Biscay, Rhône, CELTS, Massilia, ETRUSCANS, ITALY, Volaterrae, Arretium, Cortona, Volsinii, Tarquinii, Metapontum, Tarentum, Corcyra, Epidamnus, Apollonia, Potidaea, Dodona, EPIRUS, MACEDONIA, Acanthus, Thasos, Mende, Torone, Abdera, THRACE, Aenus, Danube, SCYTHIANS, Ophiusa, Olbia, Dnieper, Istrus, Odessus, Tomi, Callatis, Mesembria, Apollonia, Perinthus, Selymbria, Sestus, Lampsacus, Byzantium, Chalcedon, Astacus, BITHYNIA, Heraclea Pontica, PAPHLAGONIA, Sesamus, Cytorus, Sinope, Black Sea, Theodosia, Panticapaeum, Phanagoria, SARMATIANS, Don, Dioscurias, COLCHIS, Phasis, Trapezus, PONTUS, Amisus, GREECE, PELOPONNESUS, Achaea, Locris, Delphi, Leuctra, Chalcis, EUBOEA, Eretria, Megara, Corinth, Olympia, Athens, Mytilene, Phocaea, Assus, Cyzicus, PHRYGIA, Dascylium, MYSIA, LYDIA, Ephesus, Samos, Miletus, Didyma, CARIA, Asia Minor, PERSIAN EMPIRE, Thera, CRETE, Rhodes, Xanthus, LYCIA, PAMPHYLIA, Phaselis, Side, Nagidus, Soli, Celenderis, CILICIA, Posideium, CYPRUS, Citium, Aradus, Byblos, Sidon, Tyre, PHOENICIA, Joppa, Ascalon, Gaza, Ashdod, Gerar, Gath, EGYPT, Nile, Naucratis, Sea

World religions

Before the 1st millennium BC, polytheism was the dominant form of religious belief throughout Eurasia, with individual communities worshipping their own gods. As the empires of the ancient world emerged, a number of major religions, each characterized by a single doctrine and claims to universality, largely replaced these myriad cults, although elsewhere innumerable other creeds survived without making the transition to world religions.

All the great world religions originated in Asia, and three of them – Judaism, Christianity and Islam – developed in the same small region. Moreover, several were either established or radically reformulated at much the same time: the outstanding prophets and reformers of Hinduism, Buddhism, Judaism, Confucianism and Taoism all lived in the 6th century BC. Their appearance perhaps reflected a need in the rising empires for more universal creeds than local deities could provide, and their diffusion – particularly the spread of the great missionary religions, Buddhism and Christianity – played an important role in linking the different areas. The new religions also spread the values of those advanced cultures to people living beyond the frontiers.

All the world religions shared, to some degree, a belief in a single spiritual reality. Hinduism, the oldest of them, although it reveres

1 The diffusion of religions

- dispersion of Jews to AD 500
- spread of Christianity
- area converted to Christianity by AD 600
- spread of Buddhism
- first area of Buddhist missionary activity
- area of rise of Mahayana Buddhism
- Buddhist sites
- area of Hinduism
- area of Daoism and Confucianism
- area of Shintoism
- area of Zoroastriani
- spread of Mithraism
- Mithraic sites

A reclining Buddha from Polonnaruwa in Sri Lanka. The importance of Buddism grew after it was adopted by Mauryan emperor Ashoka and it spread throughout India. Missionary activity then brought Buddhist ideas to many places in south and east Asia. Buddhism reached Sri Lanka in the late third century BC.

numerous gods, emphasises the 'right way to live'; Buddhism, although it does not centre upon a god, instead stresses deliverance from suffering through the annihilation of desire. Originally a reformist movement within Hinduism, in its conservative, or Theravada form, Buddhism soon spread throughout India and on to Sri Lanka, Burma, Thailand and South-East Asia. It was the first and perhaps the greatest of all missionary religions, spreading to China by the 1st or 2nd century AD, Korea in the 4th century, and Japan in the 6th century.

Judaism spread mainly because of the persecution of the Jews by more formidable neighbours, beginning with their forcible removal to Babylon (586-538 BC). This led to a change in the emphasis of the faith from temple observance and ritual to morality and righteous living. Rebellion against Roman rule (64 BC) led to the destruction of the temple in Jerusalem (AD 70), and Jewish groups migrated until Judaism, too, became a worldwide religion. It was also associated with the origins of two other major creeds: Christianity (page 44) and Islam (page 50).

In East Asia, the 6th century saw the rise of the ethical system of Confucius (551-479 BC) and the mystical religion of the Tao, or 'the Way', associated with the shadowy figure of Lao-tzu. Zoroastrianism, the other great religion of the period, originated in Persia and saw life as a battleground between the forces of good and evil. It spread widely through the Roman world in the form of Mithraism, with shrines as far afield as northern Britain. Mithraism was ultimately suppressed in favour of Christianity while most Zoroastrian areas came under the control of Islam.

Most of the world religions spread along the trade routes, diffused by soldiers, administrators, merchants and ordinary travellers as well as by missionaries; and most tended to prosper under strong governments that brought peace. The development of larger, more centralized states and empires and the rise of these religions and codes thus went hand in hand, the new religions either becoming associated with or adopted by the great empires of the ancient world: Zoroastrianism with the Persian empire of Cyrus and Darius the Great; Buddhism with Ashoka's Indian empire; Confucianism and Taoism with China under the Chou. The world religions also provided the bonds that eventually linked areas of the world previously separate.

264 BC–AD 565
Rome

Rome, a city-state governed by aristocratic families leading an army of peasant soldiers, came to control an empire that stretched from the Atlantic to the Euphrates and from the English Channel to the Sahara. But military success brought social disorder; rivalries between warlords led to civil war; and republican institutions became an autocracy.

In the 6th century BC Rome was just a small fortress-town in central Italy commanding both the lowest crossing point on the river Tiber and a salt route between the mountains and the sea. By exploiting quarrels with its neighbours, the Roman Republic emerged as the dominant power first in central Italy and then in the whole peninsula. By 264 BC Rome controlled the whole of Italy and challenged the other major power in the western Mediterranean: Carthage. After three savage wars Rome defeated Carthage to acquire Sicily (241 BC), Spain (206 BC) and North Africa (146 BC). At the same time, conflict with the Hellenistic kingdoms further east resulted in the conquest of Macedon, Greece and Western Anatolia. In this way, almost by accident, Rome became an imperial power with far-flung possessions.

Administration of these provinces overstrained the Roman constitution, which had not been designed to manage an overseas empire, and the Republic finally collapsed in a series of civil wars. The last of these brought to power Octavian, who established himself as *Princeps* ('first citizen'), accepted the title Augustus (in 27 BC), reshaped the constitution, and extended and strengthened the frontiers (map 1).

While maintaining undivided power in his own hands, Augustus allowed the Senate – the traditional government of Rome – to take a share in running the empire, with responsibility for several provinces. Thus, in theory, the Republican forms endured, and administration remained in civilian not military hands. Under his successors, Roman rule expanded further still, but the Senate lost most of its power. Nevertheless, strong central control

ensured peace for over two centuries and population expanded, trade flourished and cities grew. In the mid-3rd century AD, however, Germanic invasions in the west and Persian victories in the east brought the empire temporarily to its knees. A series of strong emperors between AD 268 and AD 284 restored a semblance of orderly government to the empire, but Diocletian (AD 284-305) realized that a single ruler could no longer hold the whole edifice together. He divided power between himself and a joint Augustus,

An equestrian statue of the emperor Marcus Aurelius (161-80). Preoccupied for much of his reigns with wars against the Parthians and the Germans (who in 170 invaded Italy), Marcus Aurelius maintained, but did not expand the Roman frontiers. He was the author of the *Meditations*, espousing stoicism as his philosophy in the face of adversity.

with two deputies (Caesars), and split the empire into four prefectures and twelve dioceses (map 2). By now the military had triumphed over the civilian, and a new basis had to be found for imperial authority. Under the influence of eastern ideas, the *Princeps* became *Dominus* (lord), an absolute ruler, at the head of a vast bureaucracy. Gradually the centre of Roman power shifted eastwards: Diocletian's successor Constantine (305-37) established a new capital at Byzantium (330), which he renamed Constantinople.

Although theoretically governed by joint rulers, the empire gradually broke into eastern and western halves, and when the western provinces crumbled before a new wave of Germanic invaders in the early 5th century, little help arrived from the east. Rome itself was sacked in 410 and 455, and the Ostrogoths created their own kingdom in Italy in 493. Justinian (AD 527-565) briefly recovered some of the western provinces but failed to reunite the empire.

Nevertheless, the Byzantine (East Roman) empire survived for another millennium, and many Roman traditions continued in the West. The Latin tongue, although developing into the derivative 'Romance' languages, long remained the language of churchmen and scientists; Roman Law forms the basis of most modern Western legal systems; many feats of Roman engineering genius survive to this day; and the Roman church lives on as a direct link with the past.

2 The Roman empire, AD 305–565

- - - - frontier of the Roman empire, AD 305
——— boundary of dioceses under Diocletian
▨▨▨ territory reconquered by Justinian, 533-54

Praetorian prefectures, c. 405:
- Praefectus Praetorio Galliarum
- Praefectus Praetorio Illyrici, Italiae, Africae
- Praefectus Praetorio per Illyricum
- Praefectus Praetorio per Orientem

1 The Roman empire, 31 BC–c. AD 250

- under administration of the Senate
- imperial provinces
- public provinces
- provinces added after AD 14, with date
- - - - later subdivisions of provinces, with dates

China: the first empires

From the 16th to the 11th century BC China's first historical dynasty, the Shang, presided over a confederation of clans in the Yellow River valley. Around 1027 BC the Chou replaced them and extended their authority over the Yangtze valley as well, investing their supporters with fiefs to create a feudal hierarchy sustained by the services, food and clothes produced by peasant communities. Then in 771 BC western invaders sacked the Chou capital, and the feudatories seized the opportunity to break away. Over 100 belligerent political units sprang up. In the 5th century BC, however, bronze technology gave way to iron, animal power and irrigation transformed agriculture, increasing both food production and population, while warfare reduced the number of states. By 300 BC seven states still competed for hegemony; by 221 BC only one of them remained – Ch'in.

The Ch'in organized their subjects into groups which bore collective responsibility to maintain public order, and to provide manpower both for construction works (above all roads, canals and fortifications) and for the army (which was composed primarily of infantry). The defeated nobles suffered demotion and, instead of performing labour services to their lord, the peasants now paid taxes to the conqueror. A savage penal code, administered by a professional bureaucracy, enforced the new system.

In 221 BC Prince Cheng of Ch'in, took the title Shih Huang-ti (meaning 'first emperor'); ordered the construction of a national network of roads and canals, centered on his new capital at Hsieng-yang; rebuilt and strengthened the Great Wall; introduced a uniform coinage whose distinctive shape (circular with a square hole in the centre) remained standard until 1911; and took steps to standardize the written language throughout the empire. Small wonder that his dynasty gave 'China' its name.

The burdens imposed by the autocratic first emperor provoked civil war shortly after his death in 206 BC; but before long a new dynasty, the Han, reunited China. At first they worked through feudal principalities allocated to their family and supporters, but by 100 BC the fiefs had again come under strong central control. The Han also extended the Great Wall far to the north-west, undertook several military expeditions against the nomad Hsiung-nu in the north, invaded northern Vietnam and Korea, and for a brief period after 59 BC controlled the Tarim basin. They also eliminated the Min-Yüeh kingdoms of the south-east coast. A lively export trade, mainly in silk, began to Parthia and to the Roman empire.

Terracotta warriors from Sian (Xian). Discovered in 1974, close to the mausoleum of the first Ch'in emperor, thousands of terracotta warriors have since been excavated. Each figure was individually produced, and the varying uniforms, badges, weaponry and styles of armour provide information on the organization of the Ch'in army. By around 250 BC the Ch'in state was as large as all the other Chinese states put together. By 221 BC all the remaining states were absorbed by the Ch'in creating, for the first time, a unified China under Shih Huang-ti (the 'first emperor'). Although Ch'in rule collapsed in 206 BC, the Han dynasty inherited their unified kingdom.

Lake Balkhash

to Sogdiana
(K'ang-chu)

centre of Former Han
protectorate 59 BC–AD 23

Issyk Qul

to Ferghana

Kashgar (Shu-le)

Kud

Takla Makan D

Yarkand (Sha-ch'e)

Guma (P'i-shan)

Chero
(Chie

to Bactria
(Ta-hsia)

Khotan (Ho-t'ier

HSIUNGNU TRIBES

residence of the
Hsiungnu King

western extension to wall
built by Han emperors
117–100 BC

Li Kuang-li expedition 92 BC

Li Ling's expedition 99 BC

Wei Ch'ing's expedition 128 BC

Ho Ch'u-ping and Wei Ch'ing 119 BC

put under Chinese administration 109–106 BC

Karashahr
(Yen-ch'i)   ⊞Turfan
             (Kao-ch'ang)
-lei   ● Chiao-ho

Lo-lan
Lop Nor   Yü-men Kuan   ⊞ Chuyen

-hsün   Yang Kuan   *Gobi Desert*
                                               Chang-yeh
                                                             Great Wall rebuilt and strengthened
          Chiu   Wu-wei   by Ch'in emperors 220–210 BC
Tarim Basin Tun-huang -ch'uan

**CHIANG
TRIBES**

brought under Chinese
administration 117–115 BC

1 The expansion of Han China

	China, 207 BC
	territory added under Former Han
—	maximum extent of Former Han empire
	territory of Chinese protectorate of Western Regions, c. 59 BC
←	journey of Chang Chien, envoy of Han emperor, 138–126 BC
—	trade routes
⊞	administrative centre under Later Han from AD 126
⊡	centre of Later Han protectorate, AD 73–126
—	territory added under Later Han
←	new route opened by General Pan Chao for Later Han
←	expeditions against Hsiungnu (Huns)

Yellow River
Ch'ang-an ● Lo-yang   *Mount Yi*
      ● Sian

**CH'IN EMPIRE
(221–207 BC)**

Yangtze

*Yellow
Sea*

KOREA

(first explorations from 136 BC)
expeditions against Tien:
109 BC kingdom suppressed

86 BC ⎫ expeditions to far
82 BC ⎬ southwest

MIN-YÜEH
defeated 100 BC

**KINGDOM OF NAN-YÜEH
(206–113 BC)**

under Chinese
administration
after 111 BC

*South
China
Sea*

VIETNAM

A census in AD 2 revealed some 57 million people in the empire. Great cities abounded, the largest – Ch'ang-an, the capital – housing 250,000 people. The heart of the empire remained the Yellow River plain, where population densities in some areas approached 150 per square mile (see map 2). Shortly afterwards, however, court families and great feudatories increased their influence, while agrarian unrest mounted. Real power lay in the hands of the regional commanders and warlords and the last Han emperor abdicated in 220. The Han empire fragmented into three regional states and a century later the Hsiung-nu burst through the Great Wall and overran northern China (see page 40). China was to remain politically fragmented until AD 589.

Yellow River

**2 The population of
China, AD 2**

	very dense settlement, approx. 150 per sq. mile
	heavily settled, approx. 100 per sq. mile
	lightly settled, approx. 30 per sq. mile

The transformation of the ancient world

By the 3rd century AD, a continuous web of large states stretched across the southern half of the continents of Europe and Asia. In the West, Rome controlled the whole Mediterranean world and much of Europe; in China, the Han ruled a state that equalled the Roman empire in population and extended from the Pacific to the Takla Makan desert in central Asia; in between lay the Persian empire. The co-existence of these great states brought to vast areas of the Old World internal peace and centralised government, conditions that made possible commercial and cultural interchange on an unprecedented scale.

But this 'imperial zone' formed only a narrow corridor, flanked to the north by the domain of nomadic tribes, expert horsemen who possessed in war a speed and striking power that their sedentary neighbours could rarely match. In

the 4th and 5th centuries AD, numerous nomad groups launched devastating attacks against all the major civilizations. A confederation known as the Hsiung-nu from Mongolia broke through the Great Wall of China in AD 304 and within a decade reached the Yellow River, sacking the ancient Han capital Ch'ang-an (AD 316). A succession of invaders from the steppes dominated northern China for the next three centuries.

At the same time another nomadic people, the Huns, swept south-westwards through Asia, causing a chain reaction among the Germanic peoples along the Black Sea and the Danube. To escape them the Visigoths, perhaps 80,000 strong, forced their way into the Balkans and in AD 378 defeated a large Roman army outside Adrianople. Next, they moved into Italy and in AD 410 captured and sacked Rome itself. Meanwhile other Germanic tribes crossed the Rhine. The Vandals, the Alans and the Suevi invaded Gaul in AD 406 and plundered it for three years before passing on to Spain and north Africa. In their wake, the Franks, the Burgundians and the Alemanni also invaded Gaul, while the Picts from Scotland and marauders from the continent ravaged Britain. The empire's only success came in AD 451 when, with the aid of the Franks and Visigoths, a Roman army defeated and drove back the Huns, led by Attila, at the battle of Châlons.

In AD 480 another branch of the Huns invaded India and destroyed the Gupta empire (page 28) before attacking the Persian empire, where they defeated and killed its ruler in AD 484. Finally, around AD 550, warlike nomads from central Asia – the Avars – moved west and within a generation ravaged Gaul and the Balkans. They were followed by the Slavs and Bulgars, who also invaded the Balkans, and by the Lombards, who occupied northern Italy.

By AD 600 the great cities of Eurasia – Rome, Ch'ang-an, and countless others – were in serious decline. Yet the process, once seen as 'collapse', formed part of an ongoing transformation in which new power structures replaced the old. In many areas, traditional learning and skills were retained and adapted to changing conditions. In India and northern China, the invaders adopted native methods of government and co-operated with local elites, taking on their customs and culture as they did so. In Europe, too, the Roman tradition was modified rather than supplanted by the imposition of rulers of Germanic origin: the Franks in France; the Visigoths in Spain; the Ostrogoths in Italy. The deposition of the last Roman emperor in the west in AD 476 marked only a minor step in the transformation of the west from classical to medieval. The Latin tongue survived almost everywhere, while Christian monasteries and Islamic scholars transmitted knowledge of classical culture to future generations.

1 The collapse of the ancient world

→ Hsiung-nu and Huns
→ Juan-juan (Avars)
→ Goths and Vandals
→ other peoples

Roman Empire, c.AD 454
Gupta Empire, c.AD 410
Sassanian Empire, c.AD 261
Han Empire, c.AD 100

ллл fortified frontiers

550 Juan-juan (Avars) drive westwards out of Mongolia by Blue (Celestial) Turks

Great Wall of China in AD 220

Hsien-pi invade north China by 440

north China reunified under Toba Wei

1st century AD Hsiung-nu broken by Han China and move westwards

Hsiung-nu renew attacks on China, sacking capital Loyang 311, Changan 316

expansion of Tibetans

480 White Huns destroy Gupta empire

L. Baikal
L. Balkhash
Takla Makan
Lena
Yenisey
Amur
Yellow R.
Yangtze
Mekong
Ganges
Indus
Hindu Kush
Mathura
Pataliputra
Ch'ang-an
Lo-yang

MONGOLIA
MANCHURIA
SINKIANG
TIBET
Himalayas
CHINA
INDIA

A helmet from the Anglo-Saxon ship burial at Sutton Hoo. Dating from around AD 650, the grave is testament to a period of transition in England between paganism and Christianity.

TWO
The World Fragmented

After AD 500 the narrow chain of empires extending from Rome to China crumbled under attacks from nomads from the Asian steppes. Contacts between China and the West, between north Africa and Italy and between Byzantium and western Europe dwindled as each region fell back on its own resources and had to fend for itself.

In Eurasia, two phenomena dominated: the expansion of Islam after 632; and the emergence of the Mongol empire after 1206. Meanwhile, the Maya, Aztec and Inca civilizations appeared in America, the empires of Sri Vijaya and Majapahit grew in southeast Asia, and the empires of Ghana, Mali and Songhay developed in Africa. Europe, by comparison, remained backward until, in the second half of the 15th century, a series of path-breaking voyages of exploration laid the foundations for overseas expansion. Even then, however, Europe's achievements remained overshadowed and threatened by the expanding power of the Ottoman Turks for another century.

Death strangling a plague victim,
from the 14th-century Stiny Codex (Prague University)

The spread of Christianity

Christianity began as a Jewish splinter movement in Roman Palestine. Its founder, Jesus of Nazareth, claimed to be the Messiah, or Saviour, sent to prepare the Jews for 'the kingdom of God' but, after an initial, short-lived success, he was executed as a revolutionary (AD 29). Jewish orthodoxy rejected his message, but his followers turned instead to the conversion of non-Jews and by AD 200, despite repression and persecution, communities of Christians (as the followers of Jesus came to be called) flourished in several cities of the Roman empire (especially Antioch and Edessa). In AD 313 the Emperor Constantine granted the new faith toleration and in AD 325 at Nicaea presided over the first ecumenical council, representing the whole church, which defined beliefs for all Christians. A full ecclesiastical organization developed, with a hierarchy of bishops and a framework of patriarchates, provinces and dioceses throughout the empire (map 1).

The council of Chalcedon (451) attempted to enforce orthodoxy on the Christian world, but instead alienated the Monophysite (or Coptic) Christians of Egypt, Syria and Armenia, and the Nestorians who, expelled from Edessa, took refuge in Persia. Meanwhile the disintegration of the Roman empire in the West (page 36) undermined the position of the church. But salvation came from the periphery. The Coptic church of Egypt, with a strong monastic tradition, sent missionaries down the Nile from the 4th century, converting the peoples of Nubia and Ethiopia; while from the 7th century, the Nestorians of Persia expanded south into Arabia and east to China. In the west, the impetus for revival came from the monastic missionary church of Ireland, which evangelized first its Celtic neighbours in Britain and Brittany, and then in the 7th and 8th centuries the pagan tribes of continental Europe (map 2).

As the Muslim onslaught devastated the Christian Mediterranean (page 50), both Rome and Constantinople launched missions northwards among the Slavs. Russia opted for Orthodox Christianity, and in 988 the Russian prince Vladimir was baptized, while Poland (966) and Hungary (1001) chose Catholic Christianity. Although rivalry

between the two patriarchates resulted after 1054 in schism, the popes increased their authority by sponsoring Christian counter-offensives in Iberia, the Baltic and West Asia: the crusades (page 48). The attempt to restore Christianity to Palestine proved a costly failure, but the crusades made great advances elsewhere. Meanwhile, within Europe, monks and (from the 13th century) friars joined the expanding network of parish clergy in Christianizing the countryside and combating heresy. In 1387 Lithuania, the last remaining pagan state in Europe, converted to Catholicism, just as persecution by Timur and other rulers (page 60) extinguished the faith in Asia, the continent of its birth.

1 The early Christian churches

- main areas of Christian growth, to AD 300
- areas largely Christian by AD 600
- important Christian communities of the 1st century
- other important Christian centres, by AD 600
- ☧ the five patriarchates
- + important bishops with dates of episcopate
- ◆ other important figures, with dates

2 Christianity in medieval Europe

- ▨ Roman-rite Christians, c. 1400
- ▨ Byzantine-rite Christians, c. 1400
- ▨ Monophysite Christians
- ▨ Islam
- ── extent of Catholic (Frankish) Christianity (c. 700)
- ╍╍ maximum extent of crusader states in the east in the 12th century
- ● important bishoprics
- (743) date of foundation of a bishopric or of conversion of a region to Christianity

Trondheim (1029)
FINLAND (13th cent.)
Bergen (1070)
Turku (1220)
Uppsala (1164)
Novgorod (1135)
Aarhus (948)
Riga (1198)
Polotsk (1113)
Moscow (1326)
Armagh
York
North Sea
Lund (c. 950)
LITHUANIA (1387)
Smolensk (1128)
Canterbury
Bremen (788)
Hamburg (834)
PRUSSIA (14th cent.)
Gniezno (1000)
Rouen
Magdeburg (958)
POLAND (10th cent.)
Kiev (988)
Paris
Rheims
Mainz (743)
Prague (973)
MORAVIA (9th cent.)
Cracow (1004)
Tours
Regensburg (739)
HUNGARY (10th cent.)
Lyons
Salzburg (798)
Gran (1001)
Santiago de Compostela (c. 840)
Avignon
SERBIA (c. 870)
Kherson
Lisbon (1147)
Saragossa (1118)
Black Sea
Toledo (1085)
Valencia (1238)
Rome
BULGARIA (c. 870)
Ochrida (c. 870)
Constantinople
GRANADA (1492)
Salonica
ICELAND (1000)
Antioch
Mediterranean Sea
Acre
Jerusalem
Alexandria

Sirmium
Singidunum
Black Sea
ARMENIA
Artashat
Serdica
+John Chrysostom (398–404)
+Nestorius (428–31)
Sinope
Neocaesarea
Sebastea
PERSIA
Gangra
Constantinople
Ancyra
+Basil (370–7/9)
Amida
Philippi
Nicomedia
Nicaea
Caesarea
Cappadociae
Melitene
Edessa
Nisibis
Beroea
Thessalonica
Cyzicus
Pergamum
Asia Minor
Nyssa
Samosata
Nazianzus
Nisibis
Troas
Thyatira
Antioch
Iconium
Cyrrhus
+Ephrem (306–73)
Smyrna
Sardes
Philadelphia
Lystra
Derbe
Tarsus
Antioch
Dura-Europos
Gondeshapur
Athens
Ephesus 431
Hierapolis
Laodicea
+Ignatius (d. c. 112)
Corinth
Patmos
Myra
Laodicea
Palmyra
Seleucia-Ctesiphon
Salamis
SYRIA
Damascus
Mediterranean Sea
Tyre
Pella
+Eusebius (d. c. 339)
Caesarea
+Cyril (c. 350–86)
Jerusalem
Diospolis-Lydda
Gaza
Bethlehem
Pelusium
Ptolemais
Cyrene
Alexandria
Thmuis
+Origen (c.185–254)
EGYPT
+Arius (d. 336)
+Athanasius (328–73)
+Cyril (412–44)
Oxyrhynchus
Red Sea
Lycopolis
Chenoboskion

A stone slab of the Apostles Peter and Paul from the sepulchre of the child Amellus dating from after 313 (below). Following the conversion of Constantine, Christian art became more public and explicit representations of Christ and the saints were common. Portraits of Peter and Paul from Rome proudly allude to the connection of the two leading apostles with the city and its powerful bishops. In this example, they are depicted as Roman gentlemen of high social status, as the purple stripe of their togas attests.

PETRVS
PAVLVS

581–1279
China

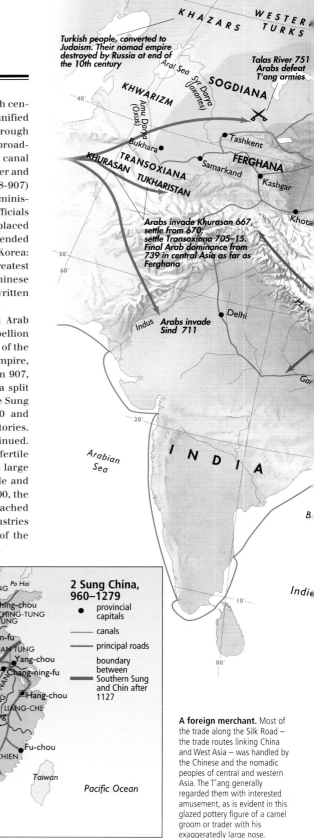

TIMELINE

581-617
China reunified under the
Sui dynasty

618-907
The T'ang dynasty

960
Coup d'état of General
Chao K'unag-yin, who
becomes first Sung emperor

963-79
Sung reunite China

1126-7
Tatar Chin conquer northern
China

1211-34
Mongols conquer northern
China

1235-79
Mongols conquer southern
China

After the barbarian invasions of the 4th and 5th centuries (page 38) the Sui dynasty (581-617) reunified China. They consolidated their empire through standardized institutions, a state-supported broad-based Buddhism, and the construction of a canal system linking the Yangtze with the Yellow River and the Lo-yang region. The T'ang dynasty (618-907) continued the process, creating a uniform administrative organization of prefectures, in which officials recruited through an examination system replaced the traditional aristocracy. The T'ang also extended their control to the Tarim basin and northern Korea: in the 660s, the Chinese empire reached its greatest extent and 88 Asiatic peoples recognised Chinese overlordship, adopting its culture, its written language and its political institutions (map 1).

In 751, however, at the Talas River, an Arab army defeated the Chinese, while a major rebellion rocked T'ang power in 755-62, causing many of the new conquests to be abandoned. Within the empire, power began to pass to the provinces until in 907, following a wave of peasant uprisings, China split into ten separate regional states. Although the Sung dynasty reunified the country between 960 and 979, they failed to regain the new territories. Nevertheless, Chinese economic growth continued. A massive movement of population into the fertile Yangtze valley and southern China produced large agricultural surpluses which stimulated trade and economic development. Between 750 and 1100, the population of the empire doubled; trade reached new heights; and a great concentration of industries arose around the capital, K'ai-feng, centre of the canal system and of the eastern road network.

2 Sung China, 960–1279
- ● provincial capitals
- canals
- principal roads
- boundary between Southern Sung and Chin after 1127

A foreign merchant. Most of the trade along the Silk Road – the trade routes linking China and West Asia – was handled by the Chinese and the nomadic peoples of central and western Asia. The T'ang generally regarded them with interested amusement, as is evident in this glazed pottery figure of a camel groom or trader with his exaggeratedly large nose.

powerful unified Turkish kingdom in 6th century, split into Eastern and Western groups c.585. Eastern Turks conquered by T'ang 630, but re-emerge from 681 and 699–715 are re-united with Western Turks. In 715 Western Turks break away: Eastern Turks finally destroyed 744

KIRGHIZ

Shih-Wei

AMUR

MALGAL

powerful kingdom on the T'ang model set up by remnants of Korean ruling clan of Koguryo. Independent from 710. Destroyed by Khitan 934

TURKESTAN

DZUNGARIA

Turfan

Kucha

Tarim Basin

Hami

under T'ang control 645–763

Tun-huang

to Tibet 763–843

KANSU

TURKS to 744

UIGHURS
Uighurs replace Turks in the steppe 745–840; more stable, less anti-Chinese than Turks. Destroyed by Kirghiz

KHITAN (LIAO)
proto-Mongol people, raid T'ang border from 695, sometimes vassals of Turks. Set up own empire (Liao) in Manchuria in early 10th century

Gobi Desert

NINGSIA

Yellow River

PO HAI (PARHAE)

still occupied by Emishi aboriginal peoples

T'ang occupation 668–676

SILLA

Sea of Japan

Ch'ang-an

T'ANG

Lo-yang

Po Hai

EMPIRE

Yang-chou

JAPAN

Kyoto

Nara

TIBET

Himalayas

NEPAL

Brahmaputra

unified kingdom c.600. Expansion after 650; under Chinese cultural influence until c.750 then Indian influence. Central control collapsed c.840

Ch'eng-tu

Yangtze

OF

CHINA

Ning-po

independent politically; increasing Chinese cultural influence from 6th century. In 7th century a strong centralized kingdom developed, based on T'ang institutions

before 660 there were three states in Korea: Koguryo, Paekche and Silla. The T'ang destroyed Paekche in 660, Koguryo in 668 and occupied N. Korea. Strong resistance led to Chinese withdrawal in 676, leaving all Korea under Silla, a powerful, centralized state on T'ang lines

NAN-CHAO
kingdom formed by federation of tribal groups organized on T'ang model

850–70

Canton

ANNAM

Chiao-chou

South China Sea

PYU

Pagan

Sukhothai

c.800

f Bengal

Indianized Buddist kingdom invaded by Nan-chao in 8th and 9th centuries

cean

KHMER

CHAMPA

Hue

Mekong

kingdom under strong Indian/Hindu influence

kingdom centred on Hue. Strong Indian influence

1 The Chinese world, 7th–8th centuries

- under permanent T'ang civil administration
- area of temporary occupation during 7th century
- under T'ang military control
- zone of Chinese cultural dominance
- trade routes → Tibetan expansion
- canals → advance of Islam

northern heartland of China. Population continued to increase rapidly; trade and industry boomed; and the new capital, Hang-chou, became the world's largest city. This was also a period of great cultural achievement. The visual arts, literature, philosophy, science and technology all reached new heights; education became more widespread, aided by the dissemination of printing, which had been invented in T'ang times and now became commonplace. Merchants formed guilds and partnerships, setting up a complex commercial organization with banks, credit systems and paper money. The government was run by a mandarinate of career bureaucrats.

But their days were numbered. Between 1211 and 1234 the Mongols (page 60) had overrun the Chin empire, causing widespread devastation, and in the 1270s the forces of Kublai Khan – 'the most powerful man since Adam' according to a European visitor – annexed the entire Sung empire. For the first time, all of China lay under foreign rule.

In 1126-7 the Chin, a powerful nomadic state north-east of the Great Wall, invaded and conquered all of northern China, with terrible devastation. The Sung now controlled only the centre and the south, but stood constantly on the defensive, maintaining huge armies and paying vast subsidies to their aggressive neighbours (map 2). Even after the Chin invasion, however, the Sung state remained immensely prosperous, since its southern territories proved far more productive than the old

The Byzantine world

Almost from its inception, the Roman empire's centre of gravity moved to the east, first pulled by the lure of economic wealth in Egypt and western Asia; then pushed by the loss of the western provinces to Germanic invaders (page 36) and by the pressure of Sassanid Persia on its eastern frontier. Except during the reign of Justinian (page 37), the west was neglected and the Roman empire became an eastern, Greek-speaking state – normally known, from the reign of Heraclius (610-641), as Byzantium.

Heraclius ended the long contest with Persia victoriously, capturing Nineveh in 628, but almost at once Byzantium faced two even more redoubtable foes: Islam (page 50) and the Slavs. However, after the failure of two long Arab sieges of Byzantium (674-8 and 717-18), the empire launched a succession of vigorous counter-offensives. Basil II (976-1025) even managed to advance the imperial frontiers close to their earlier limits: the Arabs retreated into Palestine; the Russians met defeat at Silistra on the Danube; the Bulgars, who had advanced to within 60 miles of Constantinople, became imperial subjects; plans were laid to recover the former Byzantine territories in Italy. However, the constant campaigns imposed heavy financial strains, as well as profound and debilitating social change, and in spite of further phases of recovery, the frontiers steadily shrank (map 1).

The crucial development was the emergence, in the 11th century, of the Seljuk Turks (page 50), whose crushing victory over Byzantine forces at Manzikert in 1071 induced Emperor Alexius I (1081-1118) to call on the west for help, thus initiating the sequence of events that led to the First Crusade (1096-9). It proved

a disastrous move since the Franks were less concerned to aid Byzantium than to set up their own principalities in Palestine and Asia Minor; the Normans, already in control of Sicily and Byzantine Italy, coveted lands in Greece; and the Italian cities, led by Venice, strove to increase their share of Mediterranean trade. After a century of mounting tension, the soldiers of the Fourth Crusade in 1204 conquered and pillaged Constantinople, partitioned the Byzantine empire, and established Latin states all over the Balkans (map 2).

The Latin Empire proved short-lived – its Greek-speaking subjects resented it and a new dynasty, the Palaeologi, restored the Greek empire in 1261 – but the new Byzantine state was only a shadow of its former self and when, shortly afterwards, the Ottoman Turks established themselves first in Asia Minor and then advanced into Byzantium's European territories, its fate was sealed. The capital of the east Roman empire fell in 1453 (page 70).

Nevertheless, the history of Byzantium includes both greatness and lasting achievements. For centuries it transmitted Roman culture back to areas from which earlier invasions had largely effaced it. It also passed on its culture and its religion to the Balkan peoples and to Russia. 'Two Romes have fallen', a Russian monk wrote shortly after 1453, 'but the third is still standing and a fourth shall never be.' He referred to Moscow (page 56), now emerged as the heir to the Byzantine inheritance.

The emperor Constantine IV Pogonatus and his brothers hand privileges to the Ravenna church of San Apollinare in Classe and to archbishop Mauro. During his reign Constantinople withstood a four year siege by Arab armies (674–8), although much of the Balkans was overrun by Slav tribes and the Bulgars.

Vero
Bonor
Genoa
Florent

Corsica

Sardinia

Caralis

Valentia

Balearic Islands

Carthago Nova

Carthage

AFRICA

1 Byzantine greatness and decline

Imperial frontiers

— c. 628
— c. 1030
— c. 1143
— 1328

special areas:

Exarchate of Ravenna to Lombards, 751

Exarchate of Africa to Arabs from 670

Catapanate of Italy to Normans from 1071

temporary reconquests:

Africa, 685–710
Syria, 975–6
Sicily, 1038–43
Ani, 1054
Edessa, 1052
Rum, c. 1118

general territorial losses:

to Arabs, 636–641
to Arabs after 641
to Seljuk Turks from 1065
Sultanate of Rum from 1071

CUMANS

CUMANS

Venice

Adriatic Sea

DALMATIA

SERBIA

Ragusa

Vidin

Danube

Serdica

BULGARIA

Philippopolis

Mesembria

Black Sea

Sinope

EMPIRE OF TREBIZOND

Theodosiopolis

Manzikert

Kastamuni

Adrianople

Ochrida

Prilep

Vodena

Tzurulum

Constantinople

Nicomedia

Ancyra

Sebastea

SELJUKS OF RUM

Dyrrhachium

Thessalonica

Cyzicus

Nicaea

EMPIRE OF NICAEA

Tigris

Bari

Berrhoea

Adramyttium

Prusa

Dorylaeum

Halys

Caesarea

Brundisium

Avlona

Castoria

Lemnos

Pergamum

Amorium

Samosata

KINGDOM OF SICILY

Corfu

Larissa

Aegean Sea

Sardis

Philomelium

Tyana

Marash

Edessa

Nicopolis

Smyrna

Iconium

Heraclea

Tarsus

Carrhae

Cephalonia

Chios

Athens

Meander

Chonae

Sozopolis

Antioch

Aleppo

MOREA

Corinth

Attalia

Euphrates

Zacynthus

Modon

Cos

Rhodes

Cyprus

Homs

LEVANT

Monemvasia

Crete

Tripoli

Mediterranean

Sea

2 The West attacks Byzantium

.... the Norman attack, 1084–5   ------► the Norman attack, 1185

──► routes of the First Crusade, 1096–9

......► the Norman attack, 1147

──► route of the Fourth Crusade 1204

──── imperial frontier in 1180

territory lost to other powers, 1180–1214

despotate of Epirus (est. 1204)

imperial territory in 1214

Latin Empire in 1214

Venetian territory in 1214

other Greek states

Venice

Bosporus

ABASGIA

IBERIA

Ravenna

ISTRIA

Sava

MOESIA

Singidunum

Danube

Nicopolis

✕ *Silistra 971*

Odessus

Chersonesus

Black Sea

Sinope

Trebizond

LAZICA

Tiflis

ALBANIA

Ani

Iadera

Salonae

DACIA

Serdica

PONTUS

Halys

Neocaesarea

Manzikert 1071 ✕

erusia

DUCHY OF SPOLETO

Ragusa

Scupi

Philippopolis

THRACE

Adrianople

PAPHLAGONIA

Sebastea

L. Van

ome

Adriatic Sea

Dyrrhachium

Nicomedia

Constantinople

GALATIA

Caesarea

CAPPADOCIA

Samosata

Tigris

Mosul

DUCHY OF BENEVENTO

Barium

NEW EPIRUS

MACEDONIA

Salonica

BITHYNIA

Cotiaeum

Edessa

Nineveh 628 ✕

Naples

Brundisium

Tarentum

ANCIENT EPIRUS

Larissa

PHRYGIA

PISIDIA

Iconium

ISAURIA

CILICIA

Tarsus

Beroea

Euphrates

PERSIA

DUCHY OF NAPLES

THESSALY

Smyrna

LYDIA

PAMPHYLIA

Antioch

Palmyra

Tyrrhenian Sea

Panormus

Messana

Aegean Sea

Ephesus

Miletus

Tripolis

Sicily

Syracuse

Patras

Athens

Ionian Sea

Rhodes

Cyprus

Damascus

Bostra

to Byzantium 965

Caesarea

PALESTINE

Jerusalem

Gaza

Petra

ARABIA

to Byzantium 961

Crete

Mediterranean Sea

Tripolis

TRIPOLITANIA

Apollonia

Ptolemais

PENTAPOLIS

Damietta

Pelusium

Alexandria

EGYPT

Mareotis

Nile

Memphis

Arsenoe

Tabuk

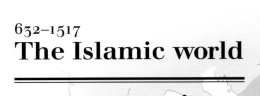

632–1517
The Islamic world

The rise and expansion of Islam ranks as perhaps the most significant development in world history between the fall of Rome and the European invasion of the Americas. Within a remarkably short time, a new world religion created a dynamic civilization which now embraces one-seventh of the global population: 600 million Muslims, spread from Morocco to Indonesia, and from Siberia to Zanzibar. 'Islam', which means 'submission to the will of God', was conveyed to humankind through the Koran, a volume of prescriptions on behaviour as well as belief, revealed by God to Mohammed his prophet, who was born in the religious and commercial centre of Mecca about 570. As Mohammed's followers grew in number, they aroused the hostility of the merchants of Mecca and in 622 the group withdrew to the neighbouring town of Medina (the *hijra*). But Mohammed returned to Mecca in triumph in 630, transforming it into the focal point for the new faith of Islam, and when he died in 632 his authority extended over the Hejaz and much of central and southern Arabia.

For the next century Islam expanded rapidly: Arab armies defeated Latin Christian, Byzantine, Persian, Indian and Chinese armies to spread the new faith from the Himalayas in the east to the Atlantic in the west (map 1). In 711 they crossed over the Straits of Gibraltar and conquered Spain. Until 656 political control over the empire remained with Mohammed's relatives, but then a split occurred, with some Muslims following Ali, the Prophet's cousin and son-in-law (the Shi'ites), and others – the majority – accepting the rule of the Umayyad dynasty from Mecca who claimed to represent the Sunna or traditions of the Prophet. The Umayyads ruled from Damascus in Syria between 661 and 750, followed by the rival Abbasid dynasty, who created a new capital at Baghdad in Mesopotamia and opened government to non-Arab Muslims (known as *mawali*).

Gradually, the Muslim world lost its political unity and split into a number of local dynastic entities, some Sunnite and others Shi'ite (map 2). In 1055, however, the centre of the Islamic world was strengthened when the Seljuk Turks established themselves in Baghdad and shortly thereafter drove the Christians from most of Anatolia (page 48). Despite invasions from the west in the 12th century (the Crusades: page 49) and from the east in the 13th (the Mongols: page 60), Islam retained its hold over West Asia, while missionaries and merchants carried the faith eastwards to Malaysia, Indonesia and the Philippines, and southwards both to the sub-Saharan states and the cities of the Swahili coast of Africa (page 58). For a millennium after the birth of Mohammed, Islam remained the western hemisphere's leading and most extensive civilization.

2 The Muslim world, 786–1260

— Abbasid caliphate at greatest extent during rule of Haroun al-Rashid, 786–809

  areas recognizing Abbasid sovereignty, c. 1090

  disputed between Seljuks and Byzantine empire, c. 1070–c. 1180

  Zaidi Imams

  Almohads, c. 1160

→ lines of nomadic advance

The mosque at Córdoba with its ornate exterior decoration bears witness to the great wealth of Islamic Spain. The mosque was built by 'Abd ar Rahman I, a member of the ruling Umayyad family in Syria, who escaped their overthrow by the Abbasids to found a new Umayyad dynasty in Spain. Seizing power in 755, he made Córdoba his capital and resisted all attempts by the Abbasids to unseat him.

Map 2 labels
MPIRE · Aral Sea · Jaxartes · Urgench · KHWARIZM · QARAKHANIDS · Kashgar · SELJUK TURKS · Bukhara · Samarkand · TRANSOXANIA · Oxus · Merv · Balkh · Kabul · KASHMIR · Nishapur · Tus · KHURASAN · Herat · Ghazni · GHAZNAVIDS · Lahore · AFGHANISTAN · Rai · Hamadan · manshah · Zaranj · SEISTAN · Kandahar · PUNJAB · Isfahan · Yazd · Multan · Indus · PERSIA · Shiraz · Siraf · Ormuz · SIND · INDIA · Basra · Tiz · Daybul · BAHRAIN · Persian Gulf · Muscat · OMAN · ARABIA · baku · abil · ZERBAIJAN · Caspian Sea

1 The spread of Islam

  growth under Mohammed

  growth under Abu Bakr, (632–4)

  growth under Omar, (634–44)

  growth under Othman (644–56) and Ali (656–61)

  expansion of Umayyad Caliphate, (661–750)

  expansion under the early Abbasids, (750–850)

→ routes of advance

638 date of Muslim conquest

Map 1 labels
YEMEN · Aden · KHAZAR EMPIRE · Don · Dnieper · Caspian Sea · Derbent · TRANSOXANIA · Talas River 751 · FERGHANA · Aral Sea · Oxus · Bukhara 710 · Samarkand 710 · Tiflis · ARMENIA · AZERBAIJAN · Ardabil · Tabriz · GURGAN · Merv ✕651 · Nishapur 651 · Balkh 651 · Hindu Kush · PUNJAB · Kabul 664 · Black Sea · Constantinople besieged 673–78 · 717–18 · Erzurum · MESOPOTAMIA · Mosul 641 · Tigris · Jalula · Rai · Herat · KHURASAN · PERSIA · Multan 712 · SEISTAN · Indus · SIND · EMPIRE · Tarsus · Antioch · Edessa · Euphrates · Kerbela 680 · Baghdad · Nihavand 642 · Isfahan · FARS · KIRMAN · MAKRAN · Cyprus 649 · SYRIA · Damascus 635 · Yarmuk 636 · Fihl · Al Qadisiyya 637 · Kufa · Sus · Persepolis (Istakhr) 648 · Basra 656 · des · 654 · Jerusalem 638 · PALESTINE · Ajnadain 634 · Ramla · Persian Gulf · BAHRAIN · OMAN · Muscat 654 · Alexandria 643 · Heliopolis 640 · Tabuk · YAMAMA · RENAICA · Fustat (Cairo) 670 · EGYPT 640 · Nile · HEJAZ · Medina · ARABIA · Hiji · Badr 624 · Mecca · flight from Mecca, 622 · NUBIANS · Red Sea · Najran · HADHRAMAUT · Dongola · KINGDOM OF AKSUM · YEMEN · Aden

Franks and Anglo-Saxons

Within a century of the Germanic invasions, settled kingdoms had grown up in western Europe, but not in Britain, where invaders from the continent met with resistance. During the 7th century, however, seven separate important kingdoms – which are traditionally known as the Heptarchy – emerged in England. Geographical obstacles seem to have prevented the states in the south-east (Sussex, Kent, Essex, East Anglia) from expanding, and leadership at first passed to Northumbria, whose progress benefitted from its early conversion to Christianity. Mercia led the opposition, sometimes in alliance with the 'Britons' on the periphery, and by the time of Offa (757-96) its pre-eminence was unquestionable: it controlled the four southeastern kingdoms, and even Wessex recognized Mercian overlordship.

On the continent, the Franks (whose original power base lay in what is now northern France, the Low Countries and the Rhineland) converted to Christianity under Clovis (481-511) and began to expand south and east. From their new capital at Paris, Clovis and his sons and grandsons defeated the Visigoths, conquered Burgundy and Provence, and extended their overlordship in Germany as far as the middle Danube.

Most of the new lands served to maintain the loyalty of the Frankish warriors, however, and when the conquests ceased in the mid-7th century the kings had to reward their followers and endow the Church by granting away their own estates and revenues. In doing so they diminished their resources and, in time, power passed to the families which had benefitted from royal favour. Eventually Pippin of Herstal, from a leading Austrasian family, achieved prominence, and at Tertry (687) defeated his chief rivals.

Pippin and his son Charles Martel (from whom the dynasty took the name 'Carolingian') restored Frankish fortunes and inaugurated a second surge of territorial expansion (map 2). Charles Martel (714-41) defeated the Arabs at Tours in 732, halting their rapid incursion into western Europe, while his son Pippin the Short (d. 768) expelled them from southern France. In 751, with the sanction and support of the pope, Pippin made himself king of the Franks. His son Charles the Great or Charlemagne (768-814) conquered Lombardy (774) and established Frankish rule in much of Italy. He won great victories over the Frisians (784-5), Bavarians (788) and Saxons (finally subdued in 804); and created a march, or boundary province, across the Pyrenees

An image of Charlemagne from his tomb at Aachen. The tomb was endowed by Frederick Barbarossa in the 12th century. The masterpiece of gold enamels and gems shows that, for the later emperor, Charlemagne was a saint and a personal patron, able to confer political legitimacy.

between 795 and 812. In 800 the pope in Rome crowned him emperor of the west.

However, Frankish custom called for the royal domain to be partitioned. Charlemagne's father had divided it between his two sons – Charlemagne only inherited the whole when his brother died in 771 – and the new emperor likewise planned in 806 to partition his possessions among his three sons, a scheme frustrated only by the early death of two of them. This made it possible for the survivor, Louis the Pious (814-40), to inherit the whole empire. After his death, however, the treaty of Verdun (843) created three kingdoms: one in the east, one in the west, and a 'middle kingdom' which ran from the North Sea to Italy.

The Carolingians ruled through direct agents, rather than through Gallo-Roman bishops and counts as their predecessors had done; and throughout the 8th century these men generally remained loyal. After Charlemagne's death, however, their descendants tended to identify with the particular interests of their own localities, at the expense of the whole. Frankish hegemony in western Europe was thus disrupted by fragmentation just as it came under attack from the Vikings and Magyars.

1 Anglo-Saxon England, c. AD 800

Mercia and subordinate kingdoms under Offa (757–96)

allied with Mercia

British kingdoms

2 The empire of Charlemagne

Frankish realm 714

added to Frankish empire by 814

Frankish dependencies (with date of formation)

⚜ Frankish royal residences

☩ archbishoprics

⊕ important monasteries

GASCONY 769 province with date of acquisition

A carved wooden head from the Oseberg cart (c. 800) depicts a fearsome Viking warrior. Viking success was in large part achieved not through superior organization or tactical skill, but depended on their greater mobility. They were able to launch lightning attacks on undefended coastal settlements and penetrate far inland in shallow boats or on horseback.

Three separate groups of invaders in the 9th century shattered the relative stability achieved by Charlemagne in western Europe and by Offa of Mercia in England (page 52). The Saracens occupied the islands of the western Mediterranean and raided Italy and France; the Magyars of Hungary devastated northern Italy and Germany; the Vikings from Scandinavia not only plundered settlements around the European coast as far as the Mediterranean, but also created trade routes through Russia to Byzantium (page 56) and settled substantial parts of Britain, Ireland, northern France, Iceland and even Greenland.

The invasions disrupted royal authority and caused political fragmentation. In the Carolingian empire, the Frankish kings virtually capitulated to the Vikings, leaving defence to the local magnates who swiftly created their own power bases. In England, although determined resistance by Alfred the Great of Wessex (871-99) held the Danes at bay,

a second wave of Scandinavian invasions a century later proved irresistible. However in the eastern half of the Frankish empire, Otto I's defeat of the Magyars at the Lechfeld (955) proved a turning point, and Germany became the first country in Europe to recover from the invasions. This achievement assured its predominance in Europe for almost three centuries.

German rulers rarely sought to assert control over the west Frankish lands but, as heirs to the Carolingians, they claimed the imperial title and the right to rule over Italy and the lands of the former "middle kingdom" (page 53). In 962 Otto's coronation as emperor sealed the connection between Germany and Italy, and in 1034 his successors annexed Burgundy. However the emperors became increasingly dependent upon the wealth of Italy, and this embroiled Frederick I of Hohenstaufen (1152-90) with both the papacy and the populous fortified cities of the Lombard plain, which all saw Imperial power in Italy as a threat to their independence. The conquest of Sicily by Frederick's son Henry VI in 1194 made the Hohenstaufen the richest rulers in Europe; but the prospect of total encirclement once more alarmed the papacy and the Lombard towns, leading to a long and costly struggle with Henry's son Frederick II (1212-50). After his death, the Imperial position in Italy steadily deteriorated, and the last Hohenstaufen prince met defeat and death at the battle of Tagliacozzo in 1268.

Meanwhile, in Germany, the princes took advantage of their rulers' preoccupation with Italy both to consolidate their power and, on the eastern frontier, to direct a major expansion. The Slavs were driven out or enslaved, in favour of German settlers who, by 1250, had increased the German kingdom by about one-third and shifted its centre of gravity from the Rhine to the Elbe. The empire might no longer have been the strongest or richest polity in Europe, but it remained the largest.

2 The German empire to 1250

- eastward spread of German peasant settlement, 12th century
- German settlement, 1200–1250
- city with over 10,000 inhabitants
- member of Lombard Leagues of 1167 and 1226
- member of 1167 League only
- member of 1226 League only
- main royal routes
- German invasions, 1190–94
- Henry VI's Genoese and Pisan fleet, 1194
- main Hohenstaufen palaces and castles
- monasteries

The first Russian state: Kievan Russia

Three factors shaped the early history of Russia: the eastward movement of Slav settlers; the impact of the Vikings (who were known to the Slavs as Varyagi or Varangians) from the north; and, most important of all, the division of the region into forests (in the north and centre) and treeless steppe (in the south). Before the arrival of the Vikings in the 9th century, the Slavs had begun to settle the central river basins, clearing the forests and living by agriculture, hunting, trapping and the fur trade, while nomadic tribes from Asia, such as the Pechenegs, occupied the grasslands of the south. At first the Slavs resisted the Varangians, but in 862 they called in 'Rurik the Viking' to protect them from Pecheneg raiders.

Since most of the rivers of Russia follow a north-south axis, great potential existed for trade between the Baltic and the Black Sea, and the Vikings sought to dominate and exploit these waterways and the territories adjoining them (map 2). Rurik therefore occupied Novgorod, and his followers soon pushed south to Smolensk and then down the Dnieper to Kiev (882). The principal trade route established by the Vikings ran from the Gulf of Finland up the river Neva, through Lake Ladoga to the river Volkhov, thence by portages to the Dnieper and on across the Black Sea to Byzantium.

Grand Prince Svyatoslav (962-72) campaigned to the south and east, greatly extending the frontiers of the Kievan state, which forged strong links with Byzantium, its chief trading partner; and from Byzantium it received the Christian faith during the reign of Vladimir Svyatoslav (980-1015). At the same time Kiev retained numerous connections with the West: one of Vladimir's granddaughters married the king of France, another the king of Hungary and a

A scene from Novgorod's victory over Suzdal in 1169. Novgorod was the capital of the Rus until Oleg moved his capital to Kiev in 882. In 1019 Iaroslav I granted Novgorod a charter of self-government, and thereafter the town elected its own prince. Grown rich on the trade in furs, Novgorod became pre-eminent in northern Russia. During the 12th century it came into conflict with the growing power of Vladimir-Suzdal to the south. However Novgorod defeated Vladimir-Suzdal in 1169 and 1216. It avoided the Mongol destruction and defeated the Germans and Swedes in 1240–2. A struggle for supremacy with Moscow in the 14th and 15th centuries saw the eclipse of Novgorod.

third the king of Norway. Half a century later, however, dynastic conflict and administrative inefficiency brought weakness and a new wave of Asiatic nomads, the Polovtsy, broke through the defences built by Svyatoslav and Vladimir. In 1093 they sacked Kiev itself.

A great northward exodus ensued to safer regions between the Oka and the Volga, where many new towns were founded (such as Vladimir, Suzdal, Rostov and Tver) and several new states developed – notably Vladimir-Suzdal, which included the fast growing commercial centre of Moscow (first mentioned in 1147), and Novgorod, which built up a fur-trading empire that reached to the Arctic and the Urals. Meanwhile, further south, Novgorod-Seversk, Vladimir-Volynsk and Galich broke away from Kievan rule (map 1).

Mongol invaders struck the final blow to the old order (page 60). In 1237-8, moving along the frozen rivers, they struck north and sacked the wealthy towns of Vladimir-Suzdal; in 1239-40 they advanced through southern Russia, systematically destroying settlements, including Kiev. Meanwhile Novgorod, although it escaped the Mongol onslaught as the onset of spring thawed the frozen rivers, faced repeated attacks by both Swedes and Germans in the Baltic region until Prince Alexander decisively defeated the former in 1240 on the river Neva (thus earning the title 'Nevsky') and the latter in 1242 on the ice of Lake Peipus. Despite these successes, however, even Novgorod had to recognize Mongol overlordship, exercised by the Golden Horde on the lower Volga, while the Lithuanian state expanded into the old Kievan heartland.

The Mongol invasion had other lasting economic, social and political effects. The destruction of so many towns decimated both trade and industry, while the elimination of the urban middle class smoothed the path of an autocracy which imitated its overlords in ruthless terror and extortion. The fall of Kiev destroyed the cultural centre of medieval Russia, with its rich Byzantine-based literature and art, while the Mongol forces, controlling the grasslands around the Caspian and the Black Sea, prevented almost all contact with Byzantium. Russia therefore inevitably developed a distinctive culture, society and political system of its own.

2 Varangian Russia, 862–1054

- Varangian territory, c.980
- *Ulichi* East Slav tribes
- KHAZARS Finno-Ugrian and Asiatic people
- → Varangian (Viking) trade routes
- --→ Varangian raids on Constantinople, 907, 944
- → Svyatoslav's campaigns, 964-71
- → Pecheneg raids

Trade and empire in Africa

By the end of the first millennium AD great changes had taken place in Africa. The rise of a culture based on iron-working (page 26) led to the appearance of extensive states and empires based on trade. In the south, Zimbabwe, with its monumental stone buildings, exported gold and copper via the port of Sofala; in the west, the Kongo state carried on an important trade. Further north, Arab traders developed the trans-Saharan trade routes and so assisted the growth of major sub-Saharan states. Although Ghana rose to prominence before the Islamic era, its successors, Mali and Songhay, owed much of their wealth and culture – described in glowing terms by Arab travellers – to the impact of Islam. So did the Kanem-Bornu empire around Lake Chad and the Hausa city-states. In the east Arab merchant colonies also spread down the Swahili coast as far as Kilwa and Sofala, bringing this part of Africa into an Indian Ocean trading complex. The staple exports in all cases were gold, ivory and slaves (map 1).

The arrival of the Portuguese in the 15th century at first made little impact on Africa. Their immediate object was to share directly in the gold trade, previously dominated by Muslim middlemen; the slave trade remained a secondary interest. However, with the development of labour-intensive sugar-plantations in the Americas (page 86), the slave trade attracted others. By the 18th century, nine European states maintained almost 50 fortified trading posts on the west coast, from Arguim to Lagos, to handle this burgeoning commerce, while the Portuguese continued to export slaves further south from Angola and Mozambique. Of some 15 million Africans shipped abroad by Europeans between 1450 and 1870, almost 90 per cent went to South America and the Caribbean, most of them during the 18th century. Muslim traders exported perhaps as many more again northward across the Sahara and from the Swahili coast. The effects on Africa of this appalling trade in human beings are impossible to quantify, not least because the loss of population was not evenly divided. Some states, such as Kongo and Lunda, suffered disproportionately, while others seem to have profited. Thus, after the destruction of the powerful Songhay empire by Moroccan troops in 1591, the forest states of Asante, Dahomey and Benin, having direct access to the Atlantic and thus to European slave-traders, increased in importance and political power (map 2).

1 The emergence of states, 1000–1500

▦	Islamic states or influence, 1000
▨	Christian states, 1000
▢	other states, 1000
▤	new states by 1300
- - -	limit of Islamized areas, 1500
——	Christian Ethiopia, 1500
▢	new states by 1500
IFAT	states that disappeared by 1500
▦	major gold producing region
■	Muslim settlement
⬔	gold
M	musk
⌣	slaves
◣	bananas
◗	rice
◆	cattle
C	copper
⬓	salt
◑	millet
⛏	ivory

Apart from the Portuguese in Angola and Mozambique, and the fortified posts along the west coast, only the Dutch attempted to create a European colony in Africa before 1800: in the far south, around Cape Town. In the north-east, Islam continued to spread, but the Christian kingdom of Ethiopia still held its own. In the north, the Ottoman empire (page 70) maintained only nominal suzerainty over the states from Morocco to Egypt. In 1800, almost all of Africa thus remained independent of foreign control: a world unto itself, the 'dark continent'. However, precisely because of its autonomy, it would lack the ability to compete with the technological dynamism of the West in the 19th century (page 110).

2 Developments in trade and empire, 1400–1800

→ movement of peoples

→ spread of Islam

area of Islamic influence by 1800

→ trade routes

→ slave trade routes

Granada **Algiers** **Tunis**

Tangier
Fez
Marrakesh
ALGIERS
Sijilmassa
Wargla **Tripoli**

MOROCCO
Morocco ruled by Sharifian dynasties 1553–1912
Cape Bojador
Taghaza
Ain Salah
Ghadamès
Murzuk
Arab trans-Saharan slave trade route
Alexandria
Cairo
EGYPT
Ottoman conquest 1517

Arguin (Portuguese 1482)
Wadan
KAARTA *18th C*
Awdaghost
Walata
SONGHAY
Tadmekka
AIR
Agadès
Bilma
Ghat
Tamanrasset

S   a   h   a   r   a

St. Louis
Gorée
SENEGAMBIAN STATES
Gambia
Cacheu
SEGU *18th C*
Timbuktu
Gao
Jenne
HAUSA STATES
Katsina
Kano
Zaria
BORNU
KANEM WADAI
DARFUR
Sennar
FUNJ *16th C*
Suakin
Massawa
ETHIOPIA
Zeila
Berbera
SHOA
ADAL
SOMALI

Bunce Island
Freetown
MOSSI STATES
BORGU STATES
NUPE
DYOLA (TRADERS) *18th C*
ASANTE DAHOMEY OYO *17th C*
Accra **Lagos**
BENIN
NIGER DELTA STATES *18th C*
Old Calabar
KWARARAFA
TIKAR
BAMUM
BAMILEKE
BANDA
AZANDE
NZAKARA
NGBANDI
MANGBETU
NILOTES
PARANILOTES
NILOTES
GALLA
Mogadishu
Brava
Lamu
Malindi
Pemba

west Africa – arrival of Portuguese 15th C and 16th C. Dutch, English and French 17th C.

PYGMY
TEKE
MONGO
BUNYORO BUGANDA
ANKOLE KARAGWE
RWANDA
BURUNDI
KIKUYU
Mombasa
Zanzibar
Swahili Coast
Arab slave trade

LUANGO
KONGO
Ambriz
Luanda
KUBA TETELA
LULUA
LUBA *15th–16th C*
COKWE
LUNDA *16th–17th C*
KETE
SANGA
BEMBA
BISA
Kilwa Kisiwani
Benguela
LUENA-LOVALE
LOZI
OVIMBUNDU
LAMBA
LENJE
MARAVI
Tete
Sena
MWENEMUTAPA *16th C*
Quelimane
Mozambique
MADAGASCAR
HOVA MERINA
ANGOLA
OVAMBO
TONGA
HERERO
ROZWI
Sofala
Great Zimbabwe
KARANGA
TSWANA
SOTHO
XHOSA
SOTHO

CAPE COLONY
Cape Town

settlements of mainland African slaves
Portuguese slave trade

→ Spanish offensives against Algiers and Tunis, 16th century

— Morocco to 1591

→ Moroccan military expeditions

--- Saladian extension of Moroccan territory, c. 1591

— areas of Ottoman control in Africa by 1574

coastal settlements

○ Dutch   ● Ottoman
● French   ● British
● Portuguese   ◐ Spanish
● Danish   ● Brandenburger

From around the 10th century the cattle-herding peoples of the Zambezi region built large stone buildings or 'zimbabwes' for their kings. These gradually became larger and more sophisticated. The most extensive is at Great Zimbabwe, built over a period of 200 years. Its high granite walls were abandoned by 1500, but still served as a shrine.

(left inset map)

Alexandria **Cairo**
EGYPT
AYYUBIDS 1171–1250
MAMLUKS 1250–1517
Aidhab
Dongola
DONGOLA
Napata
Meroë
Adulis
Soba
ALWA
Sennar
FUNJ
AGAU
Zeila
DANAKIL
ETHIOPIA
ADAL
Berbera
Ras Hafun
El Fasher
Ain Farah
SIDAMA
OROMO (GALLA)
SOMALI
PLAINS NILOTES
Mogadishu
RIVER LAKE NILOTES c.1400
INTERLACUSTRINE STATES
HIGHLAND NILOTES c.1000
Lamu
Lake Victoria
KITARA
MASAI
Malindi
Mombasa
Pemba Is.
LATE IRON AGE HERDERS
Lake Tanganyika
Zanzibar
LUBA
Ivuna
Kilwa Kisiwani
UNDA
C
LOZI
Lake Nyasa
MANGANJA
MARAWI
Ingombe Ilede
TONGA
SHONA
MUTAPA
ZIMBABWE
Sofala
Zambezi
Great Zimbabwe *stone buildings*
Mapungubwe *stone buildings*
C
Phalaborwa
Limpopo
Kalahari Desert
Iron Age peoples
Orange

Indonesian expansion from east coast into interior bringing bananas and rice

Cape Colony established by Dutch East India Company in 1652. Gradual spread of white settlers inland. Occupied by Britain 1795

migrations of Bantu speakers to Madagascar bringing cattle and millet

MADAGASCAR
Fort Dauphin

59

The Mongol empire

The Mongols, a nomadic people from the grasslands of Central Asia, staged a sudden and devastating irruption into world history in the first half of the 13th century (map 1). Theirs was not the first empire of the steppe, however. In the 7th century AD, in the wake of the upheavals that destroyed the ancient world (page 40), a confederation of Turkish tribes had managed to dominate the plains of Asia from the Great Wall of China to the Black Sea; but by 750 their rule had collapsed and the area disintegrated into feud and faction. Thus it remained for four centuries, when a charismatic leader, Temujin (1167-1227), gained recognition as supreme ruler and in 1206 took the title Genghis Khan, 'prince of all that lies between the Oceans'. Under his leadership the Mongols first invaded the Chin empire in north China and then turned against the Islamic states to the west. By the time of Genghis's death, his empire stretched from the Pacific Ocean to the Caspian Sea. His successors continued the tide of destructive conquests: Kievan Russia (1237-40); the Abbasid Caliphate (1256-60); Sung China (1271-9). Europe and Japan were also threatened: one Mongol army reached the gates of Vienna while another defeated a German-Polish army at Liegnitz in 1241; two amphibious expeditions unsuccessfully attacked Japan in 1274 and 1281.

However the vast empire lacked coherence and stability, and the Mongols failed to develop appropriate institutions. On hearing of the death of Genghis's successor Ogedei in 1241, the victorious commander of the Mongol forces in Europe withdrew eastwards with his army, in order to take part in choosing a successor. They never returned. Likewise in 1260, on

2 The conquests of Tamerlane, c. 1360–1405

Mongol brutality in war did not end with Genghis Khan. In this late-16th century Mughal miniature *(right)*, the troops of Tamerlane are shown demolishing the fort of Mikrit in the Hindu Kush, and using the defenders' heads to erect a tower of skulls.

1 The Mongol empire

- ——— the Mongol empire by 1259
- ——→ campaigns under Genghis Khan
- ——➤ campaigns of his successors
- ‖‖‖ Mongol incursions and limited Mongol control
- *OIROTS* Mongol tribes around 1220
- ——— empire of Kublai Khan, 1260–94
- **CUMANS** other peoples

hearing of the death of Ogedei's successor, the victorious commander of the Mongol forces in the Near East decided to return to the Mongol heartland, leaving only a skeleton force behind him. This soon became known in Cairo, and the Sultan of Egypt marched to the defence of Islam, still reeling from the sack of Baghdad, the capital of the Caliphs, two years before. At Ain Jalut on 3 September 1260 the Mongols suffered a defeat and withdrew to Persia.

The Mongol empire now fragmented. The title of Great Khan went to Kublai who, although never forgetting that he was the grandson of Genghis, spent most of his long reign (1260–94) seeking to reunify China and conquer Japan. The other Mongol states – the Golden Horde in the west; the Il-Khans in Persia; the Chagatai empire in the traditional Mongol heartland – went their own way.

Despite the widespread destruction of the Mongol onslaught, their temporary unification of Eurasia permitted the exchange of goods and ideas between the far east and the far west on an unprecedented scale.

For over a century the 'Silk Road' of ancient times revived: silver and gold from Europe and the Near East reached China while Chinese silks and porcelain circulated in Europe. But the Black Death (see page 66) and the rise of Timur, or Tamerlane, (1336-1405) changed all that, for he destroyed the Chagatai khanate, dislocated the Golden Horde, defeated the Ottoman empire at the battle of Ankara in 1402 (page 70), and initiated a policy of religious intolerance. However Timur died in 1405 before he had created the institutions and traditions required to ensure the survival of his vast empire (map 2). Instead, Mongol power in the west steadily lost ground to Russia (see page 84), and crumbled in China with the rise of the Ming dynasty (see page 94). Mongolia itself came under Chinese dominion in 1696.

The Muslim empires of India and Persia

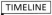
Delhi, founded in the 8th century by a Rajput chief, remained the focus of north Indian politics and also the centre of Muslim culture from the 13th to the 19th century. It served as the capital of the six Muslim dynasties, all of Turkish or Afghan extraction, who sought (unsuccessfully) to extend their rule into the Deccan between 1206 and 1526; and, after the defeat of the last of the Sultans of Delhi at Panipat (1526) by Babur – a descendant of Timur (page 60) – it became the headquarters of his descendants, the Mughals.

Babur's grandson, Akbar (1556-1605), extended the frontiers of the empire to Bengal in the east, to Gujerat and the river Godavari in the south, and to Kashmir in the north. New territories were added under Akbar's grandson, Shahjahan (1627-56) and his son Aurangzeb (1656-1707), who annexed Bijapur and Golconda in the south, and Orissa in the east. However, these achievements depended absolutely upon the acquiescence of the 150 million or so Hindu peasant farmers and petty landlords who paid the taxes that supported the Mughals' 4 million warriors, and the court grandees who commanded them. It was a delicate balance, for if the peasants and landlords were overtaxed, they would revolt; and if the grandees were not rewarded with office and wealth they would desert the court. Around 1700 the Hindu Marathas began to ravage southern regions, while some Rajput states and the Sikhs rebelled. All this reduced tax yields, and after the death of Aurangzeb several frontier provinces split off from the empire (page 96).

Meanwhile, to the West, after 1500 the leader of a fanatical sect of Shi'a Muslims, Ismail Safavi, re-unified Persia – which had been in a state of chaos since Timur's invasions – and proclaimed himself Shah. However the Sunnite Ottomans under Selim I (page 70) invaded in 1514, defeated Ismail at the battle of Chaldiran and captured Tabriz, thus initiating a duel between the two powers that lasted for over a century. The conflict centred around the key cities of Mesopotamia, and Baghdad, Tiflis, Derbend and Basra changed hands repeatedly; but its intensity stemmed from the religious division within Islam between Sunnite and Shi'ite (page 50), which excited the same passions as the split between Protestant and Catholic Christians at the same time. Eventually Shah Abbas (1587-1629), with assistance from both Russia and the Christian West, managed to regain most of the lost territories; but the Turks recaptured much of Mesopotamia in the 1630s.

Both empires boasted a rich civilization. Akbar and Abbas each built luxurious new capital cities – at Fatehpur Sikri and Isfahan respectively – and attracted to their courts local and foreign writers, artists and craftsmen. Shahjahan built the magnificent Taj Mahal outside Delhi. Nevertheless, two developments threatened these achievements. On the one hand, as in all autocracies, government authority could suddenly collapse under a weak ruler. Thus in 1739 Nadir Shah, who had usurped the Persian throne three years previously, invaded India and sacked Delhi, leaving the Mughal empire fatally weakened; but in 1747 Nadir was assassinated and Persia too suffered a period of anarchy. On the other

Aral
Sea

Syr Darya

Urgench

Khiva

Tashkent

UZBEK KHANATE

Khokand

Amu Darya

Bukhara

Merv

Samarkand

Balkh

Meshed

Nishapur
*1588–9
Safavid conquests*

P·E·R·S·I·A

Herat *1506, 1588–9*

Kerman

Kandahar

andar
Abbas
1551

Ormuz
**(Portuguese
1515–1622)**

Muscat *1551*

*Gulf of
Arabia*

Kabul
Mughal conquest 1504

Attock

Khyber Pass

Peshawar

KASHMIR

SIKHS

LAHORE

Lahore

Hindu Kush

Indus

Multan

MULTAN

Panipat
1526 ✕

Samana

Delhi

SATAMIS

DELHI   *Mughal conquest 1504*

Agra

Fatehpur Sikri

Biana

Gwalior

Hindaun

JATS

OUDH

Lucknow

BALUCHISTAN

**(TATTA)
SIND**

AJMER

Ajmer

(RAJPUTANA)

Jodhpur

RAJPUTS

Ganges

Allahabad

Benares

ALLAHABAD

T·I·B·E·T

Himalayas

Patna

Kasimbazar

Rajmahal

Plassey

KUTCH

BIHAR

Dacca

Brahmaputra

BENGAL

Sarkhej

Ahmadabad

Cambay

Baroda

MALWA

Normada

I·N·D·I·A

GUJERAT

Diu *1538*
(Portuguese)

Broach

KHANDESH

Surat

Asirgarh

Assaye

Nagpur

BERAR

Deccan

Daulatabad

Ahmadnagar

Poona

Janjira

AHMADNAGAR

MARATHAS

Dabhoi

Satara

Hyderabad

Golconda

Godavari

ORISSA

Vizagapatam

Pipli

*Bay of
Bengal*

Rajapur

Kolhapur

GOLCONDA

Bijapur

Krishna

Vengurla

Goa
(Portuguese 1509)

BIJAPUR

Vijayanagar

Nizampatam
(Petapoli)

Nellore

Bhatkal

Chandragiri

Madras

Saint Thomé

Mangalore

MYSORE

Calicut

Mysore

Tanjore

Madurai

Quilon

Kayal

Tuticorin

Ceylon

Kashgar

**KHANATE OF
KASHGAR**

Much of the early part of
Akbar's reign was spent in the
conquest of the Hindu Rajputs,
who were to become important
allies of the Mughals. In this
typically sumptuous miniature of
1569, Surjan Hara, ruler of the
fort of Ranthanbhur, submits to
Akbar, offering him the keys to
the fort and many gifts.

1 The Safavid and
Mughal empires

extent of Mughal empire

☐ at Akbar's death, 1605

☐ under Shahjahan, 1627–56

☐ under Aurangzeb, c. 1700

extent of Safavid empire

—— at the death of Abbas the
Great, 1629

**Ottoman conquests from
Safavids**

☐ conquests of Suleiman I,
1520–66

⬤ conquest of town with date

☐ from 1566–1639

hand, the armed forces of various European states
established themselves around the fringes of the
empires. In the north, the Russians in the 1550s
advanced to the mouth of the Volga (page 84), gaining
access to the Caspian. In the south, the Portuguese
created fortified bases around the Indian Ocean in
the early 16th century, followed after 1600 by the
Dutch, English and French. Although the number of
Europeans in each enclave remained relatively
small, they served corporate entities – the East India
Companies – that never died. Whenever Mughal or
Safavid control faltered, the Europeans stood poised
to take advantage (page 96).

63

South East Asia

Situated at one of the world's main cross-roads, civilization developed early in South-East Asia: traces of 'Java man' date from the middle Pleistocene and remains of *homo sapiens* from c. 40,000 BC; rice cultivation in South China began about 6000 BC and bronze working in Thailand and Vietnam in 1500 BC or earlier (pages 12 and 18). Early trade routes linked India with ports along the coasts of Burma, Thailand, Cambodia and Vietnam; Hindu-Buddhist influences from India reached the area around the 2nd or 3rd century AD; and by the 5th century Buddhist images and votive tablets appeared, along with Sanskrit inscriptions. These influences never obliterated the unique character of South-East Asian civilization; instead, the next thousand years saw their assimilation to produce distinctive societies in the area. The culture of Java and southern Sumatra likewise became Indianized, but these areas also developed commercial and political links with China, which welcomed tribute missions from a growing number of states. From the 8th century temple complexes, each combining Hindu and Buddhist influences, evolved in four main areas: central Java (notably at Borobudur and Prambanan, from the 8th to 10th centuries), Cambodia (especially at Angkor, from the 9th to 13th centuries), Burma (Pagan, from the 11th to 13th centuries) and, associated with the Hindu-Buddhist

kingdom of Champa, along the coast of central Vietnam. Meanwhile Palembang (a centre of Sanskrit culture from perhaps as early as the 7th century) emerged as the capital of the maritime empire of Srivijaya, which for centuries controlled international trade passing through the straits of Malacca and Sunda, and across the Isthmus of Kra (map 1).

The great temple-states fell into decline after the 12th century. In Java, the area of Prambanan was superseded in importance by eastern Java, where three states developed in succession: Kediri (12th century), Singhasari (13th century) and finally Majapahit (late 13th-early 16th century). On the mainland, first Mongols and then Shans sacked Pagan in the 13th century, while Angkor fell to Thai attacks after 1369. Sukothai, the first of the lowland Thai cities, was itself in decline by the late 14th century. New political centres replaced the old temple cities: in Burma, Toungoo (1347), Ava (1364), and Pegu (1369), capital of a new Mon kingdom in the south; in Thailand, Chieng Mai (1296) and Ayutthaya (1350); in Cambodia, Phnom Penh and other cities along the Mekong; in Laos, Luang Prabang (1353). All were Theravada Buddhist in the Sinhalese tradition, with stupas rather than temples. Meanwhile, in Vietnam, after the failure of Chinese attempts at reconquest (despite invasions in 1075-7 and 1285-8) a

2 Cultural divisions
southeast Asia, 1500
distribution of major religions:
- Theravada Buddhism
- Mahayana Buddhism mixed with Confucianism and Taoism
- Hindu-Buddhism
- Islamic states
- places sending tribute to China between 1370 and 1440

1 Southeast Asia, AD 300–1511

● towns with inscriptions and monumental religious buildings

⚓ trading ports, no monumental buildings known

🏛 temples with inscriptions

KINGDOM OF PAGAN
11th–16th centuries

PYU KINGDOM

LAO KINGDOMS

VIETNAM
from 1471

KINGDOM OF SUKHOTHAI

MON KINGDOMS
8th–17th centuries

KINGDOM OF AYUTTHAYA

KHMER KINGDOM
7th–15th centuries

CHAMPA PRINCIPALITIES
4th–15th centuries

South China Sea

Manila

Philippines

Halin
Ava
Pagan
-eikthano
Sri Ksetra
Toungoo
Chieng Mai
Luang Prabang
Pegu
Thaton
Sukhothai
Si Thep
Phimai
Mi Son
Dong Duong
Tra Kieu
U-Thong
Nakhon Pathom
Ku Bua
Ayutthaya
Tonle Sap (Great Lake)
Angkor
Preah Khan
Vijaya
Po Nagar (Nha Trang)
Phnom Penh
Mekong
Angkor Borei
Oc Eo
Po Klaung Gerai
Chaiya
Takuapa
Ko Kho Khao
Ligor

Aceh

Straits of Malacca

Malacca

Sumatra

SRI VIJAYA
7th–13th centuries

Sri Vijaya

Java Sea

Straits of Sunda

JOLO SULTANATE
from 14th century

Celebes Sea

Borneo

SULTANATES OF TERNATE AND TIDORE
from 14th century

Ternate
Tidore

Celebes

MAJAPAHIT EMPIRE
14th–16th centuries

Dieng Plateau
Borobudur
Prambanan
Trowulan
Singhasari
Kediri

SALENDRA KINGDOM
8th–10th centuries

Java

new kingdom, called Dai Viet, emerged and gradually absorbed Champa (annexing its capital, Vijaya, in 1471). Further south, Srivijaya declined and a powerful new Muslim state developed after 1400 at Malacca, commanding the narrow straits through which most east-west trade passed. By that time the east Javanese empire of Majapahit was in decline, and the west Javanese kingdom of Pajajaran also collapsed before Muslim pressure from the northern coastal ports in the early 16th century.

Islam had began to influence northern Sumatra just before 1300; now it spread further, often under Malaccan influence, to the north Javanese trading ports, the Spice Islands, Borneo and, in the 16th century, the Philippines (map 2). When the Spaniards arrived, Mindanao had already been converted and the spread of Islam in Luzon was only halted by the Spaniards' capture of the Muslim fort at Manila in 1571 and their determined promotion of Christianity (page 80).

Meanwhile, in Vietnam, Confucian scholarship strengthened, despite the failure of another attempt at reconquest under the Ming; and all over South-East Asia the series of voyages made by the Muslim admiral Cheng Ho in the early 15th century revived and reinforced China's system of tributary relationships

(page 74). From the 1430s, however, China abandoned its interest in the wider world and South-East Asia began to assume its modern pattern of cultures and polities which even the arrival of the Europeans, starting with the Portuguese capture of Malacca in 1511 (page 80) influenced little until the 19th century.

Prambanan was built in the mid-9th century and was the largest and most ambitious temple complex ever constructed in central Java. There are three main temples dedicated to the gods of the Trimurti: Shiva in the centre; Vishnu on the north side; and Brahma on the south.

Europe

The 14th century brought to an end the rise and consolidation of national monarchies in western Europe (page 54). Though growth in population and productivity was steady until the later 13th century, both began to decline thereafter. Part of the problem lay in a sudden climatic deterioration which terminated the agricultural boom that had prevailed since 1150: crop yields fell and marginal areas brought into cultivation were abandoned. In 1315-17 Europe experienced the first of many famines; and the weakening of human powers of resistance through inadequate nourishment may have accelerated the spread of the 'Black Death', or bubonic plague, which killed perhaps 20 million Europeans between 1346 and 1353, wiping out in some areas as much as a third of the population within two years (map 1).

However, the impact of the plague was not even. Some areas escaped altogether, and Eastern Europe seems to have suffered relatively little: Bohemia under Charles IV (1333-78), Poland under Casimir III (1339-70) and Hungary under Louis the Great (1342-82) all made rapid strides – aided in part by skillful exploitation of their natural resources, such as the silver mines of Kutna Hora in Bohemia. Above all, in the wake of the Mongol invasions (page 60) Lithuania expanded into the former heartland of Kievan Russia and united in 1386 with Poland to form the largest state in Eastern Europe (map 2).

1 Famine, plague and popular unrest

— main sea-trade routes

wine important commodities

extent of the spread of the Black Death

▨	1346	▢	end 1349
▨	1347	▨	1350
▨	mid-1348	▨	c. 1351
▨	end 1348	▢	c. 1353
▨	mid-1349	▨	little or no plague mortality

social unrest

▨ areas of disturbance during Peasants' Revolt in England, 1381

● centre of urban revolt

▢ rural uprisings

⊗ defeat of lower orders in battle

religious unrest

▨ spread of Lollardy in England to death of Richard II, 1399

▧ area of Hussite influence

■ Hussite centre

Map: Eastern Europe and Iberia. Labels include: SWEDEN, Baltic Sea, HOLSTEIN, Lübeck, Hamburg, POMERANIA, Königsberg, Danzig, BRANDENBURG 1373, LUSATIA 1368, MEISSEN, Gniezno, Toruń (Thorn), Poznań, Breslau, POLAND, Prague, KINGDOM OF BOHEMIA, Kutna Hora, SILESIA 1368, Lublin, Sandomierz, Cracow, MORAVIA, Brünn, UPPER PALATINATE 1359, AUSTRIA 1282, Vienna, STYRIA 1282, CARINTHIA 1335, Graz, Pest, CARNIOLA 1335, Trieste, Venice, REPUBLIC OF VENICE, Fiume, CROATIA, SLAVONIA, Pécs, Belgrade, Smederevo, BOSNIA, Kosovo ×1389, Durazzo, Üsküb (Skoplje), SERBIAN EMPIRE under Stephen Dushan, BULGARIA, WALLACHIA, BYZANTINE EMPIRE, MOLDAVIA, PODOLIA, KHANATE OF THE GOLDEN HORDE, RUTHENIA, Halicz, to Poland 1366, VOLHYNIA, Lwów (Lvov), Kiev, Chernigov, Dnieper, Kursk, Bryansk, Novogrudok, Minsk, LITHUANIA, Smolensk, Vyazma, Pripet, SMOLENSK, Vitebsk, Polotsk, LIVONIA, NOVGOROD, TEUTONIC ORDER, SAMOGITIA to Lithuania 1422, Vilna, Carpathian Mts., KINGDOM OF HUNGARY, Danube. Spain/Portugal section: PORTUGAL, Santiago, Santander, iron, Léon, Lisbon, Tagus, wool, CASTILE, Toledo, cattle, Córdoba, Seville, Cádiz, Granada, dried fruits, Ceuta.

Annotations: "Hungarian suzerainty until 1365; independent until 1397; then under temporary Lithuanian control"; "under Hungary to 1369; Ottoman Tributary from 1389"; "Hungarian Rule 1328; independent from 1353".

Shetlands

Orkneys

SCOTLAND

Edinburgh

North Sea

Bergen *cattle* NORWAY SWEDEN

Oslo

Uppsala

Stockholm

Newcastle

Armagh

...LAND

fish

DENMARK

Visby

furs

Riga

amber ORDER

TEUTONIC

Copenhagen

Baltic Sea

Danzig

Königsberg

York *wool* Lincoln

Chester

Nexford

wool

WALES

ENGLAND

Lynn Norwich

Bury St Edmunds

London

Roosebeke 1382

Bristol

Winchester

Lübeck

Hamburg

Bremen

FRIESLAND

HOLLAND *cattle*

Amsterdam

SAXONY

POMERANIA

rye

BRANDENBURG

Warsaw

LITHUANIA

SILESIA

POLAND

Oder

Kiev

Crécy

Ypres

FLANDERS

Ghent

Bruges

Liège

Rhine

Cologne

Brunswick

Mello 1358

Rouen

Amiens

Rheims

Mainz

Frankfurt

Elbe

Prague

BOHEMIA

Cracow

UKRAINE

wheat

Meaux 1358

Paris

Trier

FRANCONIA

HOLY

Tabor

MORAVIA

Dniester

BRITTANY

salt

Troyes

wine

LORRAINE

ROMAN

Regensburg

metals

Loire

Orléans

Passau

FRANCE

Poitiers

SWABIA

Basle

Augsburg

Vienna

Salzburg

BAVARIA

AUSTRIA

EMPIRE

metals

SWISS CONFED.

Geneva

Lyons

SAVOY

Alps

Milan

Trieste

CARINTHIA

HUNGARY

Buda Pest

Belgrade

WALLACHIA

Bucharest

wheat

Danube

BURGUNDY

DAUPHINÉ

Turin

Rhône

Venice

REPUBLIC OF VENICE

wheat

ENGLISH

GASCONY

AQUITAINE

wine

Cahors

Avignon

PROVENCE

wheat

Marseilles

Genoa

Pisa

Ravenna

Florence

Siena

Ancona

BOSNIA

silver

SERBIAN

Danube

Black Sea

Bordeaux

Toulouse

wool

...RAGON

wool

Saragossa

CATALONIA

Barcelona

Corsica

PAPAL STATES

saffron

Rome

Ragusa

PRINCES

PRINCIPALITY OF ALBANIA

BULGARIA

Adrianople

Constantinople

Valencia

salt

Majorca City

Sardinia

wheat

Alghero

salt

Cagliari

KINGDOM

wool OF

Naples

Amalfi

NAPLES

Bari

Salonica

OTTOMAN TURKS

Algiers

Bougie

Mediterranean

Palermo

Messina

KINGDOM OF SICILY

wheat

Tunis

Sea

dried fruits

DUCHY OF Athens

ATHENS

ACHAEA

Rhodes

Cyprus

Crete

alum

wheat Caffa

60

50

20

30

10

Unlike famine, plague affected every social class, and the psychological impact was profound. Until the mid-17th century, scarcely a decade passed without a recurrent outbreak. The disease, spread by infected fleas carried by rats, was particularly virulent, and few who caught it ever recovered. This illustration *(left)* from the Stiny Codex shows death strangling a plague victim.

But elsewhere the setback proved more serious. All the western states had overextended themselves financially, and the economic and demographic crisis exacerbated by the Black Death – combined with the tensions caused by the fragmentation of Italy and Germany after the end of Hohenstaufen rule in 1250 (page 55) or the Hundred Years' War between England and France – produced a series of popular uprisings in both cities and the countryside: the Jacquerie (1358) in France; the Peasants' Revolt (1381) in England; urban insurrections in Spain, Italy and the Low Countries. Few rebellions achieved their aims, but they all weakened state power even further.

China and Japan

The Mongol invasion of China caused immense destruction. During the conquest of the north (1211-34: page 60) much of the land went out of cultivation, many cities and industries perished, and countless people died or became slaves. The conquest of the south (1271-9) brought similar hardships, and Mongol rule proved harsh. Popular resentment erupted in a wave of popular uprisings after 1335, exacerbated by disastrous floods in coastal regions in the 1350s. One of the rebel leaders, Chu Yüan-chang, gradually overcame his rivals and in 1368 established a new dynasty, the Ming.

The Ming rebuilt irrigation and drainage works in great numbers, reforested on a grand scale, and moved vast numbers of people to repopulate the devastated north. New crops were introduced and the canal system extended to transport produce: by 1421 the 'Grand Canal' stretched from Hang-chou to just south of Peking and carried some 200,000 tons of grain northwards every year. Thanks to these measures, the Chinese population rose from some 60 million in 1393 (40 per cent fewer than a century before) to about 130 million by 1580. The great cities of the Yangtze delta became major industrial centres, particularly for textiles, while the southern ports fitted out the enormous fleets sent by Chu's son, the Yung-lo emperor (1402-24), to the South China Sea and the Indian Ocean (page 74).

The Ming entrusted control over the vast population to a gentry class of degree-holders, who had passed through the examination system and shared the values of the bureaucracy without actually holding office. But the system discouraged innovation and was overcentralized, with all major decisions dependent upon the emperor; and few of Yung-lo's successors possessed the dedication necessary for such heavy responsibilities. Nevertheless, the early Ming engaged in an aggressive foreign policy. They restored Korea to vassal status in 1392, occupied Annam from 1407 to 1427, and invaded Mongolia (map 1). However, after a northern campaign in 1449 resulted in the capture of the emperor, the Ming reverted to a defensive strategy, strengthening the Great Wall until it ran for almost 2,500 miles, and increasing the garrisons in the north and north-west. China remained relatively stable for another century, but in the 1430s the government banned all overseas trade by sea, except under close supervision. Not surprisingly, by 1500 smuggling had become commonplace in the south-eastern provinces and by 1550 heavily-armed bands of smugglers and pirates infested the seas around China and terrorized the coastal regions from their bases in Japan.

Central authority in Japan had collapsed in the 1330s and the country became plagued by local and provincial wars – almost continuously in the century after 1467. By about 1560, some nine leading families had formed alliances that covered most of the country, and competed openly for supreme power (map 2). In 1568 Nobunaga, leader of the Oda clan, captured Kyoto, the imperial capital, and by the time he was assassinated in 1582 by a jealous rival he had forced almost all the other lords to accept his orders. Within a decade, his ablest general Toyotomi Hideyoshi had completely reunified Japan, reorganizing the tax system and redistributing land to provide sufficient funds for his ambitious policies – including the invasion of Korea in the 1590s. After his death in 1598 another of Nobunaga's generals, Tokugawa Ieyasu, assumed power and in 1603 established the dynasty of shoguns who ruled Japan until the 19th century (page 88).

The Tokugawa put an end to the pirate problem, thus easing the pressure on the Chinese coast; but at just this time a new threat arose in the north-east, where the Manchu gradually expanded their power into the areas immediately to the north of the Great Wall and (in 1637) into Korea. Ming authority now

2 Civil War in Japan, 1467–1590

spheres of influence of the most powerful Daimyo clans

boundaries of Daimyo domains

Uesugi

Takeda

Hojo

Oda

Imagawa

Sea of Japan

Kyoto

Nara

Mori

Sogabe

Otomo

Shimazu

Pacific Ocean

Sha-ch

Li-chiang

Ta-li

T'eng-yüeh

Meng-hua

BURMA

YUNNAN

Mekong

SIAM

1 Ming China

- —— major post roads
- —— minor roads
- ⊓⊔ Great Wall
- —— Grand Canal
- ◉ national capital
- ⊙ provincial capitals
- ☐ the nine frontier defence areas
- ○ prefectures and regional military commissioners
- ■ guard units
- ➡ attacks by pirates based in Japan before 1600
- ➡ Japanese invasions of Korea in 1590s

expeditions of Yung-lo against the Mongols:
- → 1st 1410
- ⇢ 2nd 1414
- ⟶ 3rd 1422
- ⋯⋯▸ 4th 1424

Onon Gol *1410*

Tuul Gol *1414*

Kerulen

Dalai Nor *1422*

Buyr Nuur *1424*

1410

1422

MONGOLIA

Gobi Desert

KHALKHA

TUMET

PEI CHIH-LI

Shara Muren

MANCHUS

The 'Willow Palisade' surrounding area of Chinese settlement in Liao-tung.

Chien-chou

Shen-yang

Liao-tung

Ming counter-attacks to defend Korea, 1592, 1597–8

Sea of Japan

Japanese invasions of Korea under Toyotomi Hideyoshi, 1592, 1597–8

Kuei-hua-ch'eng
Hsüan-fu
Pao-an
Chi-chou
Ta-t'ung · Yü
I-chou · Peking (Shun-t'ien-fu) · T'ung-chou
Pao-ting
Ho-chien · Ts'ang
Chin-chou
Chin-chou (Po Hai)

a-chou
Il-chou
Kan-chou
Liang-chou
Hsi-ning
Ning-hsia
Ling
Yü-lin
Sui-te
T'ai-yüan
Chen-ting
Chao
Shun-te
Lai-chou · Teng-chou
Hai-ning
Ching-chou

KOKO Nor
Koko Nor
T'ao-chou
P'ing-liang
Lan-chou
Ku-yüan
Yen-an
Fu
P'ing-yang
Lu-an
Chiang
Chi-nan
Yen-chou
Ts'ao
SHANTUNG

Hsi-an
Ho-nan
K'ai-feng
Ju
Kuei-te
Hsü
P'ei
NAN CHIH-LI

SHENSI
SHANSI
HONAN

Tung
Han-chung
Hsing-an
Nan-yang
Feng-yang
Huai-an

SZECHWAN
Ch'eng-tu
Kuei-chou
I-ling
Shih-chou
Hsiang-yang
Sui
Lu-chou
Ch'u
Yang-chou
Nanking (Ying-t'ien-fu)
Wu-hsi
Su-chou
Shang-hai
Sung-chiang
Hang-chou
Ning-po
Botsu
Hirado
Hakata
JAPAN

Yangtze
Ch'ung-ch'ing
Ts'un-i
Ching-men
Shih-chou
Wu-ch'ang
An-ch'ing
Hsin-an
Hui-chou
Yen-chou
Chin-hua
T'ai-chou
HUPEH
ANHWEI
CHEKIANG

Chen-chou
Ch'ang-te
Yüeh-chou
Ching-chou
Jao-chou
Ching-te-chen
Shao-hsing
Wen-chou
KWEICHOW
An-shun
Kuei-yang
Ch'ang-sha
HUNAN
Heng-chou
Nan-ch'ang
Lin-chiang
Chi-an
Shao-wu
Chien-ning
Fu-ning
KIANGSI
FUKIEN

Yung-ning
Ch'uan
Liu-chou
Kuei-lin
Yung-chou
Shao-chou
Ch'u-chou
Ch'üan-chou
KWANGSI

Nan-ning
Yung-an-chou
Wu-chou
Lien
Shao-chou
Chang-chou
Hsia-men
KWANGTUNG

Lo ting-chou
Chao-ch'ing
Hui-chou
Ch'ao-chou
Kuang-chou
Lien-chou
Macao (Ao-men)
Lei-chou
Ch'ing-hua
Chiao-tu

Hainan

Ryukyu Islands

T'ai-nan

Chu Yüan-chang (1328–98), founder of the Ming dynasty. In 1368 he proclaimed himself the founder of a new imperial dynasty, taking the title Hung-wu, meaning 'mightily martial'.

collapsed. After 1627 a wave of rebellions broke out in the wake of repeated crop failures in the north-west, and much of central and northern China soon came under rebel sway. In 1644, one of the rebel leaders captured Peking and the last Ming emperor committed suicide. Almost immediately the Manchus intervened, seized Peking, and began the conquest of China (page 94).

1300–1699
The Ottoman empire

The overthrow of the Abbasid Caliphate by the Mongols in 1256-60 (page 60) left the Muslim world in disarray for half a century. One of the centres of recovery lay in north-west Anatolia where, around 1300, a Turkish leader named Osman founded a state which became the core of the future Ottoman empire (map 1). The damage to the structure of the Byzantine empire caused by the Fourth Crusade in 1204 (page 48) facilitated the Ottomans' rapid advance in the 14th century. By 1354 the Turks had crossed the Dardanelles to Gallipoli, and their victories at Kosovo (1389) and Nicopolis (1396) left them masters of the Balkans. The invasion of Timur (page 61) and his destruction of the Turkish army at Ankara (1402) gave the hard-pressed Byzantine empire some respite, but the renewal of expansion under Murad II (1413-51) and Mohammed II (1451-81) sealed its fate. In 1453 Constantinople fell, and Mohammed went on to extend control over Moldavia, the Crimea and Trebizond, thereby turning the Black Sea into an Ottoman lake.

Selim I (1512-20) defeated the new Safavid rulers of Persia (page 62) and conquered the Mamlukes, and his son Suleiman the Magnificent (1520-66) annexed much of Hungary and besieged Vienna (1529), making the Ottoman empire one of the

world's largest powers. It now extended over one million square miles, with some 14 million inhabitants; and its capital, Istanbul, had become the largest city in Europe with 500,000 inhabitants. Suleiman's son, Selim II managed to add Cyprus (1570-1) and Tunis (1574), although his fleet of galleys met with defeat at the hands of a Christian coalition at Lepanto (1571). However the wars of his successors against Persia (1578-90 and 1607-39) and against the Austrian Habsburgs (1593-1606) resulted in the loss of the Caucasus to the former and of annual tribute for Hungary from the latter.

The end of expansion, coupled with rapid price inflation (from 1584), a rising population and a static economy provoked a spate of popular and military uprisings between 1596 and 1610 in the Anatolian heartland of the empire (map 2). Nevertheless, Mesopotamia was regained from Persia in the 1630s and Crete conquered from the Venetians in the 1660s; and in 1683 a great army laid siege once more to Vienna. But it failed, and a Christian counter-attack drove the Turks out of Hungary by 1699 – although the Turks still remained a formidable power, controlling the entire Arab world east of Libya and most of the Balkans until the 19th century.

2 The Ottoman empire, 1520–1639

- Ottoman empire, 1520
- Ottoman vassal states, 1520
- conquests of Suleiman I, 1520–66
- ⊙ Ottoman conquest, with date
- ⊡ Ottoman siege, with date
- ✗ major battle
- vassal state under Suleiman I
- expansion of Ottoman empire, 1566–1600
- ○ administrative centres of major beglerbegliks
- → major Ottoman campaigns, 1520–1639
- ↓ revolts against Ottoman rule

TEUTONIC ORDER

LITHUANIA

HOLY ROMAN EMPIRE

POLAND

RUSSIA

Moscow

Danube

Cracow

Kiev

Dniester

Cossack settlements

Vienna (Beç)

Buda

Carpathian Mountains

Suceava

Yaş (Jassy)

Dnieper

KHANATE OF THE CRIMEA

Sava

Zagreb

HUNGARY

TRANSYLVANIA

BOGDAN (MOLDAVIA) 1455

Akkerman (1484)

(vassal 1475)

Azov

Don

BOSNIA

Jajce 1463

1528

Bosna Saray (Sarajevo)

Belgrade

Semendire 1444

EFLÄK (WALLACHIA) 1396

Vidin

BUJAK

Kilia

Bükres (Bucharest)

Bakhchesaray (Bahçesaray)

Kerç

Sea of Azov

CERKES (CIRCASSIA)

VENETIAN REPUBLIC

HERZEGOVINA (1463-83)

SERBIA 1389

Kosovo 1389

Nish

Yergögü (Giurgiu)

Danube

DOBRUJA

Kefe (Caffa)

Dubrovnik

REPUBLIC OF DUBROVNIK Ottoman vassal 1430-1804

Sofia

Filibe (Philippopolis)

BULGARIA 1393

Edirne (Adrianople) 1361

Varna

Black Sea

Caucasus Mountains

Elbasan

Manastir (Bitoli)

M A

Gelibolu (Gallipoli) 1354

Constantinople 1453

Kastamonu

Sinop

Samsun

Trabzon (Trebizond) 1461

Tiflis

Selanik (Salonica) 1430

Bursa 1326

CANDAR (KASTAMONU) 1393 1461

Otranto temporary Ottoman occupation 1480

Corfu

Yenisehir (Larissa)

KARASI 1345

Söğüt 1265

Eskisehir 1289

Ankara 1402

EMPIRE OF TREBIZOND 1461

Amasya

Cephalonia

Aegean Sea

Izmir (Smyrna)

SARUHAN 1390 1405

GERMIYAN 1380 1428

ANATOLIA

SIVAS 1398

Sivas

Erzurum

Otluk-Beli 1473

Zante

Negroponte (Euboea) 1470

to Genoa

MOREA 1460

Athens

AYDIN 1390 1426

HAMID 1381-90

MENTESE 1390 1426

Konya

Kayseri

KARAKOYUNLU

Lake Van

Modon (Ottoman 1500)

Naxos

TEKE 1391 1427

KARAMAN 1390 1468

DHU'L-QADR 1398 1515

AKKOYUNLU

Diyarbakir

Çaldiran 1514

Knights of St John

Rhodes

Adana

Marj Dabiq 1516

Aleppo 1516

Tigris

Mosul

Tabriz 1514

Lake Urmia

Crete

Cyprus (Venetian 1489, Ottoman tributary 1517)

Raqqa

Euphrates

SAFAVID EMPIRE (from 1501)

Tripoli

MAMLUK EMPIRE

Beirut

Damascus 1516

Jerusalem

1 The rise of the Ottoman empire, 1301–1520

- probable extent of Ottoman state, c. 1300
- conquests of Osman, c. 1300–26
- conquests of Orkhan, 1326–62
- conquests of Murad I, 1362–89

TEKE 1390 absorbed Emirates with date of first absorption

- conquests of Bayezid, 1389–1402

✕ major battles

1398 dates of Ottoman control

Venetian territories, 1510

◉ successive centres of Ottoman state, with dates of conquest

reduced frontiers of Ottoman state after Tamerlane's invasion and civil war of 1403–13

● Emirates restored by Tamerlane, 1402

1427 final reincorporation into Ottoman empire

boundary of Ottoman state at the accession of Mehmed II, 1451

vassal states, 1512

Ottoman empire, 1512

western frontiers of Safavid state, c. 1512 including tributary states

Ottoman sphere of influence, c. 1520

The fall of Constantinople, in 1453, came as no surprise to observers in the east. Sultan Mehmet II had managed to close the Bosphorus by building castles at its narrowest point; the city was now cut off from western naval assistance and from its traditional sources of food and supply. When the final siege began, on 6 April, there were only some 7000 Christian defenders facing and Ottoman army of more than 80,000. On 29 May a final assault took the city within a few hours.

Precolumbian America

Two major civilizations confronted the Spaniards when they arrived on the American mainland in the early 16th century: the Aztec Empire in Mexico, with a subject population of perhaps 12 million, and the Inca empire in Peru, ruling some 6 million. The rest of the continent remained sparsely inhabited – perhaps 1 million people lived north of the Rio Grande with another million in the rest of South America – divided among more than a thousand small tribal societies with distinct languages. Few regions, particularly in the north, had reached the stage of settled agriculture, despite some contacts in the north-east with Europeans around the year 1000 (map 1).

The Aztec and Inca Empires differed markedly in character, and no evidence exists of any contact between them. Like the Toltecs, who between 968 and about 1170 controlled much of the valley of Mexico from their capital at Tula, the Aztecs came from the north. In 1325 they arrived in the valley and settled on a group of islands in the swampy margins of Lake Texcoco, where they built their capital,

Tenochtitlán (site of Mexico City). Serving at first as mercenary warriors for neighbouring towns, by 1428 they had overthrown them all and, led by a priest-king and an hereditary warrior aristocracy, embarked upon an ambitious programme of conquest. When the Spaniards arrived in 1519, the Aztecs controlled the greater part of Mexico and had entered Maya territory in Yucatán (map 2).

The Inca formed one of the numerous tribes of Quechua stock inhabiting the central Andes, but until the accession of Pachacuti Inca in 1438 they played only a minor role. Within 45 years, however, Pachacuti's conquests extended Inca control from Lake Titicaca to Huánaco in the north, while his son Topa pushed north into Ecuador and south to Chile, and from the Pacific coast to the Upper Amazon. This created an empire 200 miles wide and 2500 miles long, held together by an impressive system of highways, post-stations and relay runners (map 3).

The Incas created a genuine imperial system, with an hereditary dynasty of absolute, 'divine' Incas, a Quechua aristocracy, and a highly trained bureaucracy. All land was state-owned, with a complex system of irrigation. The ordinary Inca subject spent 9 months working for the state, but in return received protection from

2 The Aztec empire to 1519

- Post-Classic Maya area
- area of Aztec domination, 1519
- → Post-Classic trading routes

famine (through state-owned food stores) and support during sickness and old age. The Aztec Empire, on the other hand, exercised harsh military dominion over vassal peoples who enjoyed political autonomy provided they paid heavy tribute to Tenochtitlán in food, textiles and other goods – increasingly in humans for ritual sacrifice to the Aztec gods (up to 50,000 a year by 1510). These demands help to explain why so many people in the valley of Mexico welcomed the Spaniards, just as a recent succession dispute provided allies for the European invaders in Peru. Although both the Aztec and Inca polities expanded faster than any 15th-century state in Latin Christendom, neither empire proved as stable as it seemed. Mexico fell to a force spearheaded by under 2,000 Europeans in 1519-22, Peru to a band of less than 200 in 1531-3 (see page 86).

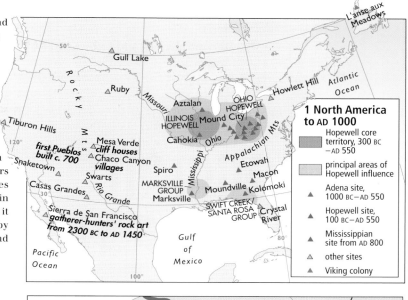

1 North America to AD 1000

Hopewell core territory, 300 BC –AD 550

principal areas of Hopewell influence

▲ Adena site, 1000 BC–AD 550

▲ Hopewell site, 100 BC–AD 550

▲ Mississippian site from AD 800

△ other sites

▲ Viking colony

An Aztec or Mixtec sacrificial knife. The Aztecs believed that the continuation of human society required that the sun and earth be nourished with human blood and hearts. War was necessary to provide the sacrificial victims, whose hearts were removed with knives such as this. It is 12 inches long with an inlaid handle in the form of a warrior costumed as an eagle, or *quauhtli*, which was also a name for the sun.

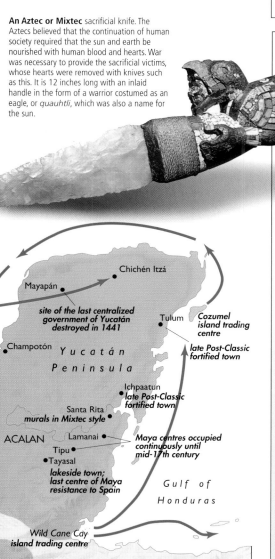

site of the last centralized government of Yucatán destroyed in 1441

Cozumel island trading centre

late Post-Classic fortified town

Yucatán Peninsula

late Post-Classic fortified town

murals in Mixtec style

ACALAN

Maya centres occupied continuously until mid-17th century

lakeside town; last centre of Maya resistance to Spain

Gulf of Honduras

Wild Cane Cay island trading centre

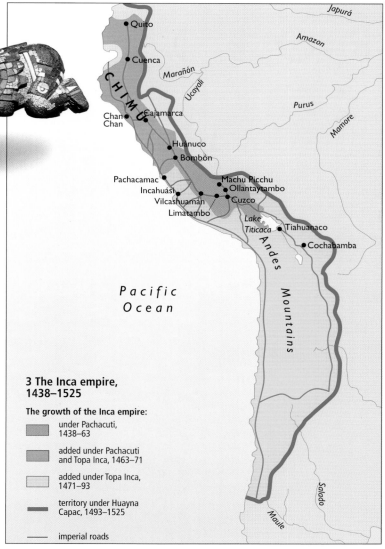

3 The Inca empire, 1438–1525

The growth of the Inca empire:

under Pachacuti, 1438–63

added under Pachacuti and Topa Inca, 1463–71

added under Topa Inca, 1471–93

territory under Huayna Capac, 1493–1525

imperial roads

The world circa 1492

The central feature of world history since the 1490s has been the expansion of Europe and the spread of European civilization throughout the globe. Until then, the world had, on the whole, pressed in on Europe; thereafter the roles became reversed. In the 16th century, however, Europe continued to stand on the periphery of the civilized world, eclipsed by Ming China (the most powerful and advanced state of the period, with over 100 million inhabitants – equal to the whole of Europe) and by the rising Ottoman, Safavid and Mughal empires of the Middle East. Meanwhile Islam won converts in central and South-East Asia, and among the peoples of sub-Saharan Africa.

The total area occupied by the major civilizations, roughly co-terminous with the area of plough cultivation, nevertheless remained relatively small. Almost 80 per cent of the world's surface was inhabited either by food gatherers or herdsmen (as in Australia and most of Siberia, North America and much of Africa) or by hand cultivators (especially in South-East Asia, West Africa and Central and South America). But plough cultivators proved far more productive, and the relatively small area that had been brought under the plough probably supported between two-thirds and three-quarters of the global population (map 1).

Until the 1490s, worldwide racial segregation prevailed. Although Christians and Muslims from all over Eurasia made pilgrimages to their Holy Places in the Middle East, they seldom settled; and although merchants travelled widely across and around Asia, their numbers remained few. In the early 15th century a succession of Chinese voyages, commanded by the Muslim admiral Cheng Ho, secured tribute and extended recognition of the new Ming dynasty; but they led to no lasting interchange of population.

Until the 1490s, therefore, the Negroids remained concentrated in sub-Saharan Africa and a few Pacific islands; the Mongoloids in Asia and the Americas; the Caucasoids in Europe, North Africa, the Middle East and India; and the Australoids in Australia (map 2). By 1800, however, the pattern had fundamentally altered as the result of six inter-continental migrations: from Europe and Africa to the Americas; from northern Europe to Africa and (later) Australasia; from Russia into Siberia; from China to South-East Asia; and from India to Africa, South-East Asia and the Caribbean. By far the greatest change occurred in the Americas, where the native population declined dramatically in the

century following the first contact with the Europeans – in some cases by 90 per cent – to be replaced by Europeans, Africans, and in some parts of Latin America by a mixed race of mestizos (map 2).

Nevertheless, the tempo of change must not be exaggerated. Although in America the Aztec and Inca empires collapsed suddenly in 1521 and 1533 respectively (page 72), elsewhere the political impact of Europe remained limited until the 18th century. China and Japan survived intact, and India kept the Europeans at arm's length for 250 years following the arrival of Vasco da Gama in 1498. There, as in Africa and South-East Asia, the European presence long remained confined largely to trading stations and fortresses along the coast.

1 The economies of the world, c. AD 1500

non-agricultural economies

generalized gathering, hunting and fishing

specialized hunting

agricultural economies

root crops dominant

grain crops dominant

nomadic pastoralism

▲ dromedary □ horse/reindeer ○ cattle

limit of plough cultivation

Cheng-ho's voyages, 1405–33

Arctic Ocean

A S I A

AUSTRALIA

Indian Ocean

A pepper harvest in Malabar. Pepper accounted for over 70 per cent by volume of the world spice trade in the 16th century. The most valuable variety, *piper nigrum*, shown here, was native to India and hard to transplant successfully. Demand from Europe and China spread it to selective parts of the East, but Portuguese efforts to introduce it in Africa and America in the 17th century met with little success.

The cultural influence of Europe was even more negligible: Christianity made little headway, except when imposed by the conquerors (as in the Americas and the Philippines), until it received the backing of western technology in the 19th century.

The comparative fragility of the Aztec and Inca civilizations in the Americas, and of the African kingdoms immediately south of the Sahara, despite their outstanding achievements, may be partially explained, first, by their geographical isolation and relative lack of external stimulus and, second, by their dependence on hand cultivation. After 1492, when all the continents came into direct contact with each other for the first time, many of these non-Eurasian civilizations proved unable to offer more than a feeble resistance to outside aggression. To be sure not until the 19th century, with the opening of the Suez Canal and the construction of the transcontinental railways in North America, Siberia and Africa, did areas that had previously been separate finally blend into a single world economy; but the first stages of global integration were completed in the three centuries following 1492.

2 The Diffusion of races

◻ Mongoloid ◻ Caucasoid ▨ Australoid ▩ Negroid

before 1492

after 1492

NORTHERN EUROPEANS
SOUTHERN EUROPEANS
AFRICAN SLAVES
NORTHERN EUROPEANS
INDIANS
INDIANS
INDIANS
RUSSIANS
CHINESE

THREE

The Rise of the West

Before 1500, civilization had been essentially land-centred, and contacts by sea relatively unimportant; thereafter direct sea contact linked the continents. This resulted not only in the growth of a global system of regions which hitherto had developed in isolation, but in a challenge to the traditional land-centred balance between the civilizations of Eurasia.

Nonetheless, the impact of European expansion should not be exaggerated. To many Europeans, the Ottoman, Mughal and Chinese empires exemplified civilized living. Industrialization put Europe ahead; but the fruits of that process – some of them poisonous – were only garnered in the 19th century. Until then, for all its thrusting novelty, Europe remained closer to its agrarian past than to its industrial future.

Between 1815 and 1914 Europe expanded and inaugurated the process of transformation throughout the world which dethroned agricultural society as it had existed for thousands of years, replacing it with an urban, industrialized, technocratic society.

Marble bust of Louis XIV
by Bernini, 1665

European exploration

In 1480 European shipping remained largely confined to the North Atlantic, the Baltic and the Mediterranean, while the West African coast had been explored cursorily, and only very recently by Europeans; Indian, Persian, and Arab vessels plied the northern Indian Ocean; Chinese and Indonesian junks sailed in the western Pacific, but rarely went beyond Japan, the Philippines and the Indonesian archipelago; and local craft navigated the Caribbean and the coasts of Peru and Ecuador. No shipping used the southern Indian Ocean, the South Atlantic, or the main basin of the Pacific. In the course of the next 150 years, however, European navigators opened all the seas, except in the regions of circumpolar ice and the South Pacific, to European ships. Initially, in the 15th century, two series of voyages sought a sea passage to southern Asia in the hope of initiating direct trade in spices. One series, mounted from Portugal, sailing by a south-eastern route and employing local navigators in the East, eventually reached their declared destinations: the entrance to the Indian Ocean (1488), Malabar (1498), Malacca (1509), and the Moluccas (1512-13). The other series, mounted from Spain and sailing west or south-west, proved less successful in its immediate purpose but more fruitful in incidental discovery: the Spaniards hit upon the West Indies (1492) and the Spanish Main (1498). Eventually they too reached South-East Asia (1521), but by a route too long and arduous for commercial use – for to reach the Pacific they had to circumnavigate an immense land-mass which, although it was initially thought to be a peninsula of Asia, by the 1520s had been recognized as a new world. They immediately began to settle the area (page 72). Taken together, the Spanish and Portuguese discoveries proved that all the oceans of the world, at least in the southern hemisphere, were connected.

For most of the 16th century, by the use and threat of force, the Iberian powers managed to prevent other Europeans from using the connecting passages, except for occasional raids. The third great series of voyages, therefore, mostly by English, French and Dutch navigators, searched for alternative routes to Asia in the northern hemisphere, in the west, northwest, and northeast. Although unsuccessful in their primary purpose, they revealed another continental land-mass with a continuous coast extending from the Caribbean to the Arctic, and opened the way for the European exploration and settlement of eastern North America (page 86).

VOYAGES INTENDED FOR SOUTH ASIA BY SOUTH-EAST ROUTE:

1/Dias 1487–8 (outward) discovered open waters of Cape Agulhas; entered Indian Ocean; reached Great Fish River.

2/Vasco da Gama 1497–8 (outward) made best use of Atlantic winds on way to Cape of Good Hope; reached India, guided by local pilot.

3/Cabral 1500 (outward) second Portuguese voyage to India; landed in Brazil, probably accidentally.

4/First Portuguese voyage to Malacca, 1509.

5/Abreu 1512–3 visited Moluccas.

6/First Portuguese visits to Macao, 1516.

VOYAGES INTENDED FOR CHINA AND SOUTH ASIA BY WEST OR SOUTHWEST ROUTE:

7/Da Mota, Zeimoto and Peixoto 1542–3 Portuguese reach Japan.

8/Columbus 1492–3 (outward and homeward) visited Bahama group, explored north coasts of Cuba and Hispaniola; found best return route.

9/Columbus 1493–4 (outward) explored south coast of Cuba; reported it as peninsula of mainland China.

10/Columbus 1498 (outward) explored Trinidad and Venezuela; recognized coast as mainland.

11/Columbus 1502–4 explored coast of Honduras, Nicaragua and the Isthmus.

12/Ojeda and Vespucci 1499–1500 (outward) reached Guiana coast, failed to round Cape São Roque, followed coast west to Cape de la Vela.

13/Coelho and Vespucci 1501 (outward) followed coast south from Cape São Agostinho to 35°S.

14/Solís 1515 entered River Plate estuary and investigated north bank.

15/Magellan and Elcano 1519-22 discovered Strait of Magellan, crossed Pacific, reached Moluccas via Philippines; first circumnavigation.

16/Saavedra 1527 discovered route from Mexico across Pacific to Moluccas.

17/Urdaneta 1565 found feasible return route Philippines to Mexico in 42°N. using west winds.

18/Schouten and Le Maire 1616 discovered route into Pacific via Le Maire Strait and Cape Horn.

VOYAGES INTENDED FOR ASIA BY NORTHWEST AND NORTHEAST ROUTE:

19/Cabot 1497 (outward) encountered Newfoundland, first sighted by Norsemen 11th C.

20/Corte-Real 1500 visited Greenland.

21/Verazzano 1524 traced east coast of North America from (probably) 34°N. to 47°N.; revealed continental character of North America.

22/Cartier 1534 and 1535 explored Strait of Belle Isle and St Lawrence as far as Montreal.

23/Willoughby and Chancellor 1553 rounded North Cape and reached Archangel.

24/Frobisher 1576 reached Frobisher Bay in Baffin Island, which he took for a 'strait'.

25/Davis 1587 explored west coast of Greenland to the edge of the ice in 72° N.

26/Barents 1596–7 discovered Bear Island and Spitsbergen; wintered in Novaya Zemlya.

27/Hudson 1610 sailed through Hudson Strait to the south extremity of Hudson Bay.

28/Button 1612 explored west coast of Hudson Bay, concluded Bay landlocked on the west.

29/Baffin and Bylot 1616 explored whole coast of Baffin Bay; concluded no navigable northwest. passage existed in that area.

1 Major European voyages of discovery, 1480–1630

→ voyages intended for Southern Asia by southeast route

→ voyages intended for China and south Asia by west or southwest route

→ voyages intended for Asia by northwest and northeast routes

⇨ approximate prevailing winds (shown for the first quarter of the year)

⇨ alternating monsoons

A 17th-century Spanish painting of Columbus's fleet *(below)*. Under the sponsorship of the Spanish monarchs Ferdinand and Isabella, Columbus made his first voyage across the Atlantic in 1492. Making landfall on Haiti, Columbus believed he had found a westward route to Asia. He made three further voyages to the Americas.

European overseas expansion

TIMELINE

1480
Portuguese found and fortify Elmina

1507
Portuguese occupy Mozambique

1510
Portuguese capture Goa

1511
Portuguese capture and occupy Malacca

1515
Portuguese occupy Ormuz

1557
Portuguese established at Macao

1600
English East India Company incorporated

1602
Dutch East India Company incorporated

1619
Dutch East India Company established at Batavia

1652
Dutch settlement at Cape of Good Hope

By 1492, Portugal already possessed several archipelagos in the Atlantic and the Gulf of Guinea, some fortresses in Morocco, and a few trading stations in West Africa (above all the castle at Elmina). In the next half century she established some 50 forts and trading posts around the shores of the Indian Ocean, as well as coastal enclaves in Angola and Brazil. Strategically, the most important bases were Mozambique (1507), a port of call for fleets sailing to India; Goa (1510), headquarters of Portuguese Asia; Malacca (1511), a major market on the strait connecting the Indian Ocean with the South China Sea; and Ormuz (1515), a key entrepôt of the international spice trade. East of Malacca the position of the Portuguese was far more precarious and their activities remained purely commercial. A few bases, some fortified, grew up in the Moluccas; a clandestine settlement developed at Macao on the Chinese mainland after 1557; and from 1580 Jesuit missionaries held a lease on the Japanese port-city of Nagasaki (map 1).

In Africa and Asia the Portuguese generally sought to control trade rather than production; and though they could not eliminate the commerce of others in the Indian Ocean, they forced many ships to use harbours under their control, and extorted tolls or duties from the rest. The Spaniards in the Americas, by contrast, embarked on a deliberate policy of conquest and colonization: from the 1490s in the Caribbean islands; from the 1520s in Mexico; from the 1530s in Peru; and from the 1570s in the Philippines.

Few dared to challenge the Iberian monopoly – apparently enhanced by the union of Portugal and Spain in 1580 – before the 17th century. However, the

2 Commercial expansion to the East, c. 1600–1700

- places under Dutch control
- places under English control
- places under French control
- places under Portuguese control
- areas under Portuguese control

trade routes
→ Dutch
→ English
→ French
→ Portuguese

Manila to Acapulco with silk

MEXICO

Charcas

Havana

San Agostín

Santo Domingo

to Nombre de Dios via Canary Is.

Havana to Seville via Azores

Seville to Veracruz via Canary Is.

North Atlantic Ocean

Azores

proximate position of Tordesillas demarcation line

Cape Verde Islands

Elmina to W. Indies with slaves

BRAZIL

Olinda

mbuco

Recife

Bahia

Elmina to Bahia with slaves

Luanda to Bahia with slaves

Bahia to Luanda with tobacco and sugar

South Atlantic Ocean

1 Spanish and Portuguese trade and settlement by c. 1600

principal Portuguese trade routes

principal Spanish trade routes

areas under effective Portuguese control

areas under effective Spanish control

Portuguese-controlled towns

Spanish-controlled towns

seat of Audiencia (Spanish admintraive division)

Manila galleons with silk

Manila galleons with silver

Sea of Japan

JAPAN

Nagasaki

CHINA

Canton

Macao

Lisbon

Seville

Canary Islands

Alexandria

Cairo

Ormuz

Diu

Hooghly

INDIA

Goa

Calicut

Cochin

Ceylon

Colombo

Maldives

Arabian Sea

Red Sea

Laccadive Islands

AFRICA

Bab el Mandeb

Aden

Elmina

Guato

Gulf of Guinea

São Tomé

Luanda

ANGOLA

Malindi

Mombasa

Pemba

Zanzibar

Kilwa

Mozambique

Sofala

Madagascar

Réunion

Indian Ocean

Luzon

Philippines

South China Sea

Manila

Cebu

Ternate

Moluccas

Spice Islands

Ambano

Timor

Malay Archipelago

Borneo

Celebes

Malacca

Sumatra

Java

Lisbon to Goa (alternative route, second half of year)

CONQVISTA
CORTALE·LA·CAVESA·A
ATAGVALDA·INGA·VMATACVCHV

foundation of East India Companies by the Dutch, the English and (later) the French brought the Portuguese under increasing attack. Dutch forces first established independent bases in the East (above all at Batavia, the heavily fortified headquarters of the Dutch East India Company) and then between 1640 and 1660 wrested Malacca, Ceylon, most South Indian ports and the lucrative Japan trade from the Portuguese. In 1652 they also created a useful south African base on the route to the East at Cape Town. The English and French also established modest settlements in India, and developed a promising trade with China. Even the Spaniards undermined the Portuguese, exporting Chinese goods after 1572 through their colony in the Philippines (map 2). Elsewhere in Asia, however, Europeans during this period traded in competition with local merchants on terms laid down by local rulers, and their efforts constituted but a fraction of Asia's total commerce.

The murder of Atahuallpa *(right)* in November 1532 set the seal on Spain's conquest of the Inca empire. Although there were perhaps only 180 Europeans in Peru, most of them young men in their twenties, their brutal murder of the 'divine Inca' broke the resistance of the Peruvian peoples. This vigorous illustration of the deed comes from the *Royal Commentaries* published between 1609 and 1616 by Garcilaso de la Vega, the son of a conquistador and an Inca princess

The expansion of France

In 1415 English troops invaded France and by 1429 had established suzerainty over almost half the kingdom. In the 1440s, however, with the aid of a powerful artillery train, Charles VII (1422-61) began a rapid reconquest which by 1453 had expelled the English from all but the port-city of Calais, and doubled the size of the royal domain. His successors annexed Burgundy (1477), Brittany (1491) and Bourbon (1527) by force, and inherited Anjou and Provence (1481). Several other semi-independent fiefs came to the crown at the accession of Louis XII (1498), Francis I (1515) and Henry IV (1589) (map 1).

After Henry's death in 1610, continuing religious division, costly foreign wars and aristocratic faction, culminating in the Fronde revolt (1648-53), brought France to the brink of dissolution again. However Henry's grandson Louis XIV (1643-1715) restored order and made France the dominant state of Europe. During the relatively peaceful years between 1659 and 1672 the king and his ministers struggled to develop the French economy (agriculture, manufacture and trade), to extend overseas possessions, and to expand the army and navy. They also developed commercial harbours and sponsored public works, such as the Languedoc Canal connecting the Atlantic and the Mediterranean. The richness of resources available to the French, including a population of perhaps 20 million (the largest of any 17th-century European state), undoubtedly played a part in these achievements; but so did the ceaseless efforts, directives, and resources emanating from the Court (map 2).

Despite France's gains at the peaces of Westphalia (1648) and the Pyrenees (1659), Louis still feared Habsburg encirclement (page 92). He sought both to secure territories that might plug the gaps in his frontier (in wars fought in 1667-8 and 1672-8 which brought the acquisition of territory from the Spanish Netherlands and of Franche-Comté), and to erect an 'iron frontier' of state-of-the-art fortresses, thickest on the ground in the north and east, to create a defence in depth that would prevent any enemy forces from penetrating to the heart of the realm as the English and the Habsburgs had done in the past. Perhaps his success in this endeavour made him too bold, for in 1700 he accepted the will of the childless Spanish Habsburg Carlos II which bequeathed to Louis's grandson Philip the entire Spanish empire – Spain, Spanish America, the South Netherlands and half of Italy – even though he knew this sudden concentration of territory in the hands of the Bourbon dynasty would provoke a general European war. After some initial French victories (1702-3), followed by a string of searing defeats (1704-9), the 'iron frontier' showed its worth and forced France's exhausted enemies to conclude the compromise peaces of Utrecht (1713) and Rastatt (1714), by which Philip retained Spain and Spanish

1 The reunification of France 1440–1589

- lands recognizing English suzerainty, 1429
- frontier of France, 1492
- Royal domain, c. 1475
- lands annexed from Burgundy, 1477
- lands of René of Anjou, annexed 1481
- lands of Duke of Brittany, annexed 1491
- lands brought to the crown by Louis XII, 1498
- lands brought to the crown by Francis I, 1515
- lands of Duke of Bourbon, annexed 1527
- lands brought to the crown by Henry IV, 1589
- other fiefs annexed, with date
- fiefs still independent at the end of the 16th century

Calais *1558*
ARTOIS *(lost 1493)*
ST POL *1477*
BAR *1477*
PICARDY
NORMANDY
BRITTANY
ALENÇON *1525*
PERCHE *1483*
VALOIS
RETHEL
Verdun
CHAMPAGNE *1552* Metz
BAR *1552*
Toul *1552*
MAINE
ORLÉANAIS
VENDÔME
NEMOURS *1503*
ANJOU
BLOIS
TOURAINE
BERRY
NEVERS
POITOU
LA MARCHE
BOURBON
BURGUNDY
CHAROLAIS
Habsburg possession from 1493
ANGOULÊME
FOREZ
LIMOGES
PÉRIGORD
AUVERGNE
DAUPHINÉ
ALBRET
GUYENNE
ROUERGUE
COMTAT VENAISSIN *papal state*
GASCONY
ARMAGNAC
BÉARN BIGORRE
ASTARAC
COMMINGES
LANGUEDOC
PROVENCE

In the vast palace of Versailles, seen in the background behind Jean-Baptiste Tuby's bronze sculpture of Apollo rising from the waters *(right)*, Louis XIV directed the fortunes of France. The complex served as the king's court, the centre of his government and a source of inspiration – and envy – to monarchs throughout Europe.

America, while Savoy, Britain and the Austrian Habsburgs partitioned the rest (map 3).

Louis had thus secured the integrity of France's frontiers, and ended for ever the threat of Habsburg encirclement; but the ruinous cost of his wars created a legacy of financial disorder and internal discontent which served to hamstring his successors. Although Louis XV (1715–74) managed to incorporate Lorraine in 1766, and his successor Louis XVI (1774–93) assisted the successful rebellion of the American colonies against Great Britain (page 104), both monarchs sacrificed (as Louis XIV had done) France's overseas possessions and accumulated such monstrous public debts that, in 1789, the government summoned a representative assembly, the States-General, to solve the financial crisis. In doing so, it unleashed revolution (page 116).

2 Administrative units and defensive fortifications

—— frontier of France 1713–14

—— administrative units of Louis XIV's reign, the *généralités* (generalities)

◉ seat of *intendants*, Louis XIV's royal commissioners

⊕ *parlement* (law courts)

ALSACE *pays d'état*

defence:

◼ fortifications (the so-called *barrière* or *frontière de fer*)

▣ fortifications built by Vauban but ceded during the reign of Louis XIV

⚓ galley port

⊞ naval port

economic:

‡ commercial harbours

major manufactures:

▤ brandy   🍶 pottery
◇ cloth   ⌐ printing
□ glass   ▤ salt
⊟ iron   ▦ silk
◗ madder   ◈ soap
   dye
▱ paper   ⊠ tapestry
                  and carpets
              ▼ wine

3 The War of the Spanish Succession, 1701–14

✕ Allied victory
✕ Bourbon (French) victory
✕ inconclusive

principal territorial changes

▨ to Spanish House of Bourbon
▨ to Great Britain
▨ to Austria
▨ to Savoy
▨ to France
▨ to Prussia

Russian expansion in Europe and Asia

After the Mongol invasion of the 13th century (page 60), the lands which had formed part of Kievan Russia fragmented. Lithuania expanded in the west, while the east and south became subject to Mongol overlords, in whose service the principality of Muscovy rose to prominence. Ivan III (1462-1505) opened another phase of expansion: in 1478 he annexed the city republic of Novgorod and in 1480 proclaimed independence from the Mongols. In 1510 his son Vassily (1505-33) overran the republic of Pskov, bringing Muscovite control close to the Baltic; and his grandson Ivan IV (1533-84) conquered the Tatar states of Kazan (1552) and Astrakhan (1556), gaining control of the Volga down to the Caspian Sea (map 1). In addition, from the 1580s, the lucrative fur trade lured enterprising Russians deep into Siberia. Crossing the Urals, they followed the River Ob until they came within portage of the Yenisey, where they built and fortified Turukhansk (1607); thence they reached the Lena river system, where they built Yakutsk (1632), and finally the Pacific, where they built Okhotsk (1649) – some 6,000 miles (9,700km) east of Moscow (map 2).

However Ivan IV failed to realise his principal territorial ambition, the acquisition of Livonia and direct access to the Baltic, while his attempt to break the power of the traditional nobility by creating a 'private domain' (the *oprichnina*) around Moscow resulted in massive depopulation. Muscovy was also still not entirely safe from the Crimean Tatars, who sacked Moscow in 1571. Then succession disputes following the extinction of the old Muscovite ruling house (the 'Time of Troubles', 1598-1613) caused the loss of much territory to Poland and Sweden.

Recovery came only in the mid-17th century, when a successful war with Poland (1654-67) brought substantial gains, including Smolensk and the Ukraine. Meanwhile the settlement of Siberia continued: 23,000 Russians lived there by 1622, 105,000 by 1662 and 230,000 by 1709. However the Amur Basin, acquired in the 1650s, had to be ceded to China in 1689 (albeit in return for useful trading concessions: map 2) and attempts to force access to the Black Sea failed. Instead, Peter I ('the Great', 1682-1725) concentrated on achieving a 'window on the west', wresting Estonia and Livonia from Sweden in 1721, acquiring the ancient port of Riga and founding the new one of St Petersburg (1703). Peter's successors reverted to his policy of expansion on the Black Sea. Catherine II ('the Great', 1762-96) annexed the Tatar khanate of the Crimea. She also acquired large parts of Poland – although the cost of her campaigns, on top of the oppressive social system which required serfs to spend almost all their time labouring on their lords' lands, provoked a major peasant uprising under Emelyan Pugachev (1773-5). The period 1772 to 1815 saw the Russian land frontier expand 600 miles (970 km) at the expense of Poland. Finally, despite a French invasion which reached Moscow in 1812, the Congress of Vienna in 1815 confirmed Russia's acquisition of Finland, Poland, Bessarabia and Transcaucasia (page 116).

The population ruled from Moscow had grown, both by territorial acquisition and by natural increase, from some 10 miilion in 1600, to over 15 million in 1725 and to almost 43 million in 1812, and the empire – the largest in the world – now stretched over 11 of the world's 24 time-zones.

2 Russian expansion in Siberia, 1581–1800

Russian territory in 1581
territory added 1581–98
territory added 1598–1618
territory added 1618–89
territory added in 1650s; returned to China 1689
territory added 1689–1725
territory added 1725–62
territory added 1762–1800

● Bratsk forts and trading posts
1630 (with date of foundation)

1 From Muscovy to Russia, 1462–1815

— boundary of all Russian territories in 1462
— Lithuania, 1462
1783 date of foundation of new town
KALMYKS native peoples

the expansion of Muscovy:
Moscow territory at end of 13th century
1478 date of acquisition by Muscovy
acquisitions to 1462
acquisitions under Ivan III, 1462–1505
acquisitions during 16th century

acquisitions during 17th century
acquisitions during 18th century
acquisitions, 1801–15
— territory ceded to Sweden 1617 and Poland-Lithuania, 1618
acquired from Poland-Lithuania, 1634
acquired from Poland-Lithuania, 1667

BARENTS SEA

PECHORA

Pechora

Obdorsk 1595
Berezov 1593
1501
YUGRA
1478

Mezen

Archangel 1584
Kholmogory
Onega
NOVGOROD TERRITORY

Solvychegodsk
Ustyug
Kama 1472
Solikamsk

FINLAND 1809
1743
Áland Islands
Ábo
Helsingfors 1721
Vyborg
Lake Ladoga
1478
Lake Onega
Kargopol
1478
1393–1425

Stockholm
Kronstadt 1704
St. Petersburg 1703
Narva 1703
1362–89
Vologda
Soligalich
1364
Galich
Vyatka
Perm 1724
Nizhniy Tagil 1724
Kungur 1724
Yekaterinburg 1725

SWEDEN
Revel
ESTONIA 1721
Novgorod
1389–1425
1364
Kostroma
Yaroslavl
1451
1489
UDMURTY
Ufa 1586
SIBERIA

BALTIC SEA
LIVONIA 1510
Pskov 1478
1389–1425
Tver
1302
Vladimir
1364
Nizhniy Novgorod
1393–45
MARI
KHANATE OF KAZAN
Kazan

Memel
Riga
COURLAND
1772
1503 Velikiye Luki
1514–21
1494
Mozhaysk
Dmitrov
Moscow
1364
Murom
Arzamas
CHUVASHI

Königsberg
Danzig
LITHUANIA
Polotsk
Vitebsk
Smolensk 1514
Vyazma
1353–59
1634 1494
1301 Kolomna
Ryazan
1393
1552
Simbirsk 1648
MESHCHERA
MORDVA
Penza 1650
Syzran 1683
Samara 1586
Orenburg 1743

Vilna
Kovno
Minsk
Mogilev 1772
1425–62
Tula
1521
Yelets 1586
Don
Tambov 1636
Saratov 1590
Ural

Grodno
Bialystok 1795
Brest-Litovsk
Pinsk
1793
Bryansk
Orel 1564
Kursk 1586
Voronezh 1586
Kamyshin
NOGAI TATARS

Vistula
Warsaw 1807
POLAND
Kalisz 1815
Lublin
Gomel 1503
Chernigov
1503 1586
1634
Belgorod 1593
Volga
Tsaritsyn 1589
KHANATE OF ASTRAKHAN
KALMYKS
Guryev 1645

Lwów
Novograd-Volynskiy
Kiev
Pereyaslav
1667
Poltava 1709
Kharkov 1654
Donets
DON COSSACKS
Don
1556
Astrakhan

AUSTRO-HUNGARIAN EMPIRE
Debrecen
Kolozsvár
TRANSYLVANIA
Brassó
Vinnitsa
Kamenets
Bratslav
ZAPOROZHYE
Yekaterinoslav (Kodak) 1786
Sech
1739
Cherkassk
Kuma
KALMYKS

Jassy
Kishinev 1791
Ochakov
Odessa 1794
Akkerman
BESSARABIA 1812
MOLDAVIA
Nikolayev 1789
Kherson 1774
1774
Taganrog 1783
Azov
1783
KUBAN COSSACKS
Stavropol

WALLACHIA
Bucharest
Ruschuk
Danube
KHANATE OF CRIMEA
Yevpatoriya
Bakhchisaray
Sebastopol 1783
Simferopol (Ak-Mechet) 1784
Karasubazan
Feodosiya (Kaffa)
Kerch
Yekaterinodar 1792
Pyatigorsk
Terek
Vladikavkaz 1784
DAGHESTAN
Derbent
CASPIAN SEA

OTTOMAN EMPIRE
Sofia
Varna
BLACK SEA
Sukhum-Kale 1810
Poti 1804
Kutaisi
1806
GEORGIA 1806
AZERBAIJAN 1805
Tiflis 1806
Caucasus
Kura
Baku 1806
1813

Erivan

PERSIA

ceded temporarily by Persia, 1723–32

Russian woodcut showing a procession of merchants carrying furs at the court of the Holy Roman Emperor c. 1570. In the early 17th century the demand for luxury furs fuelled expansion eastwards into Siberia to tap its seemingly inexhaustible supply.

The Americas

The daring conquest of Mexico by Hernán Cortés in 1519-21 and of Peru by Francisco Pizarro in 1531-3 (page 73) laid the foundations of a huge Spanish colonial empire in the Americas. By 1535, when the crown established viceregal government in Mexico and Lima became the capital of Peru, all the major centres of indigenous population in the former Aztec and Inca empires lay in Spanish hands: an area four times the size, and containing eight times the population, of the country from which the conquerors had come. Although the frontiers of colonial settlement continued to advance – with new viceroyalties in New Granada (1739) and Rio de la Plata (1776) and new military governments in Texas (1718) and California (1767) – none of these later, sparsely inhabited conquests compared with Mexico and Peru in wealth and importance. Potosí in Peru and Zacatecas in Mexico became the largest producers of silver in the world, and by 1560 silver formed America's principal export to Europe.

Elsewhere on the continent colonization proved slower. The Portuguese only settled the Atlantic coast of south America after 1549 for fear that the French might do so. By 1600, although coastal Brazil had become studded with profitable sugar plantations and mills, worked by slaves from Africa, the Brazilian interior remained the domain of native Indian tribes until the 1690s, when the discovery of enormous gold deposits in the interior provoked a new wave of colonization. In the north-west, Russian explorers and traders pressed on; but by 1819 only 19 settlements existed between the Aleutian islands and California (map 1).

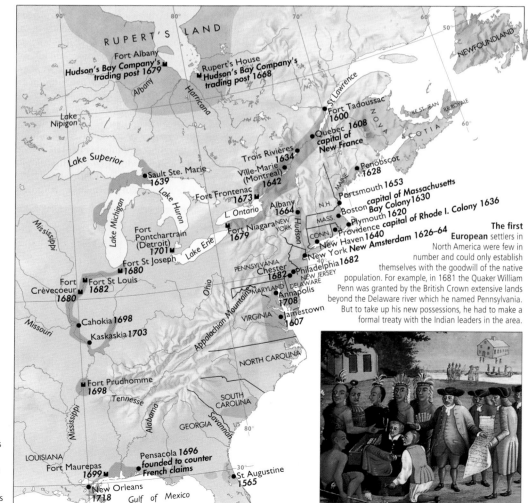

The first European settlers in North America were few in number and could only establish themselves with the goodwill of the native population. For example, in 1681 the Quaker William Penn was granted by the British Crown extensive lands beyond the Delaware river which he named Pennsylvania. But to take up his new possessions, he had to make a formal treaty with the Indian leaders in the area.

2 European settlement in North America

- early English settlements and claims
- early French settlements and claims
- early Spanish settlements

The Atlantic seaboard of north America, with its harsher climate and poor soil, also at first attracted few Europeans (who came mostly for fish and furs). Settlement only began with the foundation of Acadia (Nova Scotia) by the French in 1604, of Virginia (1607) and Massachusetts Bay (1620) by the English, and of New Amsterdam (later New York) by the Dutch (1624). Gradually, however, the Europeans pressed inland: the French advanced down the St Lawrence and (after 1682) the Mississippi, creating a chain of fortified posts all the way to the Gulf of Mexico and founding New Orleans in 1718; the English spread out around the rich fur-hunting grounds of Hudson Bay. Wars between the European states now regularly involved the Americas, with England gaining first the Dutch colonies along the Hudson (1664) and then French Canada (1763). By 1700, perhaps 250,000 Europeans lived in North America, but by 1820 that number had soared to 9 million (compared with just over 3 million in Spanish America).

The Spaniards in America relied from the first on Indian labour, both in ranching and mining, and readily intermarried; hence an extensive mestizo population developed, especially in Mexico and Peru. The British, however, who wanted land for farms and plantations, expelled or exterminated the native population: by 1820, only 600,000 lived in the English speaking areas (compared with 7.5 million in Spanish America). Instead, in Virginia, and then later in the Carolinas, where tobacco was introduced as a cash-crop, African slaves were imported to work on the plantations (like those of the sugar producers of Brazil and the Caribbean islands). By 1820, almost 2 million Africans lived in north America (compared with 800,000 in Spanish America).

Throughout the period, each mother country maintained a tight grip on its colonies. The colonists tolerated this as long as they felt insecure – whether from the threat of native uprisings or through the series of wars between the mother countries. Britain's resounding victory over France in 1763, however, brought total security to her American colonies, whose elites soon came to resent the continuing tax demands of the government in London. In 1776 they demanded their independence (page 98) and the colonies of Latin America followed suit after 1808. (page 112).

1 Colonial America

- British-claimed territory to 1763
- French-claimed territory to 1763
- Spanish territory, 1650
- ceded by France to Britain, 1763
- ceded by France to Spain, 1763
- additional Spanish territory by 1775
- Portuguese territory, 1650
- Portuguese territory, 1775
- Dutch territory, 1630
- Dutch territory, 1775
- Russian territory, c. 1775
- Jesuit missions, with date of foundation
- The United States from 1783

colonization routes
- Spanish
- Portuguese
- British
- Russian
- French
- major exports
- viceroyalty borders, 1800 (with date of foundation)

South-east Asia and Japan

In 1603 the Japanese emperor conferred the title of Shogun (military leader) on Tokugawa Ieyasu, who had established control over the state re-unified in the 1590s (page 68). The Tokugawa dynasty exercised power until 1868, giving Japan a prolonged period of political stability. A complex system of government emerged in which the shoguns in Edo (modern Tokyo) dominated or regulated the 250 or so fiefs of the feudal lords, organized society in a hierarchy of classes, and enacted a comprehensive legal code. From 1612 they banned the Christian missionaries (active in many areas since the mid-16th century) and persecuted their adherents. They also forbade all Japanese to travel abroad; limited foreign contacts to the Dutch (who maintained a trading post at Nagasaki), the Chinese and the Koreans; and until 1853 successfully repulsed various attempts by the Russians, British, French and Americans to open trade (map 1). Yet despite this isolation, Tokugawa Japan prospered: trade and cities grew rapidly; the population rose from 20 to 30 million; high literacy rates prevailed; industry and credit spread widely. By the mid-19th century, Japan was far better prepared than any other part of Asia to meet the challenge of Western expansion (page 122).

Initially, however, Western traders showed far more interest in the spices of South-East Asia. The disintegration of the empires of Srivijaya and Majapahit (page 64) left behind scores of petty states with little cohesion, opening the way to Portuguese acquisition of Malacca (1511) and footholds in the Moluccas (page 80). Their presence at first changed little: in Asia they aimed to dominate the spice trade

through a chain of fortified stations, linked by naval power, not to acquire territory. The arrival of the Dutch and then the English after 1595 (page 80) did not initially change this, for they too sought primarily to monopolize the spice trade, and even after the establishment of a fortress at Batavia (1619) the Dutch directed most of their territorial ambitions towards acquiring Portuguese and English bases, rather than to conquering native states. The only substantial European colony in the area remained the Philippines, where the Spanish authorities began to foster the cultivation of tobacco, sugar, hemp and other commercial products from the later 18th century (map 2).

The mainland monarchies of Southeast Asia – Arakan, Burma, Siam, Cambodia, Luang Prabang and Annam – had little direct involvement in European trade, and concentrated instead on extending their power at the expense of their neighbours. Over the period as a whole, Annam (Vietnam) and Siam expanded at the expense of Luang Prabang (Laos) and Cambodia. Burma almost disintegrated after the Mons rebelled in 1740, set up a king of their own at Pegu, and in 1752 captured the Burmese capital of Ava. However a charismatic leader, Alaungpaya (1735-60), defeated the Mons and established Rangoon as the southern port of a reunited Burma (1755), while his successors invaded Siam (1767) and conquered Arakan (1785).

Two factors complicated state-building in the area: the constant pressure of the hill peoples of the interior (like the Mons), always eager to assert their independence, and the steadily increasing interference of the Europeans. A group of Iberian adventurers temporarily seized power

Daimyo and their retinues enter Edo castle to participate in one of the many courtly ceremonials *(right)*. Edo, now Tokyo, was originally a fishing village, near which a castle was built in 1456. It rapidly became a powerful centre and in 1590 Tokugawa Ieyasu selected Edo for his residence, building an elaborate castle which remained the seat of the shogunate for 260 years, although it became the capital only in the 19th century.

1 Japan in isolation

- — provincial borders
- ═══ Five Highways
- ━━━ extensions to the Five Highways
- — secondary roads
- — sea routes
- ● important castle towns

feudal territories:
- major Tokugawa domains
- → American, Russian, British and other naval visits

CHINA

SAM

Noga Hills
Mogaung • Myitkyina
• Imphal
ANIPUR
Tagaung
• Bhamo
YUN-NAN

BURMA
Shwebo • Mandalay
Ava • Amarapura
Chin Hills
SHAN
STATES
naf
Myohaung
KARENNI
STATE
Magwe
An Pass
Thayetmyo
Prome • Toungoo
Lamphun
Lampang
Sawankhalok
Pegu
Thaton • Sukhothai
Bassein
Rangoon
from 1755
Syriam
to 1755
MONS
Tavoy
Moulmein
Mergui
Mergui
Archipelago
Madaman Is.

TONGKING
Hanoi • Bac Ninh
• Haiphong
Thanh Hoa
Chiang Saen
Luang
Prabang
Chiang Rai
Chiengmai
• Vientiane
Ha Tinh
Porte d'Annam
Hue
Tourane **French from 1787**
SIAM
Lopi Buri • Korat
Champassak
Ayutthaya
Stung Treng
Binh Dinh
Bangkok
Sisophon
Qui Nhon
Thon Buri
Angkor
CAMBODIA
Battambang
Kratie
Kompong Cham
Nha Trang
Chanthaburi
Phnom Penh
Saigon
**COCHIN
CHINA**
Kampot
Ha Tien
Chau
Doc
Cho Lon
Bien Hoa

Canton
Macao

Hainan

to Japan
to Japan
to Acapulco

FORMOSA
*Spanish colonies in
north Taiwan, 1626–37;
Dutch in southwest
Taiwan, 1624–61*

*Pacific
Ocean*

20°

*from
Canton
to all
major
S.E. Asian
ports*

Luzon

PHILIPPINES
• Manila

from Acapulco

*South China
Sea*

10°

Nakhon Si Thammarat
Trang
Phuket
Songkhla
Pattani

Penang
British from 1786

MALAYA

Malacca
**Portuguese 1511–1641
Dutch 1641–1826**

Singapore
British from 1819

Tiku
Fort de Kock
(Bukit Tinggi)
Padang
Painan

Djambi

Bangka
Palembang

Benkulen

Sukadana

Bantam
Batavia
(Jakarta)

Pontianak

Brunei

Balambangan

Sulu Sea

Sulu Archipelago

SARAWAK

Borneo

Karimata Strait

Billiton

Java Sea

Bandjarmasin

Strait of Macasser

Macassar

Celebes

Manado

Tidore

Halmaher

*Mola ccas
(Spice Islands)*

Buru

Ceram

Amboina

Banda Is.

Banda Sea

MATARAM
Surabaya
Jogjakarta
Bali

Sumbawa

Lombok

Flores

Timor

Sumba

10°

*Indian
Ocean*

**2 The Europeans
in southeast Asia**
European possessions, 1826
▢ British   ▢ Spanish
▢ Dutch   ▢ Portuguese

trade routes:
→ developed by Dutch and
   English East India Companies
→ developed by Arab and Gujerati traders
→ developed by the Dutch in the 17th cen
→ used by English shipping from 1786
→ used by the 'Manila Galleon'
— local trade routes
⊙ principal trading centre

Vietnamese expansion
▬ Vietnamese border, 1500
— expansion to 1611
▬ acquisitions from
   Cambodia in early
   18th century
→ Vietnamese expansion
   in 19th century
— kingdom of Luang
   Prabang, 1707
▨ area which broke away
   under Vientiane in 1707
→ Burmese conquests
→ Siamese conquests

in Cambodia in the 1590s; the French briefly
garrisoned some Siamese strongholds in the 1680s;
both the French and English East India Companies
intervened in Burma in the 1750s. Meanwhile, the
Dutch began to extend their control over Java and the
Spice Islands, and at the same time the British established their base at Penang (1786) and a free trade
port at Singapore (1819) on the Malayan peninsula.

These acquisitions led to tension between the
two colonial powers, which only abated after a treaty
in 1824 obliged the British to withdraw from Sumatra

and the Dutch from Malacca. Secure in the east, the
British now turned on Burma and, after a short war
(1824-6), annexed Arakan, Assam and Tenasserim.
The future Dutch and British colonial empires in
Southeast Asia were taking shape, but their control
remained loose and indirect. Only after the industrial
revolution, and the expanding demand for raw
materials at home, did the Europeans seriously
impinge upon the lives and fortunes of the peoples of
the region.

1517–1650
The Reformation and Catholic Reformation

Of the 250,000 or so works printed in Europe between 1447 and 1600, about 75 per cent concerned religion. The Reformation and the Catholic response would have been impossible without printing presses like this one (below), from the cover of a book printed in Frankfurt in the early 17th century.

The shattering of the unity of Latin Christendom altered the course of European history. The fall of Constantinople (page 48) allowed the Roman church to ignore the Orthodox areas; and, except in Bohemia and Moravia, heresy scarcely existed in the West. Complacent, the Papacy failed to deploy its immense wealth adequately, producing widespread pluralism and absenteeism; this, coupled with the materialism of the hierarchy, discredited the Western church in the eyes of many Christians. Some, like Erasmus of Rotterdam (1466-1536) and Thomas More (1478-1535), hoped for spiritual renewal within the church; but in Saxony Martin Luther (1483-1546) criticized clerical abuse and in 1520 called upon the German nobility to reform the church. Meanwhile, inspired by Huldreych Zwingli (1484-1531), the magistrates of the Swiss canton of Zürich renounced allegiance to Rome.

These successful protests sparked others. By 1560, seven out of every ten inhabitants of the Holy Roman Empire no longer accepted papal authority, and Protestantism (as the dissident creeds became known) also prevailed in Scandinavia, the Baltic lands, and England. Further defections from Rome came through the teaching of John Calvin (1509-64) in Geneva. Calvinism made rapid progress in France, Poland, Hungary and Scotland (where it became the official creed after 1560).

In addition, a number of more radical sects sprang up, called 'Anabaptists' by their enemies because of their belief that only adult baptism was valid. They rejected ritual, spiritual and temporal authority, and many social conventions in favour of Biblical simplicity. Many combined evangelism with social protest, and participated both in the major rising of the German peasantry in 1524-5 and in the radical government of the city of Münster in 1534-5. Both movements were brutally repressed and Anabaptism, where it survived, became a secret, separate creed.

Eventually the Catholic church reformed itself. The Council of Trent (three sessions 1545-63) condemned abuses, defined doctrine, and created a more effective and educated clergy; at the same time new religious orders (most notably the Jesuits, incorporated in 1540) targeted key areas for reconversion. By 1650 the Protestants had been expelled from Bavaria (1579), Austria (1597) and Bohemia (1628), and the number of Protestant churches in Poland had declined from 560 in 1572 to 240 in 1650. Spain eradicated its small Protestant minorities, and in 1609 expelled its substantial Moorish population. In the Holy Roman Empire, however, the Protestants fought back, provoking the savage religious conflict known as the Thirty Years' War (page 92).

1 Religious divisions in 1570

Roman Catholic	Lutheran	Islam
Orthodox	Calvinist	Anglican
Greek Catholic (Uniate)	Anabaptist	Hussite

SCOTLAND
1560
●gow
● Edinburgh

● York
Chester
ENGLAND
1
● Oxford
tol
● London

NORWAY
(Danish)
● Bergen
● Christiania
■ 1539

North
Sea

ICELAND
■ 1552
60

SWEDEN
● Åbo ■ 1528
● Helsingfors
■ 1527
● Stockholm

Reval
■ 1524
ESTONIA
RUSSIA
● Pskov

● 1561
Riga ■ 1524
LIVONIA
COURLAND
● Dünaburg

● Vilna
LITHUANIA
● Minsk

Königsberg
■ 1523
PRUSSIA
■ 1525

POLAND
● Warsaw
● Poznán
2

DENMARK
● Aarhus
● Copenhagen
● Malmö
Baltic Sea

SLESVIG ■ 1536
■ 1542
HOLSTEIN ■ 1542
Emden ■ 1526
■ 1542
■ 1529
Lübeck ■ 1531
Hamburg ■ 1549
■ 1548
● Stettin
POMERANIA ■ 1534
● Danzig

Bremen ■ 1525
BRUNSWICK ■ 1545
LÜNEBURG
Hannover
■ 1539
BRANDENBURG
● Berlin
Magdeburg ■ 1525
Wittenberg ■ 1522
Leipzig
NASSAU ■ 1528
ELEC. OF Dresden
■ 1539
SAXONY ■ 1525
DUCHY OF
SAXONY

Vistula

Breslau ■ 1524
SILESIA
Oder

● Cracow
● Lwów

NETHERLANDS
● Amsterdam
2
● Brussels
Mons ●
Cologne ●
Münster
HESSE ■ 1524
Frankfurt ■ 1530
PALATINATE ■ 1546
Metz ■ 1559
Nuremberg ■ 1528
WÜRTTEMBERG ■ 1534
Strassburg ■ 1524
Ulm ■ 1530
Munich ●
Rhine

Rouen ●
Rheims ●
Paris ●
FRANCE
Seine
Orléans ●
Tours ●
Loire
FRANCHE-
COMTÉ
Dijon ●
NEUCHÂTEL ▲ 1530
Limoges ●
26
Lyons ●

MORAVIA
Brünn ●
Prague ●
BOHEMIA
■ 1524
Elbe

Danube
Salzburg ●
AUSTRIA
2
Vienna ●
Pozsony

HUNGARY
2
● Buda
Kassa ●
Eger ●
Debrecen ●
● Kolozsvár
MOLDAVIA
● Jassy
Dniester

Graz ●
Pécs ●
Szeged ●
Temesvár ●
TRANSYLVANIA
● Brassó

WALLACHIA
● Bucharest
● Ruschuk
Danube

BASLE ■ 1523
Zürich ▲ 1524
■ 1528 ▲ 1524 THURGAU
Berne ▲ 1524 APPENZELL
SWISS ▲ 1524 SÄNKT GALLEN
VAUD CONFEDERATION ▲ 1524 GLARUS
▲ 1538 Geneva ▲ 1525 GRAUBÜNDEN
SAVOY
Turin ●
MONTFERRAT
MILAN
Milan ●
MANTUA
Venice ●
Verona ●
Trieste ●
Zágráb ●

VENAISSIN
ORANGE
Avignon ●
Toulouse ●
Marseille ●
Nizza ●
MONACO
Genoa ●
REP. OF GENOA
MASSA LUCCA
Florence ●
TUSCANY

PARMA
FERRARA
MODENA
Bologna ●
SAN MARINO
DUCHY OF URBINO
STATO DEI PRESIDI
Perugia ●
PAPAL
STATES
Rome ● 187

ANDORRA
● Barcelona

SARDINIA
Cagliari ●
10

VENETIAN REPUBLIC
Zara ●
Spalato ●
1
Bosna Saray ●
Mostar ●
MONTENEGRO
REPUBLIC OF RAGUSA

OTTOMAN EMPIRE
Belgrade ●
● Nish
● Sofia
● Philippopolis
● Adrianople
Üsküb ●
● Salonica
Janina ●

PONTECORVO
BENEVENTO
DUCHY OF CASTRO
Naples ●
Bari ●
Taranto ●
NAPLES

SICILY
Palermo ●
Messina ●
Athens ●
20

[3] delegates sent to last session of Council of Trent, (1562–3)

■ date of change from Catholicism to Lutheranism

▲ date of change to Calvinism, Zwinglianism or Anglicanism

The Habsburg ascendancy in Europe

Charles V's election as Holy Roman Emperor in 1519 created a Habsburg hegemony in Europe. He already ruled lands in Austria, South Germany and the Netherlands, and the realms bequeathed by his maternal grandparents in Spain, Italy and North Africa. Each of these inheritances soon increased. In 1526 his brother Ferdinand succeeded to the crowns of Bohemia (which included Moravia, Silesia and Lusatia) and Hungary. In 1535 Charles himself acquired both Lombardy and Tunisia, and throughout his reign he added to his holdings in the Netherlands (map 1). Moreover, in America, his Castilian subjects toppled first the Aztec and then the Inca states (see page 80). Although the central European lands (and the Imperial title) passed to Ferdinand and his successors, Charles's son Philip II also ruled a formidable inheritance. He, too, managed to extend it – adding the Philippines by conquest after 1571, and Portugal with her overseas possessions by inheritance after 1580.

Such centralization did not prove popular, however. Apart from provoking the enmity of France, which felt encircled, Charles V faced rebellions from his subjects in Spain (1520-2) and Germany (1552-5), the former provoked by taxation,

the latter arising from religious dissent provoked by the Reformation (page 90). Philip II (1556-98) contended, in the Netherlands, with the longest-lasting revolt in modern European history (map 2). The various provinces inherited or acquired by Charles V became part of a single state only in 1548. Local customs, often guaranteed by charter against central government interference, nevertheless survived and Philip II's attempts to override them – both to raise taxes and to persecute heretics – provoked insurrection. A timely display of force stifled an uprising in 1566; but in 1572 the provinces of Holland and Zeeland sustained rebellion, helped by the threat of a French invasion which made difficult a concentration of Spanish forces, until the cost of opposing them compelled Philip to withdraw his troops in 1576-7. Although forces loyal to (and maintained by) Spain reconquered many areas in the 1580s, fighting went on with the northern rebels for more than 20 years. Only in 1609 did Spain finally conclude a 12-year truce with the largely Calvinist Dutch Republic.

The Netherlands' struggle resumed during Emperor Ferdinand II's war against his rebellious subjects in Bohemia and Austria (map 3). He routed them at the battle of White Mountain in 1620.

Spain's attempts to suppress the Dutch Revolt provoked much hostile propaganda. Here *(below)* the devil crowns the duke of Alba, who led Spain's efforts 1567-1573, while a Cardinal wields bellows to fill his head with Catholic zeal. Alba holds allegorical figures of the Dutch provinces on a chain, while his agents execute Counts Egmont and Hornes, defenders of Dutch liberties. (The execution itself took place in Brussels on 5 June 1568).

2 Dutch Revolt, 1572–1648

— Netherlands, 1548
- - - - rebel areas, December 1572
— furthest extent of Dutch revolt, July 1577
— rebel areas, December 1606
▨ Dutch conquests, 1621–48
▤ Dutch Republic, 1648

North Sea

GRONINGEN
FRIESLAND
DUTCH
OVERIJSSEL
ENGLAND
HOLLAND
Amsterdam
Deventer
Zutphen
UTRECHT
The Hague
GELDERLAND
REPUBLIC
Nijmegen
ZEELAND
HOLY
Sluis
Antwerp
ROMAN
Bruges
Axel
Dunkirk
Mechelen
Leuven Maastricht
EMPIRE
Brussels Liège
Ieper
Namur
S P A N I S H
N E T H E R L A N D S

F R A N C E

Encouraged by this success, with Spanish and Papal support Ferdinand turned in 1621 against the German Protestant states, especially the Calvinists. Despite aid from Britain, Denmark and the Dutch, they lost and in 1629 Ferdinand issued an 'Edict of Restitution' by which he reclaimed Church lands acquired by Protestant rulers. Swedish military aid turned the tables against the emperor, and saved the German Protestants from collapse: an army led by King Gustavus Adolphus routed the Imperialists at Breitenfeld (1631) and drove them from much of Germany. Spain intervened to restore Habsburg fortunes but its victory at Nördlingen (1634) provoked France to declare war first on Spain (1635) and then on the emperor (1636). The war spread to almost the whole continent.

After many more years of largely unsuccessful campaigning, at the peace of Westphalia (1648) the emperor was abandoned virtually all his powers in Germany, agreed to toleration for Protestants and Catholics, and promised not to assist his Spanish cousins in their war against the Dutch rebels; by the peace of Münster (1648) Spain formally recognized the independence of the Dutch Republic (and their possession of all territories conquered since 1621); and by the peace of the Pyrenees (1659), Spain ceded all areas gained by France on the frontiers of both Spain and the Netherlands. The religious and political frontiers of central Europe which were agreed by these treaties lasted unchanged for 100 years. The Habsburg bid for European hegemony had failed.

3 The Thirty Years' War, 1618–48

- → route of Gustavus Adolphus, 1630–2
- → route of the Spanish army, 1634
- ✕ Imperial (Catholic) victory
- ✕ Imperial (Catholic) defeat
- — Holy Roman Empire
- — affected by Edict of Restitution, 1629
- ■ date region became Lutheran
- ▲ date region became Calvinist

the religious position in 1640:
- Lutheran
- Calvinist
- Catholic
- regained by Roman Catholics

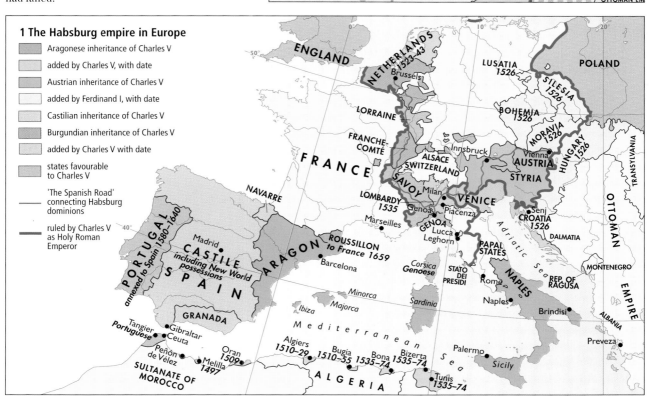

1 The Habsburg empire in Europe

- Aragonese inheritance of Charles V
- added by Charles V, with date
- Austrian inheritance of Charles V
- added by Ferdinand I, with date
- Castilian inheritance of Charles V
- Burgundian inheritance of Charles V
- added by Charles V with date
- states favourable to Charles V
- 'The Spanish Road' connecting Habsburg dominions
- ruled by Charles V as Holy Roman Emperor

1644–1911
China under the Ch'ing Dynasty

A new era in Chinese history opened in 1644 when the Ming dynasty, beset for a century by pirate raids, civil wars, and northern invaders (see page 68), fell to the forces of a Manchurian dynasty which ruled the country until 1911. The Manchu, or Ch'ing, rulers met with resistance in southern China for half a century, but quickly established a working relationship with the gentry who staffed the Chinese bureaucracy and, with its support, began a successful policy of territorial expansion which continued until the mid-18th century (map 1).

At the same time population trebled from about 100 million in 1650 to 300 million in 1800 and reached 420 million by 1850, while vast quantities of tea, silk, cotton, lacquer and porcelain were exported (mostly to Europe). But the financial strain of the wars of expansion and the pressure of the growing population on land and food caused hardships that led to recurrent unrest and revolt, not only among the ethnic minorities who were harshly exploited by Chinese and Manchus alike, but also in the heartland itself, beginning with the 'White Lotus' rebellion, 1796-1805. China remained the world's largest and most populous state, but its economic difficulties and inadequate bureaucracy prevented effective resistance to the pressures of the Western powers who sought to open the Chinese market for the goods produced by their empires.

China's defeat in the Opium War (1839-42) resulted in the cession of Hong Kong to Britain and the opening of the first five Treaty Ports (their number steadily increased)

1 Chinese imperial expansion from c. 1620

Manchu expansion Phase 1: China
- Manchu homeland
- expansion before 1644
- expansion, 1644-59
- 1644 date of incorporation

tributary states:
- before 1644
- after 1644

- ⊗ seat of main Lamaistic patriarch
- ★ risings of non-Chinese people
- sectarian risings of Chinese
- ■ official centre of foreign commerce

Phase 2: New Territories
- 1724 New Territory with date of incorporation
- → military expeditions
- border of China under the Ch'ing dynasty, at its greatest extent

R U S S I A N   E M P I R E

TANNU TUVA

Russian protectorate 1912

Lake Balkhash

ILI PROTECTORATE

to Russia 1871–81

Manchouli

to Russia 1860

MARITIME PROVINCE

Aigun

Harbin

Suifenho

occupied by Russia 1897–1905; Japanese influence after 1905

Changchun

Mukden

Hunchun

Vladivostok

M O N G O L I A
tributary territory;
autonomous 1912

Yellow River (Huang Ho)

Kalgan

Newchwang

Antung

Peking

Sea of Japan

S I N K I A N G
tributary territory

Tientsing

Taiyüan

Dairen

Port Arthur

to Russia 1898
to Japan 1905

Chefoo

Weihaiwei
to Britain 1898

KOREA
to Japan 1910

C H I N A

Tsinan

Tsingtao
to Germany 1898

J A P A N

T I B E T
tributary territory;
autonomous 1912
under British influence

British protectorate 1817

-ISH -IA

NEPAL SIKKIM BHUTAN

ASSAM
to Britain 1826

Ichang

Nanking

Chinkiang

Soochow

Wusung

Shanghai

Wuhu

Hangchow

Yangtze

Chungking

Kiukiang

Ningpo

Changsha

Yochow

Wenchow

Ryukyu Is.

to Japan 1872

Kunming

Tengyueh

Santuao

Foochow

Amoy

Tamsui

Taiwan
to Japan 1895

Mengtze

Manhao

B U R M A
to Britain 1886

New Territories
to Britain 1898

Nanning

Lungchow

Canton

Macao
to Portugal 1557

Kowloon to Britain 1898

Hong Kong
to Britain 1842

T O N G K I N G

Haiphong

Pakhoi

Kwangchowwan
to France 1898

Kiungchow

LAOS
to France
1893

S I A M

FRENCH
INDO
CHINA
1884

Hainan

In the Sino-Japanese war of 1894–5 the carefully modernized Western-style Japanese army disastrously routed the ill-led Chinese forces.

恢復天津

Treaty of Nerchinsk, 1689: Russia recognizes Chinese border along the Argun and Amur rivers

Amur

M A N C H U R I A

1629–30
-KHORCHIN

Mukden
(capital, 1625–44)

KOREA
Manchu invasions,
1627, 1636–7
vassal status
1637

1645
SHANTUNG

Eight Trigrams
rising, 1813

1645
KIANGSU

-45
-HWEI

1646
CHEKIANG

-52
-GSI

1646
FUKIEN

TAIWAN
Dutch, 1624–62; Ming
loyalists, 1662–83;
occupied by Ch'ing,
1683

-rising of Heaven
and Earth
Society, 1787–8

-Vietnamese
-pirate raids,
1800–9

**2 The dismemberment
of the Ch'ing empire,
1842–1911**

— boundary of Ch'ing empire in 1850
— states formerly tributary to China
— area affected by Taiping rebellion, 1850–64

colonial
possessions

spheres of
influence:

Russian

British

Japanese

French

German

railways:
— — — Russian   .... French
- - - - British   ⊢⊢⊢ German
—··— Japanese   +++++ Chinese

Treaty ports and towns:
⊘ 1842 Treaty of Nanking
⊗ 1858 Treaty of Tientsin
⊙ 1860 Peking Convention
◐ 1876 Chefoo Convention
▲ 1897 Sino-French Trade Convention
○ additional ports opened by 1911
● other towns and cities

in which foreigners enjoyed extra-territorial rights. More seriously, it served to weaken imperial authority and encouraged the Taiping rebellion (1850-64), the most serious of the many revolts that shook Manchu power. The Taiping and Nien uprisings alone left 25 million dead. These grave disorders also convinced the Western powers that Ch'ing China stood on the verge of collapse and encouraged them to secure a share: Russia gained the Amur basin, the Maritime Province (1858-60) and, temporarily, the Ili valley in Turkestan (1871-81); France occupied Indo-China (1884-5); Britain took Burma (1886); Japan annexed Taiwan (1895) and Korea (1910) (map 2). These losses convinced many Chinese that radical changes were inevitable, and when in 1911 a small mutiny broke out among the Manchu army, disaffection spread rapidly throughout the whole country and the imperial government collapsed (page 130).

India

TIMELINE

1707
Death of Aurangzeb: decline of Mughal power begins

1761
Capture of Pondicherry: British destroy French power in India

1765
British granted revenues of Bengal by Mughal emperor

1803
British defeat Marathas at Delhi; Mughal emperor accepts British protection

1824
British begin conquest of Burma

1857
Outbreak of Indian Mutiny

1877
Queen Victoria proclaimed Empress of India

1885
Foundation of Indian National Congress

1935
Government of India Act: Indians gain provincial autonomy

1947
Independence of India and Pakistan

1947
Independence of Ceylon and Burma

George V was crowned King Emperor of India at a durbar, or assembly of notables, in Delhi in 1911. In an effort to placate nationalist emotions, the annulment of the unpopular partition of Bengal was announced at the durbar.

2 India in 1857

- territory under British rule in 1805
- territory under British rule at close of Lord Dalhousie's administration, 1856
- — — main area affected by Indian Mutiny, 1857
- ● main centres of rebellion

Shortly after Aurangzeb's death in 1707 (page 62), Mughal power declined. In the north, Oudh and Bengal became effectively independent, owing only nominal allegiance to Delhi; in the centre, the power of the Maratha confederacy increased; in the south the Muslim state of Mysore expanded rapidly. Meanwhile European influence in India continued to increase, with both the French and English East India Companies acquiring new territory in the southeast. Robert Clive's victory at Plassey in 1757 gave the English control over the lands and resources of Bengal, Orissa and Bihar, allowing the Company to maintain an army of over 100,000 men – most of them Indian soldiers (sepoys) trained to fight in European fashion – with which they not only destroyed France's Indian ambitions but also extended their control over the entire eastern coast of the subcontinent (map 1). Mysore went down to defeat in 1799, the Marathas in 1805, both delivering extensive new territories to British control, and most other major Indian rulers soon recognized British suzerainty.

Over the next half-century the conquest of Sind (1843) and the Punjab (1849), brought the dominions of the Company up to the country's natural frontier in the northwest, while a war with Nepal (1814-16) extended them to the Himalayas. To the east the

British clashed with the Burmese empire and in 1824-6 annexed Assam and Arakan (page 89). Within India, the 'Doctrine of Lapse' introduced by Governor-General Dalhousie (1847-56) resulted in the absorption of autonomous but dependent states, such as Oudh and several Maratha kingdoms, into the directly administered territories (map 2). Not surprisingly, this policy provoked disaffection which found violent outlet in 1857. Beginning as a mutiny of the Company's native soldiers, the revolt soon involved princes, landlords and peasants throughout northern India; but the loyalty of the Sikhs and the passivity of southern India enabled the British to restore control after 14 months of bitter fighting.

The mutiny proved a watershed in the history of British India. It thoroughly discredited the Company and in 1858 the London government assumed direct control. The subcontinent now acquired a pivotal position in Britain's Imperial system, leading to intervention in Afghanistan to block Russian expansion into central Asia (page 114), and in Burma to counter French influence in Southeast Asia. From East Africa to China, the Indian army regularly acted to advance British interests. Within India, the autonomy of the princes was henceforth respected and active steps were taken to develop the economy: the construction of first-class roads and a major rail network, together with the opening of the Suez Canal in 1869, made possible the exploitation of raw materials and the introduction of export crops, such as tea. Between 1869 and 1929 India's foreign trade increased sevenfold. However, although some modern industries developed under Indian entrepreneurs, most of the trade involved importing British manufactures and exporting raw materials; and in most areas neither the character of the economy nor traditional agriculture experienced any basic change (map 3). The

3 British India, 1931

- territory under British rule
- territories permanently administered by Government of India (mostly tribal)
- states and territories administered by local Indian rulers
- Portuguese enclave
- French enclave
- Hindu majority provinces
- Muslim majority provinces
- area of Buddhist predominance
- area of large Sikh population

manufacturing products

- cotton textiles
- woollens
- tea
- chemicals
- metals
- machinery and transport material
- tobacco
- sugar
- rice mills
- iron and steel (large scale)
- shipping
- mills (various grains)

Gross National Product increased only slowly, while from 1921 (thanks to sustained population growth) per capita income declined.

The rise of a new middle class, partly through industry but more through the recruitment of educated Indians into the colonial administration, coupled with overt British racism, awakened a new political consciousness. The Indian National Congress (established with official blessing in 1885) at first accepted British rule, but soon developed an extremist wing which questioned the foreigners' right to rule India. The decision to partition the province of Bengal in 1905 provoked mass agitation and terrorist attacks; and from 1919, under the leadership of Mohendas K. Gandhi (1869-1948), Congress fought actively for home rule and, after 1929, for independence. Profiting from the unrest caused by unemployment and the world economic depression, Gandhi launched a civil disobedience campaign (1930-4) that galvanized the Indian masses, and forced Britain to pass the Government of India Act (1935) which provided a framework for participation in central and provincial government.

By 1937 Congress controlled 11 of the 14 provincial administrations, but failed to represent adequately the interests of the large Muslim minority whose leaders in 1940 passed a resolution calling for an autonomous Islamic state in the subcontinent: Pakistan. In 1942 Gandhi launched a 'Quit India' campaign and in 1946-7, faced by massive disaffection, a naval mutiny, and strong pressure from the United States, the British drew up hasty plans for partition along sectarian lines. India and Pakistan became independent in 1947, Burma and Ceylon in 1948 (page 162).

1 The growth of British power to 1805

- territory ceded to Britain by 1805 with dates
- X British victories with dates

The age of revolution

The later 18th century saw an unprecedented wave of uprisings throughout the western hemisphere (map 1). Many reflected a long-standing desire for independence, as in Corsica (1755, 1793), Haiti (1791), Sardinia (1793), Ireland (1798), Serbia (1804) and Spain (1808). Most, however, owed something to the Enlightenment, a European intellectual movement which emphasized certain fundamental rights of human beings and rejected traditional authority. Paradoxically, this could lead to rebellions by conservative elements against reforming rulers – such as the Austrian Netherlands (1787) and Hungary (1790) against the 'Enlightened' policies of Emperor Joseph II – or the resistance of colonial societies to the centralizing policies of the home government – as in North America after 1775 (page 104) and in South America after 1808 (page 112). More commonly opposition came from the middle classes: against a closed patriarchate in the Dutch Republic (1785-7); against the absolute monarchy and its aristocratic supporters in France.

In France, between 1789 and 1791 a representative assembly, summoned to solve a financial crisis, abolished feudalism, and created a constitutional monarchy and equality before the law. The king, however, refused to cooperate and was deposed in 1792, provoking Austrian, Prussian and (from 1793) British attempts to overthrow the Republic by force. They failed: instead, the revolutionary government in Paris purged its opponents at home and, by mobilizing unprecedented numbers of its citizens, conquered the Low Countries, Switzerland and Italy, imposing satellite republics.

In 1799 a successful general, Napoleon Bonaparte, took power as military dictator. He secured peace abroad (1802), and reorganized French local government, laws and education. But Britain declared war again in 1803 and, although her command of the seas (confirmed at Trafalgar, 1805) provided immunity from invasion, Napoleon defeated her continental allies – Austria, Prussia and Russia – in a brilliant series of battles (1805-7). Next, in order to create a continental blockade against British trade, Napoleon overran Spain (1808) and extended France's frontiers to Catalonia, the Baltic and Rome (1809-10). However Britain supported his opponents in the Iberian peninsula, expelling French forces by 1814. Meanwhile Russia's refusal to cooperate in the continental blockade led to a French invasion in 1812 which, although it reached Moscow, exhausted Napoleon's resources and led to his defeat and abdication in 1814 and again in 1815 (the 'Hundred Days').

Nevertheless, despite his failure, Napoleon's achievements inspired even his enemies: throughout the 19th century, Spanish, German and Italian reformers envisaged the state in essentially Napoleonic mode (page 116), while his administrative, legal and educational reforms in France survived the restoration of royal power.

1 Revolts and revolutions in Europe and America (below and right)
— borders, 1789
areas of nationalist revolt
areas of peasant revolt
areas of anti-colonial resistance
areas of revolt against royal authority

FINLAND

NORWAY (Danish)

Helsinki • St Petersburg
Stockholm •
Revel •

SWEDEN
Gothenburg •

RUSSIAN

Edinburgh •

North Sea

Aarhus •

Baltic Sea

Riga •

Pskov •

Moscow (captured) 1812 ☒
Borodino 1812 ☒
Maloyaroslavets 1812 ☒

UNITED

Dvinsk •
Vitebsk •
Smolensk (captured) 1812

EMPIRE

Liverpool •
Dublin •

DENMARK

Copenhagen •
Malmö •
Aarhus •

to Sweden
Lübeck •

Königsberg •
Tilsit •
REPUBLIC OF DANZIG

Nieman
Berezina

Vilna •

Berezina (crossed) 1812 ☒

Krasnoi 1812 ☒

Kursk •

KINGDOM

Bristol •
London •

Amsterdam •

Hamburg •
Hannover •

Berlin •

Friedland 1807 ☒
Eylau 1807 ☒

P R U S S I A

Minsk •

Waterloo 1815 ☒
Brussels •

Rhine

WESTPHALIA

Dresden 1813 ☒
Lützen 1813 ☒
Bautzen 1813 ☒

GRAND DUCHY OF WARSAW

Poznań •
Warsaw •
Brest-Litovsk •

Laon 1814 ☒
Ligny 1815 ☒
Hanau 1813 ☒

Château Thierry 1814
Rheims 1814 ☒
Champaubert 1814

Jena/ Auerstädt 1806

Leipzig (Battle of the Nations) 1813

Paris 1814 ☒

Prague 1813

Cracow •

Montereau 1814 ☒

La Fère Champenoise 1814

Ratisbon 1809

Ulm 1805

Eckmühl/ Ebersberg 1809

Montmirail/ Vauchamps 1814

Austerlitz 1805 ☒

F R E N C H

Tours •

CONFEDERATION OF THE RHINE

Zurich 1799 ☒

Hohenlinden 1800

Vienna •
Wagram 1809 ☒
Aspern/Essling 1809 ☒

NEUCHÂTEL

HELVETIC REPUBLIC

Buda • Pest •

AUSTRIAN EMPIRE

HUNGARY

Bordeaux •

Geneva •
Lyons •

Castiglione 1796

Lonato 1796

Rivoli 1797 ☒

E M P I R E

Toulouse •

Lodi 1796 ☒
Marengo 1800 ☒
Mondovi 1796 ☒
Dego 1796

Bassano 1796 ☒
Arcole 1796 ☒

Zágráb •

Danube •

Montenotte 1796

KINGDOM OF ITALY

ILLYRIAN PROVINCES

O T T O M A N

Saragossa (captured) 1809

Marseilles •
Toulon •

LUCCA

Zara •
Spalato •

Belgrade •

E M P I R E

CATALONIA

Barcelona 1808

PIOMBINO

Florence •

Adriatic Sea

Ragusa •

Nish •

Danube • Ruschuk • Varna •

Valencia 1808

Ajaccio •

Corsica

Rome •

SAN MARINO

MONTENEGRO

Sofia •

Corfu

Danube

KINGDOM OF NAPLES

PONTECORVO
BENEVENTO

MONTEVIDEO

Bari •

Mediterranean

KINGDOM OF SARDINIA

Cagliari •

Naples •
Taranto •

A L G I E R S

Palermo •
KINGDOM OF SICILY

Messina •

T U N I S

Malta (British)

Sea

2 Napoleon and the reshaping of Europe

French territories ruled from Paris, c. 1812

states ruled by members of Napoleon's family, c. 1812

other dependent states, c. 1812

☒ French victory

☒ French defeat

☒ battles of the Italian campaign

☒ battles of the War of the Second Coalition

☒ battles of the War of the Third Coalition

☒ battles in the Austrian War, 1809

☒ battles in the Peninsular War

☒ battles of the Russian campaign

☒ battles of the War of Liberation from French rule

☒ battles in the defence of France

☒ battles in the War of the 100 Days

On 14th July 1789 a crowd of Parisians stormed the Bastille fort to release a handful of political prisoners housed there (below). The incident sparked off a more widespread revolt against the authority of Louis XVI, which led, four years later, to his imprisonment and execution. Bastille Day became the symbol for liberation struggles worldwide.

VICE-ROYALTY OF NEW SPAIN

THIRTEEN COLONIES

Boston •
New York •

War of Independence, 1775

Gabriel's slave revolt, 1800

Mexico City •
Port-au-Prince •
Panama •

HAITI Toussaint l'Ouverture's revolt 1791

Santo Domingo •

SPANISH

Caracas •

Santa Fé de Bogotá •

VICE-ROYALTY OF NEW GRANADA

Quito •

Pacific Ocean

Lima •
VICE-ROYALTY OF PERU

La Paz •

AMERICA

VICE-ROYALTY OF BRAZIL

VICE-ROYALTY OF RIO DE LA PLATA

Bahia •

Santiago •

Buenos Aires •

The industrial revolution in Europe

TIMELINE

1765
Watt develops improved steam engine

1781
Steam engine first used in Europe

1825
First steam railway opened in England

1828
First modern blast furnace (Silesia)

1849
Iron first produced from coke on the Ruhr

1855
Bessemer steel process developed by Krupp

1885
Benz develops first petrol-driven car

1890
First electric tram, Florence

1896
Marconi builds first radio transmitter

1 The pattern of industrial expansion, 1800
population per sq. mile in 1801

- under 50
- 50–100
- 100–150
- 150–200
- 200–260
- 260–390
- 390–800

- ▲ iron ore mining
- ⊂ copper mining
- – lead mining
- ⊡ tin mining
- ▱ salt mining
- ⤡ slate mining

- —— canal
- ▪ expanding port
- ● expanding town
- ░ coalfields

James Watt's rotative steam engine. In 1765 Watt developed his first steam engine, used initially to drive pumps. In 1776 it was applied to the iron industry, but with the rotative steam engine in 1781 it was possible to power machinery, making possible the shift to large scale production.

alism (page 118). Britain's precedence rested upon many factors. On the one hand, unlike much of the rest of Europe, it boasted abundant coal, iron and other basic materials, and it enjoyed an advantageous position in the Atlantic trade which generated much capital. On the other hand, it possessed several unique advantages. First, it escaped direct damage from the various wars that ravaged Europe between 1690 and 1815; second, unlike most continental states which bristled with customs barriers and internal frontiers, after the union of England and Scotland in 1707 Great Britain formed a single economic unit; third, again in contrast to continental Europe, the early disappearance of serfdom in England meant that the surplus labour released by rising agricultural productivity could move, without legal obstacles, to the growing industrial centres. Finally,

The Industrial Revolution, which began in England in the later 18th century, became the catalyst of the modern world. Nevertheless the speed of change can be exaggerated. Even in continental Europe its impact remained limited before 1850 to a few enclaves; and not until the last quarter of the century did the great surge forward occur. Outside Europe, except for the United States, industrialization took place even later (page 120). In 1895, even in Germany, one-third of the population still worked on the land, and most of eastern and southern Europe remained virtually untouched by industry.

Until 1900, when its lead began to be challenged by Germany and the United States, Great Britain remained the workshop of the world and its industrial strength, which enabled it to dominate world markets, explains its pre-eminence in the age of imperi-

England possessed a unique network of navigable rivers and canals (map 1), which proved of immense importance before the railway age for moving both raw materials and finished goods.

In its earliest phase, English manufacturers had also relied on water as a source of energy; but in the century to 1870 industrial power depended on steam, generated by the combustion of coal. At first, except in Britain and (from 1820) Belgium, steam power came only slowly, held back by political fragmentation, lack of capital and, above all, poor communications which severely limited markets. The steel firm of Krupp, founded in 1811 and later to be a giant of German industry, still employed only 7 men in 1826 and 122 in 1846. The pace of industrialization only accelerated with railway development. Between 1830 and 1870 the rail networks of Britain, Belgium and Germany became virtually complete, and construction began elsewhere. At much the same time, barriers to trade came down: France demolished her internal tariffs in 1790, Prussia followed suit in 1818 and in 1834 joined the German Customs Union, which included 17 states and some 26 million people.

A new period, sometimes called the Second Industrial Revolution, opened in the 1870s (see map 2). The new German empire (page 116) led the way, increasing its coal output from 38 million tons in 1871 to 279 million tons in 1913, and its iron output from 1.5 million tons to 15 million tons. But it also led in new areas of industrial enterprise, especially chemicals, electricity and steel. By 1910, Krupp employed 70,000 men. At a time of growing international tension (page 124), such rapid economic growth was bound to produce a reaction among Germany's neighbours and Russia began a campaign of rapid industrialization in 1890 (page 114), France in 1895 and Italy in 1905. In all these states, much heavy industry was keyed to armaments. Although the bulk of the population of Europe remained largely untouched, industrialization had both changed the face of the continent and rendered its future uncertain.

2 The industrialization of Europe, 1870–1914

- ▨ areas of industrial concentration 1870–1914
- + centres of textile industry
- ○ coalfields
- ⊞ centres of engineering, armaments and metal industries
- △ iron ore fields
- ◐ lignite fields
- ◓ potash fields
- ╷ centres of petroleum industry
- —— railway network, 1870

The emerging global economy

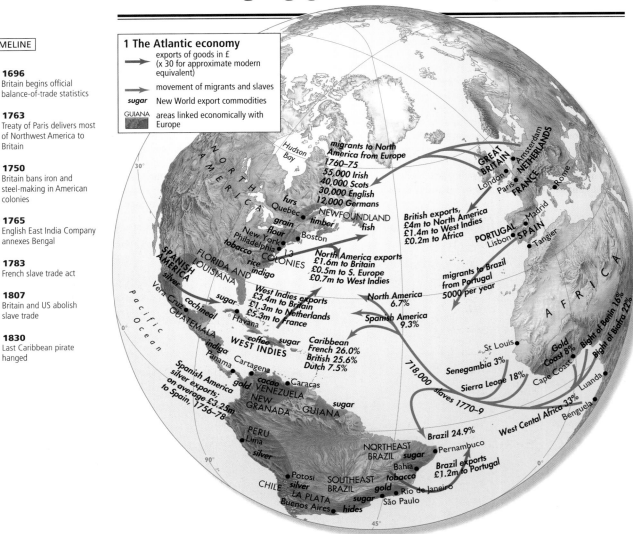

1 The Atlantic economy

→ exports of goods in £ (x 30 for approximate modern equivalent)

→ movement of migrants and slaves

sugar New World export commodities

GUIANA areas linked economically with Europe

In 1775, the areas of Spanish conquest and settlement in central and south America still ranked as the most valuable European overseas possession, thanks to the silver production of Mexico and Peru and the gold exports of Brazil, most of which went to Europe in return for manufactured goods. Along the Atlantic coast from Brazil to the Chesapeake, but above all in the Caribbean islands, plantation societies had developed to meet the rising demand both in Europe and in British North America (where over 2 million whites now dwelt) for tropical agricultural produce: cacao, tobacco, cotton and (especially) sugar. Since most plantations depended on the labour of African slaves, increased consumption in Europe meant increased shipments of slaves from Africa.

A closely integrated Atlantic economy had thus emerged. By 1775 the mainland colonies throughout the Americas were generally self-sufficient in food

and some supported limited manufacturing. But their white populations consumed prodigious quantities of imported European manufactured goods, and prosperity almost everywhere depended on the ability to export to Europe. Transatlantic commerce, in turn, contributed substantially to the economic development of Spain, France and Britain (almost 40 per cent of whose total exports in 1775 went to America).

In Asia, although the volume of European trade also greatly increased in the 18th century, it remained largely confined to ports or small coastal enclaves to which Asian merchants delivered goods. The Dutch and English East India Companies, founded in 1600-2 (page 80), still dominated trade with maritime Asia, but the shipment of spices to Europe had by the 18th century been overtaken by a boom in textiles (above all silks and cottons) and new drinks (tea and coffee). Since, however, in contrast to the Americas, few European manufactures proved competitive in Asia (except in the Mediterranean ports of the Ottoman empire), increased imports of Asian goods generally depended on shipments of American silver, either re-exported from Europe or carried across the Pacific to the Philippines and thence to China.

European trade also stimulated the demand for export commodities from, and injected large quantities of silver into, India and China; but most of Asia's economic life remained relatively unaffected by contact with the West, and much of its long-distance trade continued to be conducted by Asian merchants using their own pack-animals or ships. However, conditions were changing rapidly in two areas of great economic importance: the British had gained control of Bengal, a major centre of textile

The loading plan of a slave ship *(below)* shows how many slaves could be crammed below decks. The crowding marked a callous compromise between the slavers' desire to ferry as many slaves as possible and the need to ensure as many as possible of those embarked survived the voyage. By the late 18th century most ships lost less then 10 per cent of their human cargo. In earlier times, however, losses had sometimes exceeded 30 per cent, leading the Portuguese to refer to their slave ships as *tumbeiros* – coffins.

manufacture, in the 1760s and now used its huge tax revenues to maintain a substantial army ready to annex other areas of the subcontinent; and the Dutch in Java could impose commercial controls and receive commodities (above all coffee) as tribute.

Only Africa remained almost totally resistant to European penetration. Although the slave trade reached its apogee in the 18th century, with some 2.3 million slaves shipped out between 1770 and 1800, the prices paid by the Europeans for each slave steadily rose – suggesting that the African rulers who dealt in slaves more than held their own, despite the disruption arising from wars and slave-raiding, and the sustained loss of population.

In short, Europe's rapid commercial expansion overseas (for better or worse) hastened the economic integration of the world. The Americas outside the plantations enjoyed a degree of self-sufficiency, but Europe still determined the economic development of much of the continent. Although, except in Bengal, Java and the Philippines, the West could not yet shape the economies of Asia and Africa, with Britain now poised to conquer India (page 96) and with the Industrial Revolution underway in Europe (page 100), the stage was set for the creation of an integrated global economy.

2 The trading worlds of Asia and Africa

—— routes of European trade

—— routes of trade primarily of African and Asian merchants

coffee African and Asian export commodities

• centres of European trade in Africa and Asia

1775–1865
The United States

The disputes and difficulties leading to the American War of Independence and the foundation of the United States began almost immediately after the English victory over France in the Seven Years' War (page 86). Britain began to reorganize her vastly expanded North American possessions, establishing a huge Indian reserve west of the Alleghenies (1763) and extending the boundaries of Quebec (formerly French Canada) to the Mississippi and Ohio rivers (1774). The 'thirteen colonies' bitterly resented both this check to their westward expansion and the simultaneous insistence by Britain that its colonies should henceforth bear a greater share of the costs of their defence. Armed opposition began at Lexington and Concord in Massachusetts in 1775 (map 1). The colonies' representatives declared Independence in 1776, compelled the main British field army to surrender at Yorktown (1781), and fought on until the Treaty of Versailles (1783) recognized their sovereignty and extended the frontiers of the 'United States of America' to the Great Lakes and the Mississippi.

Expansion now proceeded rapidly. In 1783 the new republic comprised some 800,000 square miles (2,072,000 km^2) of territory, but the purchase of Louisiana from France (1803) more than doubled its size. West Florida was taken by force in 1812 and East Florida (60,000 square miles, 155,400 km^2) during the presidency of James Monroe. Thereafter extensive territories in the south and west were added, largely at the expense of Mexico (map 2), and in 1846 a compromise with Britain was reached over Oregon, increasing the number of states from 13 to 34. The population expanded from 3 million in 1785 to 31 million in 1860, fuelled by the arrival of a new wave of European immigrants, predominantly German and Irish.

These developments had important political consequences. The ruling elites of the southern states, with their plantation economy and large black slave population, felt increasingly threatened by the industrializing north and the growing Midwest. This, rather than the issue of slavery, underlay the American Civil War (1861-5); but the issues in fact proved inseparable because, with over 90 percent of

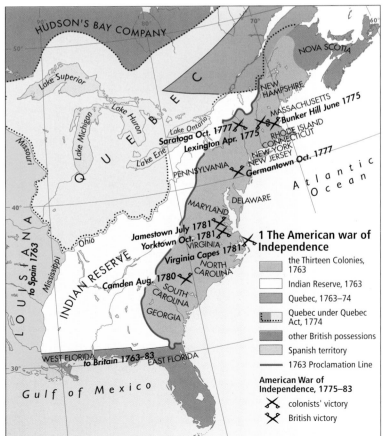

1 The American war of Independence

- the Thirteen Colonies, 1763
- Indian Reserve, 1763
- Quebec, 1763–74
- Quebec under Quebec Act, 1774
- other British possessions
- Spanish territory
- 1763 Proclamation Line

American War of Independence, 1775–83

- ✗ colonists' victory
- ✗ British victory

Dead soldiers at Gettysburg
(below). The small market town of Gettysburg, Pennsylvania, was the scene of the greatest battles of the war. Lee, advancing into the North to force Lincoln to negotiate peace on the basis of Southern independence, attacked General Meade's Union army, but in the course of a three-day battle was comprehensively beaten. The Union lost 23,000 men, the Confederacy 28,000.

the black population living in the South, the moral question was also a regional question. Abraham Lincoln, elected President in 1860 by the votes of the Northern states, was right to claim that the nation could not permanently remain 'half slave and half free'.

Soon after Lincoln's election, South Carolina seceded from the Union and was quickly joined by ten other states which came together as the Confederate States of America with their capital at Richmond, Virginia (map 4). For Lincoln the fundamental issue was whether a constitutional republic could preserve its territorial integrity; he recognized no constitutional right of secession. By 1863, however, pressure from radical Republicans added the aim of freeing the slaves in the rebel states to the commitment to restore the Union. Thanks to the superior military skill of their commanders, and to their shorter lines of communications, the confederacy fought on for four years (1861-5). The Northern strategy was to deny the South vital resources by a naval blockade, to gain control of key river routes and forts in the west and to capture Richmond. Eventually the superior demographic and economic resources of the North prevailed – albeit at the cost of 635,000 Union and 383,000 Confederate military casualties – and created the 'second American Revolution' which, by crippling the southern ruling class and liberating its labour force, determined that the thrusting, urban, industrialized North, with its creed of competitive capitalism, would stamp its pattern (for good or ill) on the entire United States.

4 Comparative resources: Union and Confederate states, 1861

Union States	Confederate States

Total pop.: 2.5 to 1	Naval ship ton.: 25 to 1	Farm acreage: 3 to 1
Male adult pop.: 4.4 to 1	Factory prod.: 10 to 1	Draft animals: 1.8 to 1
Free men 18–60 yrs in military service: 1864 44% 90%	Textile prod.: 17 to 1	Livestock: 1.5 to 1
Wealth produced: 3 to 1	Iron production: 20 to 1	Wheat prod.: 4.2 to 1
Railroad mileage: 2.4 to 1	Coal production: 38 to 1	Corn production: 2 to 1
Merchant ship ton.: 9 to 1	Firearms prod.: 32 to 1	Cotton prod.: 1 to 24

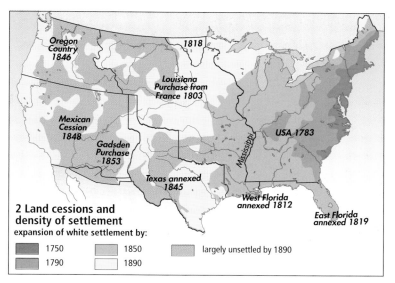

2 Land cessions and density of settlement

expansion of white settlement by:

1750	1850	largely unsettled by 1890
1790	1890	

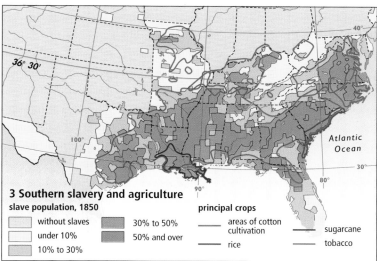

3 Southern slavery and agriculture

slave population, 1850

without slaves	30% to 50%
under 10%	50% and over
10% to 30%	

principal crops

—— areas of cotton cultivation	—— sugarcane
—— rice	—— tobacco

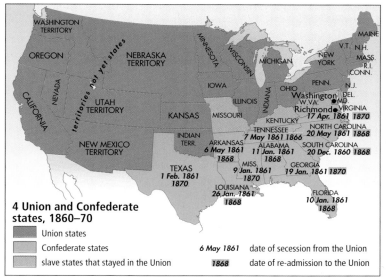

4 Union and Confederate states, 1860–70

Union states	
Confederate states	6 May 1861 date of secession from the Union
slave states that stayed in the Union	1868 date of re-admission to the Union

Australia and New Zealand

1 The European settlement and development of Australia

native land rights claims, Jan. 1997

more than 2 persons per square mile 1961 (by statistical division)

no significant use, c. 1960

■ penal settlements   ● settlements

railways
— before 1881   ---- 1901-1920
-·-·- 1881-1900   ······· after 1920

minerals
   gold   ▣ tin   zinc
   copper   U uranium   ▲ oil
   lead   ✦ blast furnace   N nickel
   ⌂ natural gas   iron ore   A alumina/bauxite
   T tungsten   silver   M manganese

Although Australia and New Zealand were reconnoitred by the Dutch explorer Abel Tasman in 1642, colonization only began in 1770 when James Cook raised the British flag at Botany Bay. New South Wales served as a penal colony from 1788 to 1839, as did van Diemen's land (later Tasmania) from 1804 to 1853, but in 1829 the British government, in order to forestall the French, claimed the whole Australian continent. Fear of France also led to the annexation of New Zealand in 1840. However, the geographical

obstacles, the lack of exportable goods (at first chiefly seal products and sandalwood), and (especially in the case of New Zealand) the opposition of the indigenous population complicated the colonization process in both territories. In 1850, the total white population of Australia still numbered only 350,000, and that of New Zealand was less than 100,000.

The discovery of gold in New South Wales and Victoria in 1851 initiated a new phase, and encouraged the growth of the inland population. Even more important was the rapid growth of sheep-farming: in 1850 Australia sent 17,000 tons of wool to Great Britain, but 134,000 tons in 1879. Nevertheless, as centralizing systems of communications and transportation developed, the dominance of the coastal cities – especially Sydney and Melbourne – increased. By the 1890s, two-thirds of Australia's population lived in urban areas along the coast (a pattern that steadily intensified throughout the 20th century.) In New Zealand, where wool remained largely a South Island product, exports rose in value from £67,000 in 1853 to £2.7 million twenty years later. The development of the North Island, which was held back by the bitter Maori Wars (1860-71), only came after the introduction of refrigeration, which made possible the export of frozen lamb, butter and cheese. Dairy farming developed rapidly, and the North Island now drew ahead of the South in population.

Political development kept pace with economic growth. In 1855 New South Wales, Victoria, South Australia and Tasmania became self-governing colonies, followed by Queensland in 1859; in 1901 they joined together to form the Commonwealth of Australia. New Zealand, which had been divided in 1852 into six provinces, each with an elected council, became a united Dominion (after measures had been taken to safeguard the rights of the Maori population) in 1876. Both countries achieved sovereign status under the Statute of Westminster in 1931. The economy of both dominions remained heavily dependent on primary exports – wool, meat, grain and dairy products – which enjoyed preferential treatment in the British market. Even the spectacular discoveries of minerals, coal, oil and gas in and about Australia after 1950 went largely into exports. However Britain's decision to join the European Economic Community and dismantle 'imperial preference' in 1973 (page 166), coupled with the conviction that the countries of the Pacific Rim would become the economic hub of the world in the 21st century, drove both Australia and New Zealand to develop new economic activities and to foster trade with countries outside the British Commonwealth.

This romanticized picture of an attack on a Maori *pa* (fort) during the first New Zealand War suggests the storming of a castle. In fact, recent research has revealed that the *pa* evolved rapidly into sophisticated trench and bunker systems which anticipated those of the Western Front by over 50 years. By the end of the conflict large tracts of Maori land had been confiscated by the colonial government.

2 The development of New Zealand to c. 1875

- ☷ pioneer sheep regions 1840s
- ☷ sheep
- ▲ timber
- ◪ gold rushes

1850 date of foundation of city

Marsden's first mission 1814

Russell *first capital 1840-1*

NORTH ISLAND

Auckland *second capital 1841-65*

Thames 1867-71

AUCKLAND

New Plymouth 1841

TARANAKI (NEW PLYMOUTH)

Cook's landfall 1769

WELLINGTON

Napier 1855

HAWKE'S BAY

Nelson 1841

Blenheim 1855

Wellington *capital since 1865*

NELSON

MARLBOROUGH

West Coast 1864-68

Hokitika

Tasman's landfall 1642

WESTLAND

Christchurch 1850

Akaroa *French colony 1840*

CANTERBURY

SOUTH ISLAND

OTAGO

SOUTHLAND

Dunedin 1848 *NZ's largest city 1861- c. 83*

Invercargill 1857

Stewart Island

3 The development of New Zealand since 1875

- ☷ major sheep regions
- ○ coal c. 1880–1914
- ⌐ dairying (periods shown)
- ◪ gold-dredging 1880s–1960
- ▲ forest products since 1950
- ♠ wine
- ⚘ horticulture
- ⊗ hydro-electricity since 1930
- ←—→ main trunk railways

Marsden Point *oil refinery 1965*

NORTH ISLAND *majority of population since 1901*

since 1920s

Polynesian migration since 1950s

Auckland *largest city since mid 1880s*

Glenbrook *steel mill 1969*

Hamilton

since 1920s

Arapuni *first major h.e. station 1929*

New Plymouth

Wellington–New Plymouth railway 1886

since 1880s

75% of Maori north of line 1980s

North Island main trunk railway 1908

since 1900

Palmerston North

Napier

Wellington–Napier railway 1891

Westport

Nelson

Picton

Wellington *urban area second largest since 1906*

Greymouth

Christchurch–Picton railway 1945

Cook Strait

rail ferry 1962, h.e. cable 1965

Lake Coleridge

first government h.e. station 1914

Cheviot

Christchurch *largest South Island city since 1895*

SOUTH ISLAND *majority of population 1861-1901*

Christchurch–Bluff railway 1879

Manapouri

N.Z.'s *largest h.e. station 1971*

Port Chalmers *first export of frozen meat 1882*

Dunedin

Edendale *first dairy export factory 1882*

Bluff *aluminium smelter 1971*

The decline of the Ottoman empire

The period between 1798 and 1923 saw the disintegration and final collapse of the Ottoman Empire, the major power in West Asia since the 16th century (see page 70). Plagued by foreign invasions, wars, and the revolts of subject peoples demanding national independence, the empire steadily lost territory.

In 1798 a French army led by Napoleon Bonaparte invaded Egypt and Syria, only to be defeated by the British. Peace was arranged in 1802 and three years later the sultan appointed Mohammed Ali governor of Egypt. Under his rule, however, the province gained de facto independence and in 1841 Mohammed was recognized as hereditary viceroy. Meanwhile, between 1830 and 1847 the French conquered Algeria, and in 1881 they annexed Tunis; the following year the British occupied Egypt. There were also wars with Russia, rebellions in the Arab provinces and almost constant revolts in the Balkans – starting with the Greek War of Independence in 1821, which resulted (following the pressure of foreign powers) in the recognition of a sovereign Greek state in 1830. Foreign intervention also

**1 The Ottoman empire,
1798–1923**

- Ottoman empire, 1798
- lost by 1886
- lost by 1914
- - - eastern limit of nominal Ottoman control, 1913
- frontiers, 1914
- lost by 1920
- Ottoman empire under the Treaty of Sèvres, 1920
- Turkey under the Treaty of Lausanne, 1923

precipitated the Crimean War (1853-6) and the Lebanese crisis of 1860-1, while Russian and Austrian demands helped secure the independence of Montenegro, Serbia and Romania by 1878. By 1882, the Ottomans had lost 40 per cent of their empire.

Their finances also deteriorated rapidly until in 1875 the state became virtually bankrupt and the Sultan suspended payment of the interest due on the Ottoman debt. In 1881, he agreed to supervision of his treasury by European bankers: the empire's survival became dependent on foreign governments which preferred the preservation of a weakened Ottoman state to the dangerous power vacuum that would follow Turkish collapse. Nevertheless, further territorial losses followed: Italy annexed Libya in 1911 and, at the end of the Balkan wars in 1913 (page 124), the Ottomans surrendered Crete, most of the Aegean islands, Thrace, Macedonia and Albania. In all, between 1908 and 1911, the Turks lost 30 per cent of their remaining possessions.

Throughout the 19th century the sultans made various attempts to modernize their empire, but not always successfully: Selim III, who aimed to create a modern army, was deposed in 1807 when his troops mutinied against the proposed reforms. The Janissaries rebelled in 1826 against reforms decreed by Mahmud II, but this provoked their abolition.

After a decade of agitation, in 1876 Sultan Abdul Hamid II introduced a constitution, and a Parliament met the following year; but it was dissolved almost immediately and only pressure by the Ottoman Society for Union and Progress (the 'Young Turks') forced its restoration in 1908. The following year Abdul Hamid abdicated, and the Young Turks came to dominate the administration. However, their nationalist policies and opposition to any further surrender of territory contributed substantially to the Arabs' willingness to seek accommodation with the Turks' enemies, once the Ottoman empire entered World War I on the side of Germany and Austro-Hungary (page 132).

Despite tenacious resistance, the Turks were eventually defeated and West Asia (despite earlier promises to the Arabs) came under the control of the victorious French and British governments. The Sultan collaborated with Great Britain after his defeat, and in 1920 agreed to the treaty of Sèvres which would dismember the empire. However, the arrival of Greek troops at Izmir provoked a nationalist uprising which crystallized around the Turks' only undefeated general, Mustafa Kemal. The sultanate was abolished and, after some reverses, Turkish forces drove back the Greeks and their allies and secured recognition of the sovereignty of the Turkish Republic at the treaty of Lausanne in 1923.

Mustafa Kemal, or Atatürk *(above),* – 'father of the Turks', as he styled himself – was an Ottoman commander in the First World War. His effective leadership of Turkish forces in 1922 led to his becoming president of the new Turkish republic that year. He was determined to turn Turkey into a modern, industrialized, Western-style secular state.

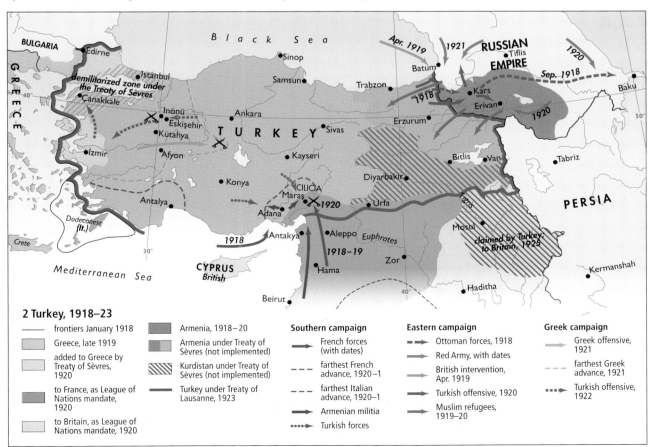

2 Turkey, 1918–23

- —— frontiers January 1918
- Greece, late 1919
- added to Greece by Treaty of Sèvres, 1920
- to France, as League of Nations mandate, 1920
- to Britain, as League of Nations mandate, 1920
- Armenia, 1918–20
- Armenia under Treaty of Sèvres (not implemented)
- Kurdistan under Treaty of Sèvres (not implemented)
- Turkey under Treaty of Lausanne, 1923

Southern campaign
- French forces (with dates)
- farthest French advance, 1920–1
- farthest Italian advance, 1920–1
- Armenian militia
- Turkish forces

Eastern campaign
- Ottoman forces, 1918
- Red Army, with dates
- British intervention, Apr. 1919
- Turkish offensive, 1920
- Muslim refugees, 1919–20

Greek campaign
- Greek offensive, 1921
- farthest Greek advance, 1921
- Turkish offensive, 1922

Africa in the 19th century

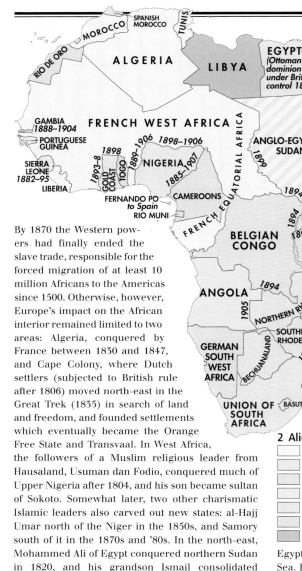

By 1870 the Western powers had finally ended the slave trade, responsible for the forced migration of at least 10 million Africans to the Americas since 1500. Otherwise, however, Europe's impact on the African interior remained limited to two areas: Algeria, conquered by France between 1830 and 1847, and Cape Colony, where Dutch settlers (subjected to British rule after 1806) moved north-east in the Great Trek (1835) in search of land and freedom, and founded settlements which eventually became the Orange Free State and Transvaal. In West Africa, the followers of a Muslim religious leader from Hausaland, Usuman dan Fodio, conquered much of Upper Nigeria after 1804, and his son became sultan of Sokoto. Somewhat later, two other charismatic Islamic leaders also carved out new states: al-Hajj Umar north of the Niger in the 1850s, and Samory south of it in the 1870s and '80s. In the north-east, Mohammed Ali of Egypt conquered northern Sudan in 1820, and his grandson Ismail consolidated

2 Alien rule in Africa, 1913

French	Anglo-Egyptian condominium
British	independent
German	
Portuguese	*1882–95* date of determination of colonial boundary
Belgian	— frontiers, 1914
Spanish	
Italian	

Egyptian control over much of the littoral of the Red Sea. Finally, in the south, the formation of the Zulu kingdom by Shaka in 1818 led to widespread disruption as neighbouring peoples moved away from the aggressive new state.

Meanwhile, the progress of industrialization in Europe (page 100) created a demand for new sources of raw materials and new markets, while the mass-production of quinine (which offered protection against the malaria endemic in Africa) and machine-guns gave the Europeans the ability to satisfy these demands by force. In the 1870s the French advanced inland from Senegal while the British began the conquest of Nigeria. In 1882 the British invaded and occupied Egypt, and the Belgians advanced up the Congo river. Next, Germany laid claim to Togoland, the Cameroons, Southwest Africa and

The Battle of Isandhlwana
on 22 January 1879 was the first major engagement of the Zulu war *(right)*. A British force of 1700 white and African troops under Lord Chelmsford was routed by 20,000 Zulu, the consequence rather of British arrogance and carelessness than of overwhelming numbers. It demonstrated the continuing possibility that African tactics and weaponry could triumph over well-armed European forces.

East Africa, each move provoking parallel actions by other powers. Portugal revived her effort to colonize the interior of Angola and Mozambique, while Britain claimed parts of East Africa (later Kenya and Uganda) and, on the initiative of the Cape politician and industrialist Cecil Rhodes, central Africa (later Zimbabwe, Zambia and Malawi).

Even larger gains accrued to the French, who swept into sub-Saharan Africa from three directions and gained control over almost one-third of the continent (map 1). With the conquest of Libya and Cyrenaica by Italy in 1911 and the partition of Morocco between France and Spain in 1912, of the 40 political units into which Africa had been arbitrarily divided, only two could claim any real independence: Ethiopia, which had defeated an Italian attempt at annexation in 1896, and Liberia, which enjoyed financial support from the United States. In little more than a generation, the Europeans had gained control over an additional 12 million square miles (31 million km²) of territory.

111

1808–1929
Latin America

Napoleon's invasion of Spain and Portugal in 1808 (page 98) enabled these countries' American colonies to gain independence. The revolt began in Argentina in 1810 and in Venezuela in 1811, helped by the decision of Great Britain and the United States to oppose intervention by the Iberian powers. The fall of Lima (1821) and Simón Bolívar's victory at Ayacucho (1824), deprived Spain of control over South America. In the North, early rebellions in Mexico were suppressed, but in 1823 a republic was proclaimed, and a last Spanish attempt at reconquest in 1829 met with defeat. Only Brazil made the transition to independence peacefully, as Portugal agreed to provide a constitution and in 1822 the Portuguese king's eldest son became Emperor Pedro I of Brazil. Only in 1889 when, following the abolition of slavery (1888), disgruntled plantation owners rose in revolt, did a federal republic replace the empire.

Independence remained in essence a political movement confined to the colonial aristocracy, who desired a transfer of authority without social change. The next half-century was dominated by military dictators who ruled in the interests of the privileged classes and squandered their assets on repeated territorial disputes. Mexico lost most, forfeiting vast territories to the United States (see page 104); but it was also the first state to introduce limited social reforms after the election of the Indian Benito Juarez as President in 1861.

A subsistence economy still prevailed in most areas. Although Brazil with its slave-operated coffee plantations offered an exception, elsewhere the great rural estates showed little interest in producing for the market. After 1880, overseas investment increased rapidly, but selectively, concentrated mainly in Argentina, Brazil, Mexico and Chile. Moreover, even there, the foreign stimulus shifted those economies sharply towards the export of primary products: grain and meat from Argentina, nitrate from Chile, coffee and rubber from Brazil, oil from Mexico, and fruit from the so-called 'Banana Republics' of the central isthmus.

Most of these countries modernized and commercialized their production, and built docks and railways to expedite the export of food and raw materials. This attracted a new wave of immigrants and created a new urban and industrial proletariat as well as a middle class prospering from the export trade; but it left the majority of the rural population in abject poverty. Mexico under the repressive regime of Porfirio Díaz (1876-1911) exemplified these trends until in 1910 the country erupted in revolution: eventually, in 1917, a constitution incorporating major social and political reforms was adopted. Elsewhere, as long as prosperity continued – that is, until the Great Crash of 1929 (see page 138) – political and social pressures remained under control (albeit sometimes only thanks to armed intervention by the United States); but rapid and unbalanced economic expansion steadily undermined the regimes that promoted it.

abbreviations to map below

A	AGUASCALIENTES	N	NUEVO LEÓN
C	CAMPECHE	P	PUEBLA
G	GUANAJUATO	Q	QUERÉTARO
H	HIDALGO	S	SAN LUIS POTOSÍ
ME	MÉXICO	T	TLAXCALA
M	MORELOS	V	VERACRUZ

(see map left)

COSTA
RICA
1838

PANAMA
1903

Cartagena
Panama
Mompos
Antioquia

Maracaibo

Caracas

Orinoco

Angostura

Georgetown

▽ Páez 1830–48

▽ Guzmán Blanco 1870–88

VENEZUELA *1830*

to Britain 1904

BRITISH
DUTCH
FRENCH

GUIANA

Cayenne

◇ violent constitutionalism

Bogotá

COLOMBIA
1830

1873

1900

□ Cabanagem 1835–40

□ Balaiada 1839

□ Confederation of
Equator 1824

▽ García Moreno
1860–75

Quito

ECUADOR
1830

ORIENTE

to Ecuador 1880

1907

to Ecuador 1880

Amazon

Manaus

RIO NEGRO
(later Amazonas)

PARÁ

MARANHÃO

CEARÁ

RIO GRANDE
DO NORTE

PARAIBA

PERNAMBUCO

ALAGOAS

SERGIPE

Guayaquil

Iquitos

Tabatinga

B R A Z I L
1822
(empire 1822, republic 1889)

PIAUI

P   E   R   U

ACRE
1899–1903

to Bolivia 1867

PIAUI

SABINADA
1837

SANTA CRUZ

□ Praieira
1848–9

Santa Cruz

▽ Castilla 1845–62

Lima

Callao

to Peru 1909

to Peru 1902

1824

Cuzco

Simón Bolívar (1783–1830)
(below) became known as 'The
Liberator' for his role in the
emancipation of South America
from Spanish rule. After partici-
pating in several unsuccessful
revolts, he and his army defeated
the Spanish at Boyacá in 1819
and organized the republic of
Gran Colombia. In 1821, he
defeated the Spanish near
Carabobo, ensuring Venezuelan
independence. Between 1822
and 1824 he also helped free
Ecuador and Peru. Southern Peru
became a new republic, named
Bolivia in his honour.

La Paz

Tacna

to Peru 1929

Arica

Potosí

BOLIVIA
1825

Corumbá

MATO GROSSO

GOIAS

Liberal
revolution
1842

BAHIA

MINAS GERAIS

Diamantina

Minas Novas

ESPIRITO
SANTO

Chilean
gains
1883

▽ Melgarejo
1864–71

1870

1870

GRAN
CHACO

PARAGUAY
1811

Concepción

SÃO PAULO

Ciudad Real

São Paulo

RIO DE JANEIRO
Rio de Janeiro

○ Batalla 1903–15

Jujuy

1874

Asunción

1874

1921

SANTA
CATARINA

□ Farroupilha revolution
1835–45

1 Latin America:
political development
from 1824 (above and left)

1818

Córdoba

RIO GRANDE
DO SUL

C
H
I
L
E

URUGUAY 1828
part of Brazil
1816–28

◇ aristocratic
presidentialism

Valparaíso

Santiago

Constitución

Mendoza

San Luis

Rosario

Buenos Aires

Montevideo

Rio de la Plata

1816

Valdivia

A
R
G
E
N
T
I
N
A

War of the
Desert
1880–81

◇ conservative
republic
1826–1910

▽ Rosas 1829–52

United Provinces of
Rio Plata 1819–25
Argentine confederation
1825–53
Argentine republic from
1853

P
A
T
A
G
O
N
I
A

settled by Argentina
by late 19th C

settled by Chile
through 19th C

FALKLAND IS.
(Islas Malvinas)

colonized by
Britain 1765–74;
claimed by Spain to 1811,
subsequently claimed by
Argentina;
British from 1833

boundary of Mexico,
1824

Mexico 1867

1821   date of independent
statehood

Republic of Gran
Colombia, 1821–30

United Provinces of
Central America,
1823–38

later Brazilian
acquisitions

areas affected by
Mexican revolution
from 1910

disputed between
Ecuador and Peru

disputed between
Bolivia and Paraguay

▽   caudillismo

○   revolutionary
movements

◇   constitutionalism

□   radical reformism

French territory

British territory

Dutch territory

Spanish territory

The expansion of the Russian empire

For 40 years after the Congress of Vienna (1815) Russia remained the strongest military power in Europe, focusing her interests on the Balkans and on the straits leading from the Black Sea. Since most Balkan subjects of the Ottoman empire were Orthodox Slavs, Russia considered herself their natural protector; and because Turkey lay in the way of Russia's access to the Mediterranean, it desired Constantinople to remain amenable to Russian influence alone. However, France and Austria also had imperial ambitions in these areas, while Britain opposed any further Russian expansion. In 1854, therefore, following Russia's invasion of Turkey's Danubian provinces and destruction of the Ottoman fleet, France and Britain (supported by Austria) declared war and invaded the Crimea, eventually forcing Russia to evacuate the Balkans and to dismantle its Black Sea fleet. A further Russian attempt to liberate the Balkan Slavs from Turkish rule in 1877-8 also failed (page 108).

Russia proved far more successful in Asia (map 1). Her forces subdued the Kazakhs (1816-54), completed Russian control of the Caucasus (1857-64) and annexed the khanates of central Asia (1865-76). The imperial frontier now reached – and sometimes penetrated – the great mountain chains that separated it from Persia, Afghanistan, India and China. The colonization of North America also continued into the early 19th century, and forts were built as far

south as California; but most were soon abandoned and Alaska was sold to the United States in 1867. On the other hand, China ceded to the Tsar the Amur basin and parts of the Pacific coast (where Vladivostok was founded in 1860), and leased Port Arthur (1898). This warm-water harbour, unimpeded by winter ice, was soon linked to the main Trans-Siberian railway (completed in 1903). But Russian expansion conflict-ed with Japanese designs. The two powers had already clashed over their interests in Korea and south Manchuria, following Japan's victory over China in 1894-5 (page 130), and in 1904-5 Japan attacked Russia, forcing her to abandon most of her gains in the Far East and to cede south Sakhalin.

This humiliating defeat fanned the flames of domestic unrest. Shaken by the backwardness exposed in the Crimean War, Tsar Alexander II (1855-81) had initiated a number of reforms in the 1860s: new local government organizations; educational improve-ments; and radical changes to the legal system. The emancipation of the serfs in 1861 was the corner-stone of the reforms (map 2). However, still confined to their villages, many peasants felt aggrieved that they often had to acquire by purchase less land than they had previously worked. From 1890 the government embarked on an industrialization programme with railways at its centre. Many of the lines aimed to facilitate the movement of troops to frontier areas in case of war, but they allowed not

1 Russia in Asia, 1815–1900

- the Russian empire, 1815
- acquisitions 1816–56
- acquisitions 1856–76
- acquisitions 1877–1900
- vassal khanates
- railway

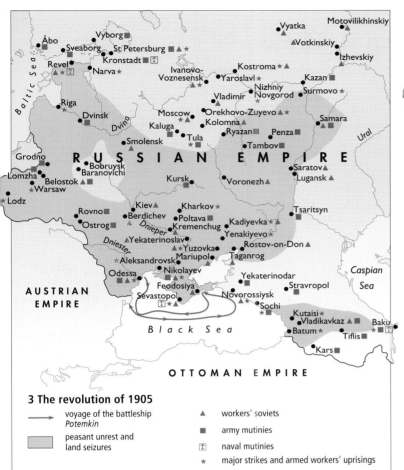

3 The revolution of 1905

→	voyage of the battleship *Potemkin*
▲	workers' soviets
■	army mutinies
(shaded)	peasant unrest and land seizures
🏴	naval mutinies
★	major strikes and armed workers' uprisings

2 Serfdom in Russia, 1860

serfs as a percentage of the population

▨	over 50	▨	10–30
▨	30–50	▢	under 10

—— boundary of Russia, 1871

serfs' obligations

◆ *obrok*: dues in kind or cash
◇ *barshchina*: labour service to landlord
⬖ both *obrok* and *barshchina* dues

only migration from overcrowded central Russia to western Siberia, but also the movement of peasants to urban areas to man a growing number of factories. Between 1863 and 1914 Russia's urban population increased from 6 to 18.6 million.

In 1905, in the wake of Japan's victory, revolutionary parties proved quick to exploit the low incomes and general hardships created by these rapid changes, while the new professional classes pressed for political reform (map 3). Unrest in the towns spread to the countryside, to the army and even to the Black Sea fleet, led by the battleship Potemkin, forcing Tsar Nicholas II (1894-1917) to grant a constitution, including a duma, or parliament; but by 1907 the government had regained full control. Nevertheless the 1905 revolution irreparably weakened the old order, and after 1912 another wave of social unrest swept the empire. Internally, Russia was in no position to meet the challenge of the First World War in 1914.

Although mobilization took place with a rapidity that took the Germans by surprise (page 132), the tsar's government proved incapable of supplying its millions of troops with equipment, munitions or (eventually) with food.

'It is better to abolish serfdom from above than wait for it to abolish itself from below,' declared Alexander II *(left)* in 1857. Four years later Alexander did indeed free the serfs. He soon found that it was one thing to emancipate them, another to feed, clothe and educate them. Radical though they were in Russian terms, Alexander's reforms failed to address the core problems facing his country.

Nationalism in Europe

Nationalism flourished in Europe in the wake of the French Revolution (page 98), but it remained confined largely to the middle classes and proved relatively short-lived. The Great Powers at the Congress of Vienna in 1815 aimed to restore Europe (as far as possible) to its pre-war condition by combating both liberalism and nationalism and by creating a barrier around France. To that end Holland received the Austrian Netherlands (later Belgium); Prussia took over Westphalia and much of the Rhineland; Sardinia-Piedmont annexed Genoa; Russia retained Finland and most of Poland; and Austria gained Venetia and Lombardy.

By 1830, however, when a new wave of liberal and national agitation arose, the Great Powers no longer worked in unison, enabling Greece (page 108) and Belgium to obtain independence. In 1848-9, when an outburst of nationalism erupted into full-scale revolution, the solidarity of the conservative powers – coupled with divisions among the nationalists themselves – still sufficed to maintain the status quo. Shortly afterwards, a new generation of statesmen began to use nationalism for their own ends. Cavour

Known as the 'Iron Chancellor', Otto von Bismarck *(above)* became minister-president of Prussia in 1862. After wars against Denmark (1864) and Austria (1866), he formed the North German confederation (1867) and after the Franco-Prussian war (1870-1) inaugurated the German empire. As German chancellor (1871-90) he played a leading role in the European alliance systems of the 1870s and 1880s.

2 The unification of Germany, 1815–71

☐ Prussia in 1815	● free city
☐ acquired by Prussia, 1815–66	▬ German Empire, 1871
▬ German Confederation, 1815	◀ Austro-Prussian forces attack on Denmark, 1864
┄ North German Confederation, 1867	◀ Prussian armies in the war with Austria, 1866
☐ Imperial territory of Alsace-Lorraine, 1871	◀ German armies in the Franco-Prussian war, 1870–71

1 The unification of Italy, 1859–70

- French from 1768, formerly Genoese
- Kingdom of Sardinia in 1815
- territory annexed 1859
- territory annexed March 1860
- territory annexed November 1860
- territory lost to France 1860
- territory annexed 1866
- territory annexed 1870
- Austrian empire, 1815
- Italian border, 1914

SWITZERLAND

AUSTRO-HUNGARIAN EMPIRE

SAVOY

PIEDMONT

• Aosta
• Bergamo
Como •
Monza •
Brescia •
Magenta 1859 × Milan
Novara 1849 × Solferino 1859 ×

TYROL
• Trent (Trento)
VENETIA
Udine •
Görz (Gorizia) •
Trieste •
Custoza 1848, 1866 ×
Verona •
Padua •
Venice •
Fiume •

LOMBARDY

• Susa
Turin •

KINGDOM OF SARDINIA

FRANCE

Alessandria •
PARMA
Parma •
Guastalla •
Ferrara •
MODENA
Modena •
ROMAGNA
• Bologna
SAN MARINO

LIGURIA
Genoa •
Pontremoli •
La Spezia •

Mantua •

Pola •

NICE
Monaco •
Nice •

Pisa •
Lucca •
Arno
Florence •
Arezzo •
Siena •

Rimini •
Pesaro •
Urbino •
Ancona •
Castelfidardo •

MARCHES

Zara •

Dalmatia

OTTOMAN EMPIRE

TUSCANY
Élba

UMBRIA
Spoleto •
PAPAL
STATES
Rieti •

Lissa 1866 ×

Adriatic Sea

Livorno (Leghorn) •

CORSICA

Civitavecchia •
Mentana •
Rome •

Tiber

Terracina •
Gaeta •
Pontecorvo •
Volturno 1860 ×
Benevento •

KINGDOM

Bari •

Sassari •

KINGDOM OF SARDINIA

Mediterranean Sea

Tyrrhenian Sea

Castellammare •
Naples •
Salerno •
Potenza •

NAPLES

Taranto •

Cagliari •

OF

THE

• Cosenza

Lipari Is.

TWO

Aspromonte 1862 ×

Messina •
Reggio •

Palermo •

SICILIES

Marsala •

Catania •

Syracuse •

sought a unification of Italy along conservative lines, in the interests of Piedmont-Sardinia, and was hostile to the more revolutionary nationalism of Garibaldi and Mazzini. Bismarck in Prussia wanted unification to achieve his aim of a conservative, Prussian-dominated German state. Both used diplomacy and war to achieve their objectives: Cavour allied with France before attacking Austria in 1859, securing the unification of Italy (except for Venetia and the Papal States) by 1861 (see map 1). Bismarck allied with Austria in order to defeat Denmark (1864), then in concert with Italy attacked Austria (1866), and finally defeated France (1870-1), achieving in the process the unification of Germany (map 2).

Liberal nationalists later endorsed both achievements, but neither satisfied the nationalism they had aroused. Italy still laid claim to the Alto Adige and Istria; Bismarck's 'Small German' solution, which excluded Austria, disappointed those who hankered after a Greater Germany.

Nevertheless, the four short wars fought between 1859 and 1871 solved the Italian and German questions, and re-drew the map of Central Europe. Moreover, the Great Powers now remained at peace for over four decades and although nationalist grievances continued to fester, territorial disputes within Europe ceased to divide most governments.

1830–1914
Imperialism

Until 1830, the search for oriental luxuries remained the driving force behind European imperialism, and (with the important exception of India: page 96) the European stake in Asia and Africa remained confined to trading stations and the strategic outposts necessary to protect trade. Thereafter two new factors transformed the situation. First came the enforced 'opening' of key markets – Turkey and Egypt (1838), Persia (1841), China (1842), Japan (1858) – to European, particularly British, commerce. Then, from the 1870s, a new phase of the Industrial Revolution (page 100) provoked a search for raw materials to feed the new industries. In the scramble for these resources between 1880 and 1914, Europe added almost 9 million square miles (23.4 million km^2) – one-fifth of the land area of the globe – to its overseas colonial possessions.

France and Britain took the lead. The former conquered Algeria after 1830, annexed Tahiti and the Marquesas in the 1840s, expanded its colony in Senegal in the 1850s and began the conquest of Indo-China in 1859. Britain, both to forestall the French and to safeguard its position in India, claimed sovereignty over Australia and New Zealand (page 106), and acquired Singapore (1819), Malacca (1824), Hong Kong (1842), Burma (1852), and Lagos (1861) (map 1).

1 Colonial penetration, 1815–70
see key right

Pacific Ocean

Russian *1900–1905*
Russian *1898–1905*
Port Arthur
Tsingtao
Weihaiwei *1898*
Shanghai
Ningpo
Foochow
TAIWAN *(to Japan 1895)*
Amoy
Canton
Hong Kong
Macao
TONGKING

JAPAN
KOREA *(to Japan 1910)*

MANCHURIA

MONGOLIA

RUSSIAN EMPIRE

C H I N A

TIBET

Marshall Is. *1888*
Marianas *(Ladrones) 1899*
Pacific Islands to Germany
Gilbert Is. *1892*
Guam *1898*
Ellice Is. *1886*

Caroline Is. *1899*
Solomon Is. *1893*
to Germany
to UK
Samoa *1888–99*

Heligoland *1814–90*
NETHER-LANDS
DENMARK
GREAT BRITAIN
GERMANY
BELGIUM
FRANCE
ITALY
AZORES
PORTUGAL
SPAIN
Gibraltar
Ceuta
Melilla
MALTA
TUNISIA *1881*
CYPRUS *(leased by UK 1878)*
OTTOMAN EMPIRE
PERSIA
KUWAIT
Aden
OMAN
ARABIA

1895
TURKESTAN
1873
1884–5

Madeira
Canary Is.
IFNI
RIO DE ORO
MOROCCO *1912*
ALGERIA
LIBYA *1912*
EGYPT *1882*

FRENCH WEST AFRICA *1876–98*
ANGLO-EGYPTIAN SUDAN *1898*
ERITREA *1889*
ABYSSINIA
ITALIAN SOMALILAND *1889–92*
BRITISH SOMALILAND *1884*
FRENCH SOMALILAND *1884–8*
Socotra *1876*

I N D I A
LAOS *1893*
UPPER BURMA *1886*
LOWER BURMA
SIAM
ANNAM *1884*
INDO-CHINA
CAMBODIA
NORTH BORNEO *1881*
BRUNEI
SARAWAK *1888*
DUTCH BORNEO

Diu
Goa
Penang
Singapore
MALAYA *1875–95*
SUMATRA
JAVA
CEYLON
Laccadive Is.
Maldives
Nicobar Is.
Andaman Is.
Cocos Is.
Chagos Archipelago

NEW GUINEA
PAPUA *(to Australia 1902–6)*
to USA
BISMARCK ARCHIPELAGO *1885*
New Hebrides *1906*
Fiji *1874*
Tonga *1900*
NEW CALEDONIA
TIMOR
Norfolk I.

COMMONWEALTH OF AUSTRALIA *1901*
NEW ZEALAND
TASMANIA

TOGOLAND *1884*
IVORY COAST *1893*
GOLD COAST *1874–96*
DAHOMEY *1890*
NIGERIA *1884–1900*
Porto Novo *1883*
CAMEROONS *1884*
FRENCH CONGO *1875–92*
CONGO FREE STATE *1885*
GERMAN EAST AFRICA *1886*
UGANDA
BRITISH EAST AFRICA *1886*
Seychelles
Comoro Is.
Mauritius
Réunion

SENEGAL
GAMBIA
PORTUGUESE GUINEA
SIERRA LEONE *1896*
LIBERIA
Fernando Po
São Tomé
Ascension I.
St. Helena

ANGOLA
PORTUGUESE EAST AFRICA
MADAGASCAR *1895–6*
NORTHERN RHODESIA *1891*
NYASALAND *1891*
SOUTHERN RHODESIA *1890*
GERMAN SOUTH-WEST AFRICA *1884*
Walvis Bay *1878*
BECHUANALAND *1885*
SWAZILAND *1895*
BASUTOLAND *1871*
UNION OF SOUTH AFRICA *1910*

Cape Verde Is.
Tristan da Cunha
Gough I.
St. Helena
South Georgia

2 The closing of the world system

major powers

British	Ottoman
French	Dutch
German	Italian
Portuguese	Spanish

Belgian	
Russian	
USA	
Danish	
Japanese	

1893 date of European control
1902 date of independence
princely states of India
○ treaty ports
----- sphere of effective

...... proposed spheres of influence
major investments of European colonial powers outside Europe
—— major sea routes

major raw materials exported to Europe

grain	jute
meat	silk
tea	rubber
cane sugar	veg oil
dairy produce	copra
cotton	wool

The same imperatives underlay British expansion after 1880, except that the number of competitors to forestall increased. Thus the French empire grew between 1871 and 1914 by nearly 4 million square miles (10.4 million km²) and 47 million people (mainly in north and west Africa and Indo-China, where Laos and Tongking were added to Cambodia and Cochin-China, but it also secured Madagascar and some Pacific islands); Germany also acquired an empire of 1 million square miles (2.6 million km²)and 14 million colonial subjects (in South-West Africa, Togoland, the Cameroons, Tanganyika and the Pacific islands); Italy obtained several outposts in Africa; the United States annexed the Philippines, Guam, Hawaii and some Caribbean islands; and Russia began to expand in central Asia. Britain too managed to acquire extensive new territories in Africa which almost linked Cape Town with Cairo, more Pacific islands (including Fiji), and parts of the Indonesian archipelago (map 2). It added 88 million subjects to her empire and, by 1914, exercized authority over a fifth of the world's landmass and a quarter of its peoples.

In retrospect, the fragility of these European empires, so hastily assembled, is obvious. None of the imperial powers possessed the resources to govern them effectively and European imperialism proved more ephemeral than anyone at the time imagined; yet it left an indelible mark on the peoples of Africa and Asia, propelling them willingly or unwillingly into the 20th century.

Advertisements often unconsciously reflect the assumptions on which societies operate. The Victorian tobacco advert *(left)* shows the wealthy European manufacturers receiving the raw material from crudely parodied native growers, to whom the finished product will eventually be resold.

North America

26 Apr. 1865
The South surrenders; end of Civil War; Reconstruction begins

1867
Canadian Federation formed; USA purchases Alaska from Russia

1869
First trans-continental railroad in USA completed

1870-1
Manitoba and British Columbia join Canadian Federation

1877
Reconstruction formally comes to an end

1885
Canadian-Pacific railroad completed

1898
USA annexes Hawaii: Cuba and the Philippines seized from Spain

1914
Canada and (1917) USA join World War I

Although the United States made a remarkably rapid recovery after the Civil War (page 104), development remained very uneven. In the defeated South, the period of Reconstruction (1865-77) proved a bitter experience. South Carolina, which in 1860 had ranked third in the nation in per capita wealth, ranked 40th ten years later; and other once-prosperous states did scarcely better. The 4 million liberated black slaves fared worst, being left (as Frederick Douglass wrote) without money, property or friends. Although the population of the Union surged from 31 million in 1861 to 92 million in 1910, most of the increase by-passed the South and concentrated wealth and power in the north-east and the upper Mid-West. Only around 1920 did cheap labour attract textile industry to the South (map 1).

The settlement of the Great Plains, made possible by the railway boom after 1870, constituted perhaps the most striking achievement of the post-war period. The track in operation increased from 30,000 miles (48,000 km) in 1860 to 163,000 (262,000 km) in 1890 (at which point it exceeded the size of the entire European rail system); the number of farms rose from 2 million in 1860 to 6 million in 1910; and the population living west of the Mississippi grew from 6 million to 26 million. Yet the bulk of the population remained concentrated in the north-east (map 3), and most of the 25 million immigrants arriving between 1870 and 1914 stayed there, providing cheap labour for American industry.

Railways played an even more prominent role in the development of Canada. The United States made no secret of its hope to absorb the provinces and thus create a continent-wide empire. After the acquisition

Pittsburgh, Pennsylvania, surrounded by huge coal-fields and beds of iron and at the confluence of two important rivers, became the leading centre of iron and steel production in the United States. So vast and dramatic was the sight of its blast furnaces and coke ovens at work that early 20th-century artists and commentators began to refer to it as 'Hell with the lid off.'

2 Canada, 1867–1929

land occupied;
- prior to 1851
- 1851–1871
- 1871–1901
- 1901–1921

population of towns, 1871;
- 25,000-100,000 people
- over 100,000 people

population of towns, 1911;
- 25,000-100,000 people
- over 100,000 people

railways 1916:
- Canadian Pacific Railway
- Canadian Northern (Main Line)
- National Trans-continental Railway
- main industrial regions

ALBERTA 1905 date of accession to Dominion of Canada

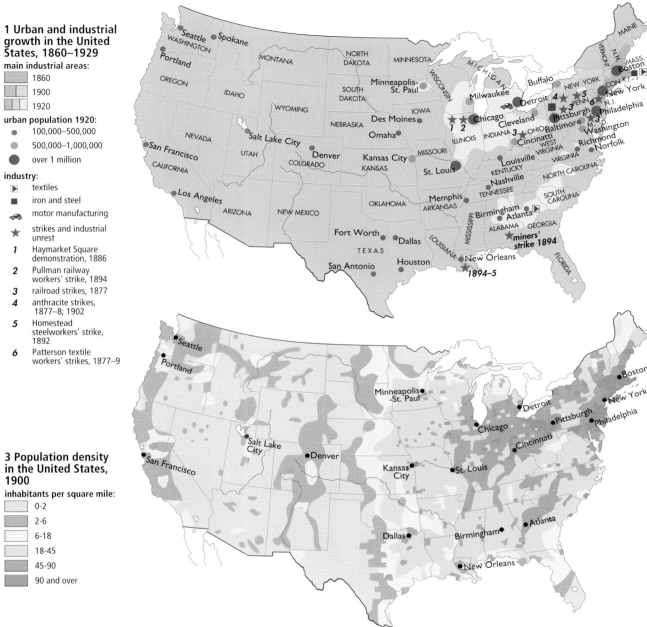

1 Urban and industrial growth in the United States, 1860–1929

main industrial areas:
- 1860
- 1900
- 1920

urban population 1920:
- 100,000–500,000
- 500,000–1,000,000
- over 1 million

industry:
- ▷ textiles
- ■ iron and steel
- 🚗 motor manufacturing
- ★ strikes and industrial unrest

1 Haymarket Square demonstration, 1886
2 Pullman railway workers' strike, 1894
3 railroad strikes, 1877
4 anthracite strikes, 1877–8; 1902
5 Homestead steelworkers' strike, 1892
6 Patterson textile workers' strikes, 1877–9

3 Population density in the United States, 1900

inhabitants per square mile:
- 0–2
- 2–6
- 6–18
- 18–45
- 45–90
- 90 and over

of Alaska by the United States (1867), this pressure grew, but the Canadians frustrated their neighbours' intentions by forming the Canadian Federation in 1867, completed by the purchase of Rupert's Land from the Hudson's Bay Company (1869) and the adhesion of Manitoba (1870) and British Columbia (1871). The great transcontinental railways – the Canadian Pacific (completed 1885) followed by the Canadian Northern and the National Trans-continental – became the lifeblood of the new Dominion, opening Manitoba and Saskatchewan, and turning Canada into one of the world's leading wheat producers. It also facilitated the exploitation of rich mineral deposits, particularly copper and nickel (map 2). Overall, Canada's industrial output increased from $190 million in 1890 to over $500 million in 1914.

This achievement was dwarfed, however, by the economic and territorial growth of the United States. Output of iron and steel increased 20-fold between 1870 and 1913, by which time steel production exceeded that of Britain and Germany combined, and the United States remained the world's leading agricultural producer. Meanwhile, in 1898 (following a successful war with Spain), the Philippines, Guam, Puerto Rico and Hawaii were annexed, the latter after many years of American encroachment in the islands' affairs; and in 1903 Cuba and the Panama Canal Zone became protectorates. The United States now possessed the political and economic might to intervene almost anywhere on the world stage: in Mexico in 1914 and again in 1916, and – on a far greater scale – in Europe in 1917-18 (page 132).

1868–1941
Japan

The Tokugawa shoguns (page 88) gave Japan over two centuries of peace and prosperity. In 1868, however, internal tensions, combined with the pressure of Western powers to open Japan to foreign trade, resulted in a revolution (known as the Meiji Restoration) which replaced the shogun and the feudal structure with a modern system of government. The new Japanese leaders implemented widespread reforms in the belief that a modern economy and military would ensure Japan's international independence and equality. They instituted a national education system (which by 1900 provided teaching for 90 per cent of children), a conscript army, and a navy with modern ships. Legal codes, largely based on French and German models, were introduced from 1882. The economic reforms were wide-reaching; the first railway opened in 1872 and by 1906 the system linked most parts of the country; up to one-third of state expenditure went on developing commerce and industry (map 1); and a land tax reform in 1873 provided a secure source of revenue for the government. The shifting structure of Japanese foreign trade (see table 3) illustrates the dramatic impact of these changes. Whereas by 1878-82, manufactured goods represented half of all imports but only 7 per cent of exports, in 1918-22 the ratio had reversed:

1 Industrial Japan
town population, 1918
- ● less than 50,000
- ● 50,000–100,000
- ◉ 100,000,–500,000
- ⊠ 500,000–1 million
- ■ over 1 million

- ⌒ railways in 1906
- ⌐ additions to railways 1906–1918
- ▬ main manufacturing areas
- KYOTO prefecture

industries:
- ■ metal
- ⚓ shipbuilding
- ✚ textiles
- ⚲ wood
- ◀ silk
- ⚱ ceramics
- ▮ chemicals
- ⚶ food
- ⊞ machinery
- ▪ manufacturing industry

minerals:
- ● coal
- C copper
- ▲ iron
- ▮ oil

The battle of Tsushima Strait, in May 1905, was one of the most complete naval victories in history *(right)*. The Russian fleet, in dire need of mechanical overhaul, was outmanœuvred by the Japanese Togo, and forced to surrender after the sinking of six of its battle-ships. The war was over – the first time that an emerging Asian power had defeated a Western one; the news resounded throughout the colonial world.

finished manufactures now accounted for over 40 per cent of sales and only 15 per cent of purchases. Moreover the total value of Japan's exports rose in this period from 30 million to 1.8 billion yen.

International recognition of Japan's new status was nevertheless slow in coming: consular jurisdiction survived until 1894, and the unequal treaties negotiated in the 1850s with the Western powers remained in force until 1911. As Japan's strength and confidence grew, however, so did nationalist and imperialist ambitions. In 1894-5 a victorious war against China, arising from disputes in Korea, ended in a treaty granting Taiwan to Japan. Russo-Japanese rivalry over Manchuria culminated in Japanese victory in the war of 1904-5. The Treaty of Portsmouth (1905) gave Japan a lease of territory in China and extensive rights in South Manchuria. In 1910 she acquired Korea. Japanese support for the victorious Western powers in World War I brought few further rewards, however, and the country's military leaders became frustrated. After 1931, under the impact of the Great Depression (page 138), Japan overran first Manchuria and then – despite strong opposition from the United States – northern China in an attempt to achieve economic self-sufficiency (map 2). Germany's victory over France and the Netherlands in 1940 offered an opportunity to expand southwards – thereby gaining control over valuable oil fields in Borneo and Burma – precipitating full-scale war with the Western powers (page 142). Paradoxically, Japan's total defeat and the ensuing American occupation propelled her even more decisively into the modern world than the Meiji restoration had done.

2 Japanese expansion from 1914

- Japanese territory by 1914, with dates of acquisition
- spheres of Japanese influence, 1918
- expansion to 1933
- expansion to Nov. 1941
- Japanese conflict with USSR
- Japanese attacks
- Chinese capitals
- Allied bases
- railways

3 Structure of Japanese trade

food, drink   raw materials   semi-manufactured goods   finished goods   other

1878-82 export import

1918-22 export import

0%   25%   50%   75%   100%

European rivalries and alliances

The unification of Germany and Italy (page 116) seemed for a time to have resolved the major questions which had disturbed the peace of Europe since 1848. Bismarck, the architect of German unification, concentrated after 1871 on building a system of alliances that would ensure the future of the new empire, mainly by isolating France, which proved unable to reconcile itself to the rise of the new German empire, and for almost 20 years he succeeded in convincing the rest of Europe of Germany's conservative and pacific intentions. In time, however, the alliances that had seemed defensive became aggressive and destabilizing.

Meanwhile, although the achievements of Bismarck and Cavour reduced nationalist fervour in central Europe, they stirred up a hornet's nest in the Balkans, where the struggles of various national groups for independence from the Turks inevitably involved the neighbouring powers, Russia and Austria (which, after its exclusion from Germany in 1866 became far more interested in the Balkans).

Revolts in the Balkans between 1875 and 1878, culminating in Russian intervention and war with the Turks, resulted in the treaty of Berlin (brokered by Bismarck) which either confirmed or established the independence of Serbia, Montenegro, Romania and Bulgaria and granted Austria a mandate to govern Bosnia and Herzegovina. In 1879 Germany and Austria signed a defensive alliance, expanded to include Italy in 1882 (map 1). Russia, satisfied that Slav interest had been met in the Balkans, turned increasingly to Central Asia, and the Far East. The main European rivalries were now between Britain and Russia in Asia, and Britain and France in Africa. Britain remained isolated in Europe, while France and Russia signed an alliance in 1894 as a counterweight to the strength of the alliance bloc based around Germany.

The situation changed after 1897, however, when Germany began to seek a 'place in the sun'. This was not unreasonable; but by then most places in the sun had been occupied by others, and German policy – which involved building a High Seas Fleet to rival that of Britain – therefore seemed to constitute a threat to the established imperial powers. As a result, Britain resolved its differences with France in 1904,

1 European alliance systems, 1882–1914

— frontiers, 1912

The Triple Alliance, 1882

The Triple Entente, 1912

The Balkan League, 1912

AUSTRO-HUNGARIAN EMPIRE

Budapest

Lake
Balaton

Sava

Banja Luka

BOSNIA-
HERZEGOVINA
administered by Austria-
Hungary 1878; annexed 1908

Sarajevo

Belgrade

Carpathian Mts

Jassy

MOLDAVIA
semi-independent
1829

Galatz

S E R B I A

principality 1817;
independent 1878

Nish

Vidin

ROMANIA
united 1859; independent 1878;
kingdom 1881

Bucharest

WALLACHIA
semi-independent
1829

Danube

Balchik

MONTENEGRO

Kotor
(Cattaro)

Cetinje

Scutari

Tirana

to Serbia
1913

Monastir

Usküb
(Skoplje)

ALBANIA
principality
1913

Koritsa

Sofia

B U L G A R I A
principality 1878
independent 1908

to Bulgaria 1913

Maritsa

EASTERN
RUMELIA
to Bulgaria 1885

Varna

Burgas

Black
Sea

Adriatic
Sea

Macedonia

Kavalla

to Bulgaria 1913

Adrianople

T h r a c e

Constantinople

EPIRUS

to Greece 1913

Salonica

Thasos

Corfu

Yannina

to Greece 1864

Preveza

Arta

THESSALY
to Greece 1881

Larissa

Lemnos

to Greece 1913

Mytilene

OTTOMAN
EMPIRE

Ionian
Sea

Ionian
Islands

to Greece
1864

KINGDOM OF GREECE
independent 1830

Patras

Tripolis

Athens

Piraeus

Aegean
Sea

Chios

Smyrna

to Greece 1913

Nikaria

to Greece 1864

CRETE
independent 1898
to Greece 1913

Candia

Dodecanese

Rhodes

occupied by Italy
1912

and with Russia in 1907,
and France settled its long-standing dispute with Italy in 1902. Thereafter,
the Triple Entente with France and Russia
became the lynch-pin of British foreign policy,
the only firm assurance against the German 'threat'.
Germany, on the other became concerned with the
danger of 'encirclement' by a hostile ring constructed
by Great Britain (map 1).

As a result, a dangerous simplification of align-
ments occurred into a bi-polar system: the Triple
Alliance and the Triple Entente drew tighter, and
Germany in particular grew closer to its only
dependable ally, Austria. When Austria annexed
Bosnia and Herzegovina in 1908, Germany gave her
qualified support, though it rekindled Austro-Russian
antagonism in the Balkans. During the Balkan wars
(1912-13), in which a Russian-sponsored Balkan
League consisting of Serbia, Greece and Bulgaria
attempted to drive the Turks out of Europe, the two
diplomatic systems still cooperated; but Austria
stood aghast at the consequent enlargement of
Serbia – which almost doubled its size – and feared
Serb agitation for an independent south Slav state
(map 2).

The assassination of the heir to the Austrian
throne in Sarajevo (Bosnia) in June 1914 provided
what seemed to the Austrian government like its last
chance to deal with Serbia before it grew too powerful, and Germany threw its entire weight behind its
ally. Russia, however, could not afford to leave Serbia

in the lurch and began to mobilize against Austria.
Germany regarded this as a direct threat, and also
began to mobilize. However, to forestall an attack
from Russia's allies in the West, German Grand
Strategy called for an immediate attack on France –
in the hope that it could be knocked out of the war
before Russia advanced in force. On 28 July, Austria
declared war on Serbia; on 1 August 1914 Germany
declared war on Russia, and two days later on
France. The diplomatic system created by Bismarck,
coupled with the volatile situation in the Balkans,
had produced a world war (page 132).

2 The Balkans, 1878–1913

- – – frontier of Ottoman empire, 1800
- ——— frontier of Ottoman empire, 1885
- ——— national frontiers after the Balkan wars 1912–13

HMS Temeraire, depicted on a pre-war postcard. Britain responded to Germany's increased warship building after 1900 with a rival programme based on the most modern Dreadnought battleships. The Royal Navy was fully mobilized for exercises at the outbreak of war.

The formation of a world economy

The integration of the global economy into a single interdependent whole formed one of the principal developments of the period 1870-1914. Europe (and to a lesser extent the United States) stood at the heart of this process, emitting the impulses that opened up the remaining areas of the globe to Western exploration and exploitation.

Three interrelated aspects deserve special attention. First came the development of better means of communication. In 1870, railways remained largely confined to Europe (60,400 miles, 97,250 km of track) and North America (56,300 miles, 90,600 km): the rest of the world could boast only 9100 miles (14,650 km). By 1911, however, the total network of tracks had increased to 657,000 miles (1.06 million km) – 175,000 miles (280,000 km) of them outside Europe and North America – and included some spectacular transcontinental links: across the United States (four between 1869 and 1893), Canada (1885), Russia (1904) and the Andes (1910). The expansion of world shipping was equally striking, with not only a spectacular rise in the total tonnage, but a shift from sail to steam which increased the speed and regularity of shipments. However, the main shipping traffic, both passenger and freight, took place among the advanced countries and the white dominions, or between them and the producers of the raw materials they required. Canal construction also continued apace – above all the Suez Canal, completed in 1869, which carried 437,000 tons in 1870 and over 20 million in 1913; and the Panama Canal, completed in 1914, which carried 5 million tons of cargo in its first year. These spectacular totals reflected the enormous savings in distance – 41 per cent for vessels sailing from Liverpool to Bombay, 60 per cent for vessels sailing from New York to San Francisco.

Finally, messages travelled around the world with increasing speed. Cables laid beneath the oceans linked the continents – between Britain and North America (1866); from Vancouver to Brisbane (1902) – followed by telephones (with international lines from 1887) and wireless stations (from 1897).

These developments paralleled a boom in commerce. Foreign trade tripled in volume between 1870 and 1914, although (again) most of the activity occurred among the industrialized countries, or between them and their suppliers of primary goods or their new markets. In 1913, only 11 per cent of the

1 The development of the world economy

foreign investment, 1914
(in $ million)

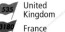

535	United Kingdom	420	United States
3180	France	1050	Germany

— busiest shipping routes
— other major shipping routes, c. 1900
— international telegraph cables

Colonial empires in 1900

Belgian	Japanese
British	Ottoman
Danish	Portuguese
Dutch	Russian
French	Spanish
German	USA
Italian	other countries

Panama canal, 1914

MEXICO 500 400 850
UNITED STATES OF AMERICA
DOMINION OF CANADA 2800 200 880
Gulf of Mexico 4250 400 950
PERU
COLOMBIA
VENEZUELA 340
CHILE 300
BOLIVIA
ARGENTINA 400 1550
PARAGUAY 200 200
URUGUAY
BRAZIL 700 500 700
North Atlantic Ocean

3 The share of world trade

1860 total $8 billion

Others
United Kingdom
USA
France
Russia
Spain
Austria-Hungary
Italy
Scandinavia
Germany
Holland and Belgium
Switzerland

world's trade took place between the primary producers themselves. Britain ranked as the world's largest trading nation in 1860, but by 1913 it had lost ground to both the United States and Germany: British and German exports in that year each totalled $2.3 billion, and those of the United States exceeded $2.4 billion.

Britain remained the world's financial capital, however, as well as its largest lender, with almost $20 billion in foreign investments by 1914 – slightly more than those of France, Germany, Holland and Belgium combined. The United States and Russia were in fact net borrowers of foreign capital. Investments within Europe and North America on the whole assisted and accelerated economic advancement, helping to create the costly infrastructure (such as railways and other public works) for developing nations that would in time repay these debts. By contrast, investments in non-industrial regions (such as the Russian and Ottoman empires) and overseas territories that lacked both the knowledge and the power to direct the capital flow, served to colonize rather than develop them, destroying native industries and creating dangerous political and economic pressures which would, in time, produce conflict between rich nations and poor nations and demands for a new economic order (page 174).

order (page 174).

Miners at the Republic Gold Mining Company in the Transvaal, South Africa, fuelled the economic engine that drove the Gold Standard. This originated in Britain in 1821, but until Germany joined the system in 1871, most other countries remained on a bi-metallicstandard, gold and silver.

2 Foreign Investment in 1914 (in $ million)

Russia	500
Belgium	900
USA	3,510
Holland	4,100
Germany	5,650
France	9,280
United Kingdom	19,935

NEW ZEALAND 300

COMMONWEALTH OF AUSTRALIA 1700

GERMAN NEW GUINEA

DUTCH NEW GUINEA

DUTCH BORNEO

SARAWAK

JAPAN 500

MONGOLIA 200

CHINA 600

INDO-CHINA 200

SIAM

BURMA

INDIA 1850

RUSSIAN EMPIRE 550 400 2400

FINLAND

investment in the rest of Europe

NORWAY 20

SWEDEN 535

GERMANY 180 1050

U K

FRANCE 750

AUST.-HUNGARY 450

ITALY

SPAIN

OTTOMAN EMPIRE 650

PERSIA

Suez canal, 1869

Mediterranean Sea

ARABIA

EGYPT 500

LIBYA

ALGERIA 200

FRENCH WEST AFRICA 100

NIGERIA

ANGLO EGYPTIAN SUDAN 200

ABYSSINIA

BRITISH EAST AFRICA 600

all of Africa

CONGO FREE STATE 500

GERMAN E. AFRICA

MADAGASCAR

RHODESIA

ANGOLA

GERMAN SOUTH WEST AFRICA

UNION OF SOUTH AFRICA 1550 from 1910

Indian Ocean

FOUR

The Modern World

By making the world one, the European powers stirred up forces that eventually caused their own eclipse. The world wars between 1914 and 1945 whittled away their resources and Europe's exhaustion benefited the Soviet Union and the United States, the two superpowers on the eastern and western flanks, whose rivalry produced an age of bipolarity. But bipolarity, too, proved to be temporary. The recovery of Europe, the emancipation of Asia and Africa, the rise of Japan and finally the collapse of the Soviet empire brought a new constellation into being, and with it the threat of confrontation between rich and poor nations and of the exhaustion of global resources through overpopulation. No one can foretell the shape of things to come. All this section can do is show, in historical perspective, how the world of the 20th century changed and chart the emergence of significant new factors.

Devastation inflicted by the first atomic bomb
Hiroshima, 1945

1 The Nationalist (Kuomintang) regime, 1928–37

- occupied by Japan by 1933
- area in which Japan attempted to establish a puppet North China state, 1935

areas of effective control of Nationalist government
- from 1928
- added 1929–34
- added 1935–7
- brought under Nanking influence, 1935–7

By 1911 the imperial government of China was thoroughly discredited (page 94) and an army mutiny led to the emperor's abdication. But the Republic proclaimed in 1912, with Sun Yat-sen as its first president, was overwhelmed by its inherited problems, and Sun was soon deposed by Yuan Shih-k'ai, the most powerful general of the old regime. After Yuan's death in 1916 power passed to provincial warlords, whose armies caused untold damage and millions of casualties. Compounding this misery were the expansionist policies of Japan and the foreign powers, based in the Treaty Ports (page 88), which interfered in the Chinese economy and in Chinese politics.

In 1919, the refusal of the Paris Peace Conference to abrogate foreign privileges provoked spontaneous urban uprisings (the 'May 4th' movement). These provided a new opportunity for Sun Yat-sen, who in 1923 reorganized his Nationalist (Kuomintang; KMT) Party, allied with the Chinese Communist Party (founded 1921), and prepared to reunite the country. But Sun died in 1925 and it was Chiang Kai-shek, the Moscow-trained general of the KMT army, who in 1926 marched northwards to eliminate the warlords. Helped by peasant and workers' uprisings along his route, Chiang proved remarkably successful, but in 1927 he turned on his allies, massacring the Communists in

Shanghai. However KMT direct rule remained limited to the lower Yangtze (map 1). Nevertheless, the Japanese, fearing the potential challenge from a reunited China, decided to reinforce their hold in the north and overran Manchuria (1931) and Jehol (1933).

Although KMT purges had virtually eliminated Communism from the cities, peasant disaffection – arising from the absence of land reform – offered an alternative constituency. From his base at Chingkang Shan, Mao Tse-Tung and others created a new centre of revitalized communism, developing a peasant-based party rather than an urban, proletarian party on the Russian model. In 1929 KMT pressure

2 The Chinese Communist movement to 1945

- abortive urban insurrections after the break with Kuomintang 1927
- position of early Communist army groups
- early Soviets (self-governing Communist areas) 1927–35
- route of the 'Long March', Oct. 1934–Oct. 1935, of Chinese Communists after Kuomintang assaults on Kiangsi Soviet area
- main Communist base area, governed from Yenan 1935–45
- area occupied by Japan end 1941
- area occupied by Japan during 1944 offensives
- 'liberated areas' dominated by local Communist groups by 1945
- railways in 1937
- main industrial areas 1937
- main industrial centres 1937
- other industrial centres 1937

USSR

MANCHURIA

Manchouli • Hailar

• Tsitsihar
• Kiamusze

OUTER MONGOLIA (independent 1921)

Harbin

Kirin

Changchun

Mukden Fushun
Chinchow Penki
Anshan
Yingkow Antung

KOREA
Japanese 1910–45

Kalgan

Paotow
• Tatung • Peking
Tangshan • Dairen
Tientsin Port Arthur (Lüshun)

SHEN-KAN-NING

Taiyuan

Yenan Pao-an: Soviet 1930–5
Tsinan
Tsingtao

Yellow Sea

Lanchow

Yellow River (Hwang Ho)
Kaifeng
Loyang Chengchow
Lienyünkang

Sian
Hsü-chou (Suchow)

4th army group, Chang Kuo-tao Hsü Hsiang-ch'ien

C H I N A

Nanking Soochow
Shanghai

Chengtu

Wuhan Hangchow • Ningpo

Chungking
Kiukiang 10th army group, Fang Chih-min

East China Sea

Nanchang Aug. 1927

Tsunyi Jan. 1935
W. Hunan
Changsha
Hengyang
Chingkang Shan, Mao Zedong and Chu Teh, 1927–9

compelled Mao and his followers to move first to Kiangsi, and then in 1934 to the north-west (the 'Long March': map 2).

Kweiyang
Jui-chin (Juikin)
Foochow
Kiangsi Soviet under Mao Zedong and Chu Teh, 1929–34

TAIWAN
Japanese 1895–1945

In 1937 Japanese forces invaded northern and central China and the KMT retreated to the interior, where they remained until the Japanese surrender in 1945. A race to occupy the liberated areas now ensued, with the Communists gaining much of the north and most of Manchuria, and the KMT re-occupying the south. In 1946 hostilities between the two sides erupted into a civil war from which the Communists emerged victorious. The People's Republic of China was proclaimed in October 1949, and soon afterwards the KMT fled to Taiwan. For the first time in a century, a strong regime controlled all of mainland China – albeit most of the country had been devastated by the warlords, the Japanese occupation and the civil war.

Kunming

Amoy

Canton Dec. 1927
Swatow
Hailufeng Soviet under P'eng P'ai, 1927–8

Hong Kong British

BURMA

FRENCH INDO-CHINA

THAILAND

Hainan South China Sea

A poster from c.1927 showing Sun Yat-sen (top centre) and Chiang Kai-shek (on horse) about to set out with Kuomintang forces on the 'Northern Expedition' of 1926–8.

All the war-plans of the Great Powers in 1914 envisaged a short war. The German Schlieffen Plan called for an attack on northern France through Belgium, leading to the rapid collapse of the French government before Russia had time to mobilize (page 125). It almost succeeded: the Germans came within 40 miles of Paris, but not before Russian armies had invaded East Prussia. Although their advance was halted at Tannenberg (August), important German reserves were diverted from the Western front just as a spirited counter-attack by French and British troops began at the Marne (September). The two sides now spread their forces out and dug in, until their trenches stretched from the Channel coast to Switzerland.

The war in the west (map 2) turned into a war of attrition. Each side launched repeated offensives, with appalling casualties but little gain, for railways were able to bring up reinforcements before the slow-moving front-line troops could make good any advantage. In 1916 the British, under Sir Douglas Haig, made a major frontal assault on German lines at the river Somme. On the first day of the battle 60,000 British casualties were mowed down as they advanced through the barbed wire. Haig threw his forces into an unwinnable conflict for another four months. Both sides experienced terrible losses and achieved little. Neither side could break the trench

stalemate by pursuing alternative strategies. The British and French attempted a series of attacks from the rear: in the Dardanelles and Mesopotamia against the Ottoman empire, which entered the war in November 1914 on the side of the Central Powers (Germany and Austria); on Austria's southern frontier after Italy declared war in May 1915; at Salonika in Greece in support of Serbia. All failed. The Germans countered by building a fleet of submarines with the express intention of bringing Britain to its knees by attacking vulnerable food imports on which Britain relied. In 1917 unrestricted submarine warfare failed to halt Britain's food supply, but provoked the United States into war with Germany.

On the eastern front, which stretched for twice the distance of that in the west, warfare remained more mobile and both Germany and Austria scored major successes. In 1915 the former overran a huge area of Poland, whose resources it ruthlessly exploited, while the latter occupied most of Serbia. In 1917 the combination of huge losses and economic chaos broke the fighting spirit of the Russian forces and provoked revolution and military collapse (page 134). At the peace of Brest-Litovsk in March 1918 Germany gained the Ukraine, Poland, Finland and the Baltic provinces.

NORWAY • Bergen • Kristiania

⚓ Scapa Flow

SCOTLAND • Glasgow • Edinburgh ⚓

UNITED KINGDOM

IRELAND • Belfast • Newcastle

• Dublin • Liverpool • Manchester

WALES **ENGLAND** • Birmingham

• Cork • Bristol ⚓ • London ⚓

NORTH SEA

naval blockade of Germany effective end 1916

1916: Battle of Jutland ★

SWEDEN • Gothenburg • Stockholm

FINLAND • Helsingfors ⚓ • Revel ⚓

• St Petersburg (Petrograd) ⚓

1918

Baltic Sea

1917: Riga offensive • Riga • Pskov

• Dvinsk • Moscow • Volga

RUSSIAN EMPIRE

1914: Russian offensive in East Prussia

• Smolensk • Tula • Kursk

DENMARK • Aarhus • Copenhagen • Malmö ⚓ Kiel

• Memel • Königsberg • Gumbinnen • Vilna • Minsk

⚓ 1914: Tannenberg counter-offensive

• Danzig • Masurian Lakes ★ Tannenberg

• Hamburg ⚓ • Bremen ⚓ • Stettin • Posen

NETHERLANDS • Amsterdam

GERMAN EMPIRE • Berlin • Hanover • Dresden

• Warsaw • Brest-Litovsk • Kiev 1918 • Kharkov

POLAND • Lodz 1914

BELGIUM • Brussels ⚓ • Cologne

LUXEM-BOURG • Rhine • Elbe

• Rouen • Paris ⚓ • Metz • Strassburg • Prague • Cracow

see inset below left • Seine • Orléans

• Nantes • Orléans • Loire

FRANCE • Bordeaux

SWITZERLAND **LIECHTENSTEIN** • Berne • Geneva • Munich • Danube

1916: Asiago offensive • Innsbruck 1917

• Vienna **AUSTRO-HUNGARIA EMPIRE** • Budapest

• Tarnow ★ • Lemberg 1917 • Gorlice • Kishinev

1915: Gorlice campaign 1916: Brusilov offensive

UKRAINE • Dnieper • Odessa

1918: Central Powers advance through Ukraine

Caporetto ★ 1917 ★ 1915 Isonzo • Kolozsvár

• Venice • Trieste 1918 • Zagreb

1915: conquest of Serbia • Sebastopol ⚓

1916: Central Powers conquest of Romania

• Toulouse • Marseilles • Nice **MONACO** • Bologna

SAN MARINO **ITALY**

Kolubara 1914 **SERBIA** • Belgrade **ROMANIA** • Bucharest

• Bilbao • Madrid • Barcelona

• Sarajevo **BOSNIA-HERZEGOVINA** • Danube **BULGARIA** • Burgas

1918: Allied advance into Serbia

MONTE NEGRO • Skopje • Sofia

BLACK SEA

Corsica • Rome • Sardinia • Cagliari

1916 ⚓ Tirana • Monastir • Salonica • Constantinople

ALBANIA • Brindisi ⚓ • Bari

SPAIN • Valencia • Cordova

Balearic Is. 10

MEDITERRANEAN SEA

1915: British land at Salonica to support Serbia

1915: Gallipoli offensive ★ Gallipoli • Smyrna

GREECE • Athens **OTTOMAN EMPIRE** • Angora

• Palermo • Messina • Naples

Sicily 20 30

Dodecanese (It.) • Crete **Cyprus (Br.)**

Instead of moving its forces across to the West, however, Germany sent its troops to occupy these new territories – even Finland – and at the same time launched a final, all-out offensive in the West, in an attempt to break the deadlock. Once again it came close to success but the Allied line held and in July, aided by tanks and reinforced by American forces and money, a counter-attack began that pushed the German army back towards the German frontier. Morale collapsed: by October 1918, with Austria close to disintegration and with Germany facing a grave political crisis at home, the Berlin government sued for an unconditional armistice, granted on 11 November 1918.

At the peace conferences held in and around Paris in 1919, the victors imposed upon Germany, Austria, Hungary, and Bulgaria notable losses of territory, huge reparations and stringent reductions in their armed forces. The draconian nature of the settlement made it inevitable that, although over 9 million men had perished in the fighting, and the financial cost of the war totalled over $186 billion worldwide, it would not be (as so many had hoped) 'the war to end all wars'.

1 The Great War in Europe, 1914–18

Entente Powers

Central Powers

major Entente Power offensives

major Central Power offensives

farthest advance by Entente Powers: (east 1914, west 1918)

farthest advance by Central Powers: (west 1914, east 1918)

★ battle

★ battle costing over 250,000 lives

⚓ naval base

The Menin Road (left), vividly recalled by the British painter Paul Nash, saw some of the Western Front's worst fighting. In the second half of 1917, a British campaign to re-capture seven miles of Flanders towards Menin and Passchendaele floundered in heavy rain and mud. The British lost 265,000 men and Menin remained in German hands

133

The USSR from Lenin to Stalin

2 Collectivization, 1923–39

- 2-10% of all farms collectivized by 1928
- 25-50% of all farms collectivized by 1933
- 50-70% of all farms collectivized by 1933
- 70-85% of all farms collectivized by 1933
- famine areas, 1932
- *Kraslag* labour camp admin. zone
- corrective labour camps, 1932

By 1917 the strain of war had fatally weakened the Tsarist government: liberals, businessmen, generals and aristocrats all plotted its overthrow. In the end sheer hunger turned a general strike and bread queues into a revolutionary movement which in February forced the Tsar to abdicate, and power passed to a provisional government of prominent *duma* (parliament) politicians. The revolutionary committees (soviets) did not disband, however, and gradually the 'peace, bread and land' programme of the Bolshevik group, led by V. I. Lenin, gained support. In October, the Bolsheviks seized control of strategic points in Petrograd (formerly St Petersburg), arrested the Provisional Government, and assumed power in the name of the soviets. The same soon happened in other cities (map 1).

No one thought they would retain power for long. The overriding need was for peace, and Lenin accepted the onerous terms imposed by Germany in the treaty of Brest-Litovsk (March 1918: page 133); but almost immediately the Bolsheviks (who now took the name 'Communists') faced massive invasions by forces loyal to the Tsar and assisted by troops from Britain, France, Czechoslovakia, Poland and other anti-Bolshevik powers. Nevertheless, by 1920 the civil war had been won, albeit at the cost of 13 million lives and immense damage to property. Lenin now introduced his 'New Economic Policy', which by 1925 allowed the Russian economy to regain its pre-war industrial level. In 1928 Lenin's successor, Joseph Stalin, introduced a Five Year Plan of industrialization, and the following year embarked on the forced collectivization of agriculture, which transformed small, individual peasant holdings into huge state collective farms. The results of the policy proved disastrous, however. It was implemented without adequate machinery, and poorly organized. Crop yields fell, and a great famine in 1932-3 claimed millions of victims. This rural catastrophe caused some 40 million people to move into the cities, where their fresh labour was used mainly for construction, making the industrial growth rates of the Soviet economy under the first and second Five Year Plans (1928-37) look both startling and unique amid the Great Depression that prevailed elsewhere.

This industrialization took place against a background of state-directed terror as Stalin consolidated the Communist dictatorship. The security forces (the NKVD) executed perhaps 12 million people, while a further 10 million suffered imprisonment in forced labour camps (see map 2). Russia survived the German invasion in 1941 (page 140), partly because over 1500 factories were moved to safety further east, but the setback remained undeniable. A further 20 million Soviet citizens died in the conflict and, although the USSR mobilized more fully than any other state in World War II, its industrial output in 1946 stood at only 70 per cent of the 1940 level.

A poster of Stakhanov, a model mine-worker who exceeded his norm through exceptional efforts. He became a hero of the Soviet State and a propaganda tool in Communist efforts to increase worker participation.

1 Russia in war and revolution

━━━━ Russian empire, 1914

╌╌╌╌ front between Russia and Central Powers, 12 Mar. 1917

✊ serious Russian mutinies, Aug. 1917

★ principal towns where Bolsheviks took power, Nov. 1917–Feb. 1918 (dates in new calendar)

━━━━ boundary of Russian territory occupied by Central Powers following the Treaty of Brest-Litovsk, Mar. 1918

⋯⋯⋯ area controlled by the Bolsheviks, Aug. 1918

▲ towns occupied Entente forces, Aug. 1918–19

╌╌╌╌ eastern boundary of area controlled by Bolsheviks, Apr. 1919

▨ area controlled by Bolsheviks, Oct. 1919

━━━━ areas controlled by anti-Bolshevik forces, May 1920

➤ White Russian armies

➤ non-Russian anti-Bolshevik forces (Entente Powers)

━━━━ boundary of Soviet territory, Mar. 1921

──── frontiers, 1923

Narvik

Norwegian Sea

Barents Sea

Entente fleet

Murmansk

White Sea

Canadians Americans

British French Canadians Italians Serbs

Finns

British French

Archangel 17 Feb. 1918

Mezen

S W E D E N

N O R W A Y

FINLAND independence of Finland recognized Dec. 1917

Åbo

Helsingfors

Stockholm

Lake Onega

Lake Ladoga

Petrozavodsk 17 Jan. 1918

Onega

Sukhona

Vologda 8 Feb. 1918

Vyatka 8 Dec. 1917

Perm 14 Nov. 1917

Nicholas II and family shot by Bolsheviks July 1918

British/French naval assistance

Revel 8 Nov. 1917

Yudenich

ESTONIA

Riga

LATVIA

Letts

Baltic Germans

Dvinsk

Baltic Sea

Königsberg

LITHUANIA

Vilna

GERMANY (E. PRUSSIA)

Petrograd 7 Nov. 1917

Novgorod 27 Nov. 1917

Kornilov's attack on Petrograd Sep. 1917

Pskov 15 Nov. 1917

Tver 10 Nov. 1917

Government moved from Petrograd Mar. 1918

Yaroslavl 9 Nov. 1917

Kostroma 15 Dec. 1917

Ivanovo 7 Nov. 1917

Nizhniy Novgorod 10 Nov. 1917

Izhevsk 9 Nov. 1917

Kazan 8 Nov. 1917

Kolchak 1918-19

R U S S I A

Yekaterinburg 8 Nov. 1917

Ufa 8 Nov. 1917

Warsaw

POLAND

Brest-Litovsk

Minsk 7 Nov. 1917

Poles

Gomel 12 Nov. 1917

Vitebsk 12 Nov. 1917

Smolensk 9 Nov. 1917

Mogilev 1 Dec. 1917

Moscow 15 Nov. 1917

Kaluga 11 Dec. 1917

Tula 20 Dec. 1917

Orel 14 Nov. 1917

B O L S H E V I K

Trans-Siberian Railway

Don

Penza 4 Jan. 1918

Samara 9 Nov. 1917

Czechs

Orenburg 31 Jan. 1918

Vistula

Volga

Cracow

Lemberg

CHOSLOVAKIA

HUNGARY

Debrecen

Kolozsvár

Brassó

Temesvár

Zhitomir 22 Jan. 1918

Kiev 8 Feb. 1918

Vinnitsa

Denikin 1919

Poltava 19 Jan. 1918

Dnieper

Kharkov 24 Dec. 1917

Yekaterinoslav 11 Jan. 1918

Kursk

Voronezh 12 Nov. 1917

Tambov 13 Nov. 1917

Don Cossacks 1917-19

Saratov 9 Nov. 1917

Don

Tsaritsyn 27 Nov. 1917

Volga

Ural

Ural Cossack Army 1918-20

Kishinev 10 Dec. 1917

BESSARABIA

Jassy

Odessa 31 Jan. 1918

Nikolayev 27 Jan. 1918

Simferopol 26 Jan. 1918

Wrangel 1920

Sea of Azov

Novocherkassk 25 Feb. 1918

Rostov 10 Nov. 1917

Cossacks

Don

Astrakhan 7 Feb. 1918

Kuma

ROMANIANS

ROMANIA

Bucharest

Danube

Ruse

BULGARIA

Sofia

Varna

Burgas

Plovdiv

Adrianople

Salonica

Constantinople

French Sebastopol 29 Dec. 1917

Novorossiysk 14 Dec. 1917

French

British

British

Black Sea

Entente fleet

Batum

Georgians 1919-20

Caucasus

Mensheviks

Tiflis

Baku 15 Nov. 1917

Caspian Sea

Angora

Trebizond

T U R K E Y

Erivan

Smyrna

Athens

GREECE

British 1918-19

Persia

1919–1939
European political problems

The collapse of the Central Powers in the autumn of 1918, and the subsequent peace treaties (page 133), brought about major frontier changes, the emergence of several new states, and the enlargement of others on the winning side (see map 1). The dismemberment of the Austro-Hungarian empire, the disarmament and the imposition of reparation payments on Germany and her allies, and the effects of the Russian Revolution and civil war (page 134) completely altered the balance of political power in Europe. In terms of population and industrial strength, however, Germany, although weakened, still had no rival in central Europe. The only hope of those who stood behind the peace treaties was the maintenance of overwhelming collective military strength against any revival of German strength. France tried to restrain Germany by signing alliances with the new states of Poland and Czechoslovakia, but Britain proved reluctant to enter into new continental commitments, and the United States withdrew into isolationism. However, Germany's formal recognition of the post-war frontier settlements with France and Belgium by the Locarno treaties (1925) inaugurated a new spirit of cooperation and it was welcomed back into the community of nations. After 1928 many nations signed the 'Kellogg-Briand Pact', which outlawed aggressive war.

But indications of stability proved illusory. Many

PLEBISCITES AND TERRITORIAL DISPUTES

1 plebiscite Feb. 1920: divided between Denmark and Germany
2 occupied by France 1923–5
3 to Belgium 1919
4 to Belgium 1919
5 evacuated 1930, remilitarized, 1936
6 League of Nations Mandate by plebiscite to Germany 1935
7 to France 1919
8 divided between Germany and Poland by plebiscite Mar. 1921
9 Allied occupation 1920–3, annexed by Lithuania 1923, autonomous 1924,
   to Germany 1939
10 to Germany July 1920
11 to Poland Dec. 1918
12 partitioned between Czechoslovakia and Poland 1920
13 to Hungary 1921
14 to Austria 1920
15 occupied by Poland 1920, annexed by Poland following elections 1922
16 to Greece from Bulgaria 1919
17 demilitarized 1924, remilitarized 1936
18 Greek-Bulgarian conflict, 1925

states, especially in eastern Europe, displayed alarming political instability; and all European participants emerged economically weakened from the World War. Italy – which had run up huge debts and lost 600,000 men in the war, but gained only 9000 square miles (14,400 km²) of new territory at the peace – soon became ungovernable, with civil war between left- and right-wing extremists prevailing in many cities until in 1922 the Fascist party, led by Benito Mussolini, took power. In other parts of Europe, the cost of the war and the defects of the peace settlements, coupled with the strains of economic readjustment and disastrous inflation, strengthened anti-parliamentary and revolutionary movements of both left and right. And with the onset of the Great Depression in 1929 (page 138), financial and economic chaos returned to the entire continent. Unemployment rose drastically, especially in Germany where after 1930 the anti-parliamentary movements of both right and left, the Nazis (National Socialists)

and the Communists, increased their strength enormously until in 1933 the Nazi leader, Adolf Hitler, became Chancellor and proceeded to absorb or abolish all the other parties.

Hitler's victory, combined with the economic weakness of Britain and the political instability of France, irretrievably damaged the precarious balance of peace in Europe. The League of Nations, created in 1920 to regulate international disputes and protect member states from aggression, remained only as strong as its members. Its failure to prevent Italy's annexation of Ethiopia in 1935-6, and Germany's remilitarization of the Rhineland in 1936 encouraged further aggression (map 2 and inset). Hitler, who rapidly increased and modernized Germany's armed forces, annexed Austria and parts of Czechoslovakia in 1938, then Bohemia and Memel in spring 1939, while Italy invaded and occupied Albania (1939). Whether an early alliance between the western democracies and the Soviet Union would have halted the aggressors is a matter of dispute. However, fearing that he might be next in line, and already engaged in hostilities with Hitler's ally, Japan, in August 1939 Stalin signed a non-aggression pact with Germany. The collapse of the unstable system created after World War I was now unavoidable.

Adolf Hitler (1889-1945) is greeted by a crowd in the Sudetenland, shortly after its occupation by Germany in 1938. Born in a small Austrian town, Hitler fought in the German army in the First World War. In 1919 he joined a small radical nationalist party in Munich. During a two-year jail sentence for his part in an unsuccessful coup in Munich in 1923, he wrote his major work *Mein Kampf*. In it he called for revenge for Germany's defeat in 1918 by building a racially strong Germany and overturning the Versailles settlement. His message proved attractive to the conservative masses in the Depression after 1929 an in January 1933 he assumed the chancellorship.

1 National conflicts and frontier disputes, 1919–36

— German empire, 1914
— Austro-Hungarian empire, 1914
— Russian empire, 1914
— post-settlement frontiers
▲ plebiscites held

new states
areas of dispute
areas temporarily autonomous or independent
areas under armed occupation
areas under League of Nations High Commissioners

2 Axis expansion, 1935–9

Germany, 1935
— frontiers, 1937

German annexations:
Mar. 1938
Oct. 1938
Mar. 1939
→ Italian campaigns 1935–6

remilitarized by Germany, 1936
incorporated by plebiscite, 1935
to Poland, 1938
client state of Germany, nominally independent from Mar. 1939
to Hungary, 1938–9
ALBANIA *annexed by Italy 1939*
conquered by Italy, 1935–6

1929–1939
The Great Depression

The New York Stock Market crash in October 1929 reflected deep weaknesses in the world economy. Commodity prices world-wide had been falling since 1926, reducing the capacity of exporters such as Australia and Latin America to buy products from Europe and the United States. Within the latter, wages lagged behind profits, impairing the development of domestic markets and limiting the potential of new industries, such as automobiles, to replace old ones, such as textiles. International finance never recovered from the strains of World War I, which caused a dramatic increase in productive capacity, particularly outside Europe, without a corresponding increase in sustained demand. Fixed exchange rates and free convertibility gave way to a compromise – the Gold Exchange Standard – that lacked the stability necessary to rebuild world trade.

In the scramble for liquidity that followed the Great Crash, funds flowed back from Europe to America and Europe's fragile prosperity crumbled. In many industrial countries one-quarter of the labour force was thrown out of work. Prices and wages plummeted, industrial production fell to 53 per cent of its 1929 level in Germany and world trade sank to 35 per cent of its 1929 value (see map 1). Early attempts to solve the problem did more harm than good. In 1930 the United States imposed the highest tariff in its history; in 1932 Britain responded with the Ottawa agreements, a series of preferential tariffs for the Commonwealth. Britain also left the Gold Standard in 1931, followed by other countries, dividing virtually the entire world into closed currency blocs which inhibited trade still further. Only Soviet Russia, largely isolated from the world economy, continued to increase its industrial production (page 134).

Economic nationalism fostered political nationalism, just as mass unemployment and the erosion of middle-class living standards fostered political extremism. In Japan, the fall of the Hamaguchi government in 1931 marked the end of constitutional democracy and the beginning of aggression in

1 The world economy, 1929–39

major currency blocs:
- gold bloc
- yen bloc
- dollar area
- sterling area
- areas of shifting allegiance due to German-American rivalry
- areas of loose currency bloc allegiance

production indices:
- 1929=100
- 1930
- 1932
- 1934
- 1936
- 1938

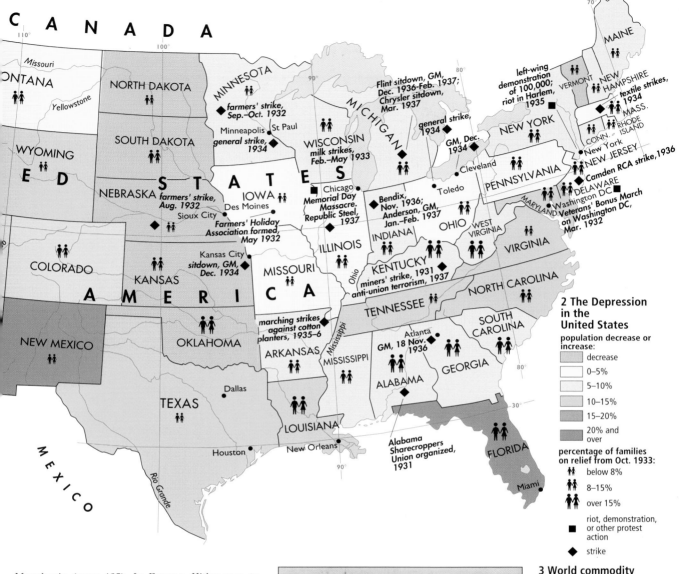

C A N A D A

MONTANA
Missouri
Yellowstone

NORTH DAKOTA

farmers' strike, Sep.–Oct. 1932

MINNESOTA

Minneapolis · St Paul
Minneapolis general strike, 1934

Flint sitdown, GM, Dec. 1936-Feb. 1937; Chrysler sitdown, Mar. 1937

MICHIGAN

MAINE

left-wing demonstration of 100,000; riot in Harlem, 1935

VERMONT

NEW HAMPSHIRE

textile strikes, 1934

MASS.

CONN. · RHODE ISLAND

WYOMING

SOUTH DAKOTA

WISCONSIN
milk strikes, Feb.–May 1933

general strike, 1934

NEW YORK

· New York

NEW JERSEY

UNITED STATES

NEBRASKA
farmers' strike, Aug. 1932

IOWA
Des Moines · Sioux City

Chicago
Memorial Day Massacre, Republic Steel, 1937

Cleveland ·

GM, Dec. 1934

· Toledo

PENNSYLVANIA

DELAWARE

Camden RCA strike, 1936

Farmers' Holiday Association formed, May 1932

ILLINOIS

INDIANA

Bendix, Nov. 1936; Anderson, GM, Jan.–Feb. 1937

OHIO
Ohio

WEST VIRGINIA

MARYLAND

Washington DC

Veterans' Bonus March on Washington DC, Mar. 1932

COLORADO

KANSAS

Kansas City sitdown, GM, Dec. 1934

MISSOURI

KENTUCKY
miners' strike, 1931
anti-union terrorism, 1937

VIRGINIA

AMERICA

NEW MEXICO

OKLAHOMA

marching strikes against cotton planters, 1935–6

TENNESSEE

NORTH CAROLINA

ARKANSAS

Mississippi

MISSISSIPPI

Atlanta
GM, 18 Nov. 1936

SOUTH CAROLINA

GEORGIA

TEXAS
· Dallas

ALABAMA

LOUISIANA

· Houston

New Orleans ·

Alabama Sharecroppers Union organized, 1931

FLORIDA
· Miami

MEXICO

Rio Grande

2 The Depression in the United States

population decrease or increase:

	decrease
	0–5%
	5–10%
	10–15%
	15–20%
	20% and over

percentage of families on relief from Oct. 1933:

below 8%

8–15%

over 15%

■ riot, demonstration, or other protest action

◆ strike

Manchuria (page 123). In Europe, Hitler rose to power in 1933 partly in response to the deflationary policies of his predecessors that raised unemployment from 3 million in 1930 to 6 million in 1932 (page 137). Even in Britain and the United States, fascist movements exercised considerable pressure. In the former, a right-wing National Government, formed in 1931, preserved democratic rule; in the latter, President Franklin Roosevelt, elected in 1932, implemented a 'New Deal' that laid the foundations for recovery. Nevertheless in 1934 some 20 billion days were lost in the US through industrial action and in 1938 over 10 million Americans remained out of work (map 2). Only World War II, and the boost it gave to production, pulled the United States out of the Depression.

By 1932 two out of every five Germans were out of work, and many of the rest were on short time. Here (*right*) the unemployed queue for newspapers carrying lists of jobs. Official efforts were made to limit the employment of women and to give preference to unemployed men.

3 World commodity production, 1926–38

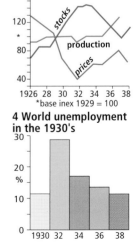

stocks

production

prices

1926 28 30 32 34 36 38
*base inex 1929 = 100

4 World unemployment in the 1930's

%
30
20
10
0
1930 32 34 36 38

The Second World War: the West

Hitler's accession to power in 1933 added a new dimension to international politics. At first his expansionist designs had to await economic recovery, but his virtually unopposed annexation of Austria and Czechoslovakia (1938-9) and the Nazi-Soviet Pact of August 1939 (page 137) led him to expect similar acquiescence when, the following month, he invaded Poland. This time he miscalculated: the western democracies declared war (though this did nothing to aid the Poles).

Over the next two years, Germany rapidly secured first Denmark and Norway, then France and the Low Countries, and finally Yugoslavia and Greece, while Italy annexed Albania and invaded Egypt (map 1). Despite the Nazi-Soviet pact, however, Hitler's ultimate goal was the conquest of Russia: his operations in the West, like the Schlieffen Plan in 1914 (page 132),

merely aimed to eliminate Germany's western enemies before the main struggle began in the east. In this Hitler failed because Britain – though defeated on the continent and subjected to sustained aerial bombing – refused to concede defeat. Nevertheless, in June 1941 Hitler launched his forces on Russia and, thanks to the

1 The Axis advance, 1939–41

- Axis territory, 1 Sep. 1939
- Axis co-belligerents
- occupied by Axis after Sep. 1939
- Vichy France and territories
- Soviet annexed territory, 1939–41
- neutral powers
- frontiers, 1 Sep. 1939
- Axis advances, 1939
- Axis advances, 1940
- Axis advances, 1941
- Axis airborne landings
- Allied forces
- Soviet advances, 1939–40
- Allied retreat and withdrawal
- major cities severely damaged by bombing

combination of strategic surprise and tactical superiority, made rapid progress, taking over 3 million Russian prisoners-of-war. But the winter killed many Germans, who had far outrun their logistical support and lay stranded outside Moscow, Leningrad and Rostov. At precisely this point, on 7 December 1941, Japan attacked the United States (page 142), and Hitler – in an act of egregious folly – also declared war.

Although Germany launched another major thrust in Russia in 1942, reaching the Volga at Stalingrad, that too failed, with the loss of a major army, and its troops fell back in the face of superior Soviet forces, supplied both by the industrial complex built up beyond the Urals (page 134) and by the United States. Meanwhile, Anglo-American troops cleared Axis forces first from Africa and then from Sicily in 1942-3, leading Italy to make peace (though German forces there fought on); partisans gradually took over Yugoslavia; and from June 1944 allied armies liberated France and Belgium before moving into Germany. They met the Soviets on the Elbe in May 1945.

The costs of the war were appalling: 15 million military personnel and 35 million civilians perished, 20 million of them Soviet citizens. The Germans murdered prisoners of war

(Canadians, Americans and Britons in the West as well as Russians in the east); they murdered all captured partisans and members of the communist party; and they murdered all Jews they could find, many in mass shootings and at least 6 million in special extermination camps. However, they also lost heavily: the Anglo-American strategic bombing offensive reduced most of their major cities to rubble, and the Soviet troops carried out a systematic campaign of destruction as they advanced in 1944-5. By war's end, almost all Europe lay in ruins, yet already the differences between the victors had appeared which would darken the post-war years (page 164).

German troops fighting on the Eastern Front in June 1943. From early in 1943 the Soviet army experienced an almost uninterrupted run of successes against the Germans. In 1944 the Red Army pushed as far west as Warsaw, and in 1945 into Germany itself. Nearly 3 million German soldiers died during the war.

2 The defeat of Germany, 1942–5
- [ ] Grossdeutches Reich, 1942
- ← Axis attacks
- ◄-- Axis withdrawals
- ← Allied attacks
- major cities under heavy air attack
- major battle with date
- partisan/resistance movements
- commando raids
- V1 launching sites
- V2 launching sites
- frontiers 1942

The Second World War: Asia and the Pacific

Japanese expansion in Asia after 1931 (page 123) stemmed from a desire for economic self-sufficiency, military security and a self-imposed leadership of East Asia. By 1940, however, with no end in sight to the Chinese war, Japan widened its ambitions to include the empires of the colonial powers – those of France and the Netherlands, recently defeated by her ally Germany, and those of Britain, at war with Germany (page 140) – as an alternative source of raw materials and markets that would free Japan from economic dependence on an increasingly unfriendly United States.

In September 1940 Japan occupied French Indo-China and the United States promptly placed an embargo on sending all iron and steel scrap to Japan. Next, following a sharp defeat in summer 1939 at Nomonhan (Kalkhin Gol), Japan concluded a neutrality pact with Russia – which had been seen as the empire's principal potential enemy since the Russo-Japanese war (page 122) – and prepared to occupy the rest of the European colonies in South-East Asia. But first she felt it necessary to forestall a counterstrike by the United States: at dawn on 7 December 1941 her aircraft attacked and partially destroyed the US Pacific fleet at Pearl Harbor, Hawaii.

Japan hoped to fight the world's greatest industrialised power to a stalemate that would result in a negotiated peace recognizing Japanese hegemony in east Asia. Within six months, her forces had conquered the American outposts of Guam and the Philippines, and occupied the British and Dutch colonies throughout South-East Asia. Their forces also overran the Bismarck archipelago and much of New Guinea, and captured most of the island redoubts necessary to create a defensive perimeter in the mid-Pacific (map

On 2 September 1945
Japanese representatives finally signed the act of surrender (below) on board the battleship USS Missouri in Tokyo Bay.

1 The Japanese advance, 1941–2

- - - Japanese empire, 1941
→ Japanese advance or strike
● Japanese base
■ Allied base
✕ battle

1). In June 1942, however, at Midway Island, aggressive tactics shaped by superb intelligence allowed the aircraft carriers of the US Pacific fleet (which had not been in Pearl the previous December) to destroy a major Japanese carrier force. The United States, although following a 'Europe first' policy in the world war, still possessed abundant resources to advance on two distinct axes against Japan: in the south Pacific, an island-hopping strategy (by-passing the major centres of Japanese resistance and executed by amphibious forces) aimed for the Philippines; in the central Pacific, carrier-borne forces advanced towards the Marianas, from whose airbases bombing raids could be launched on Japan itself. At the same time, Allied forces moved from India into Burma; and in August 1945 Russia finally broke her neutrality pact and invaded Manchuria (map 2).

But Japan, though utterly exhausted, succumbed to none of these conventional threats: rather two atomic bombs, dropped on Hiroshima and Nagasaki in August 1945, precipitated the unconditional surrender of the millions of her troops still in arms. The brief Japanese colonial adventure had caused almost as much destruction as Hitler's war in Europe; but it also unleashed forces of revolutionary nationalism that would shape events throughout Asia over the next five decades (page 162).

**Map labels:**

U S S R

Soviet army attacks 9 Aug. 1945

MANCHURIA (MANCHUKUO)

INNER MONGOLIA

Peking

Khabarovsk

Tientsin · Dairen

Seoul

KOREA · Fusan

JAPAN

Tokyo

Hiroshima 6 Aug. 1945

Nagasaki 9 Aug. 1945

Shikoku

Kyushu

fighters sweep over Japan from May 1945

Sea of Okhotsk

Kamchatka 17 Aug. 1945

Komandorski Is.

Attu · Aleutian Is.
Kiska · Amchitka

May–Aug. 1943

Kurile Is.

Hokkaido

Sea of Japan

Bering Sea

Japanese perimeter Oct. 1944

Japanese perimeter Mar. 1944

10 Oct. 1943

C H I N A

inese advance into
rma after Oct. 1943
panese offensive into
E. India Feb.–June 1944
itish offensive into
rma after Nov. 1944
ngoon retaken May 1945

Chinese counter-offensive Apr.– June 1945

Nanking

Shanghai

bombing raids from June 1944

1944 Japanese Ichi-Go Offensive

Amoy

Okinawa

Formosa

direct air attack on Japan from Okinawa from May 1945

Iwo Jima Feb.–Mar. 1945

20th Air Force begins direct air attack on Japan from 24 Nov. 1944–14 Aug. 1945

Bonin Is.
Volcano Is.

Pacific Ocean

Midway

Hawaiin Is.

Oahu
Pearl Harbor

BURMA

Kunming

Laokai
Hanoi

Canton

Hong Kong

Gulf of Tongking

Hainan

Luzon landings Jan. 1945

Philippine Is.

Manila

25 Oct. 1944
Battle of Leyte Gulf.
Heavy Japanese naval losses

Leyte
Leyte landing 20 Oct. 1944

Mindanao May 1945

Battle of Philippine Sea.
Japanese carrier aviation annihilated June 1944

Saipan
June 1944

Tinian

Guam
July 1944

Marianas

Ulithi
Sep. 1944

Palau
Sep. 1944

Caroline Is.

Truk

Eniwetok
Feb. 1944

Pacific Ocean area forces

Wake I.

Marshall Is.

Kwajalein
Feb. 1944

Majuro
Jan. 1944

Christmas I.

FRENCH INDO-CHINA

Mandalay

SIAM

Rangoon

Bangkok

Phnom Penh

Saigon

Gulf of Siam

MALAY STATES

Kuala Lumpur

edan

Singapore

BRUNEI
June 1945

SARAWAK

Tarakan
May 1945

Borneo
July 1945

Morotai
Sep. 1944

Noemfoor
July 1944

Sorong

May 1944

Halmahera

Sansapur.

Hollandia

New Guinea

Saidor
Jan. 1944

Manus
Feb. 1944

Admiralty Is.

Bismarck Arch.

New Ireland

Rabaul

Bougainville
Nov. 1943

Solomon Is.

Tulagi

Makin

Gilbert Is.

Tarawa
Nov. 1943

Abemama

Ellice Is.

Battle of Santa Cruz Oct. 1942

Eastern Solomons Aug. 1942
Japanese forces repulsed

DUTCH EAST INDIES

Sumatra

Palembang

Batavia

Java · Surabaya

Bandjarmasin

Celebes

Macassar

Amboina

Ceram

Banda Sea

Aru Is.

Tanimbar Is.

Buna

Port Moresby

Guadalcanal
7 Aug. 1942–
9 Feb. 1943

South Pacific area forces

Espiritu Santo

New Hebrides

Fiji Is.

Japanese perimeter Aug. 1945

Lombok

Flores

Sumba

Timor

Timor Sea

Darwin

Cape York

17–25 Sep. 1942
Japanese ground forces repulsed

Coral Sea

New Caledonia

A U S T R A L I A

Sydney

Melbourne

---

2 The Allied counter-offensive

→ Allied advance

✈ Allied air attack

■ Allied base

✳ atomic bomb target

● Japanese base

◉ Japanese base bypassed or neutralized

✕ battle

Japanese perimeters

········· March 1944

—·—·— October 1944

— — — August 1945

The United States since 1945

TIMELINE

1952
Eisenhower elected
president

1956
Federal Highways Act

1960
Kennedy elected president

1963
President Kennedy
assassinated; US build-up in
Vietnam begins

1968
Martin Luther King
assassinated

1973
US withdrawal from Vietnam

1974
President Nixon resigns after
Watergate scandal

1980
Ronald Reagan elected
president

1987
Stock Market crash

1994
NAFTA established

The requirements of wartime production solved the unemployment problem (page 138) of the United States at last, and the gigantic output achieved to meet the needs of army, navy, air force and allies demonstrated the economic potential which, when realized, would create an era of unprecedented prosperity for the United States. Gross National Product almost trebled in real terms between 1950 and 1990, while real income per head nearly doubled.

A number of factors brought about the economic surge: rapid population increase (from 132 million in 1940 to 281 million in 2000); technological advances coupled with the emergence of new consumer goods; the sudden spending of wartime savings between 1945 and 1948; and the rearmament programmes connected with the Cold War and the Korean War (page 164 and 154). Affluence came to seem entirely normal and business confidence was seldom less than buoyant: on this basis of wealth and hope most American people began to transform their entire way of life. The expansion of the suburbs constituted perhaps the most obvious change. Easy credit, cheap fuel (both for homes and cars), mass production of housing and automobiles, and giant road-building programmes (40,000 miles of interstate highways by 1980), all helped encourage Americans in their millions to move off the farms and out of the cities into endless miles of suburbs. So although the population of the central cities grew from 48 million to 79 million between 1950 and 1990, that of their urban fringes also rose from 21 million also to 79 million (map 1).

By 1990, less than one-third of the US population lived in non-metropolitan areas, but the flight from the farms did not reduce productivity: on the contrary, the number of people fed by one farm worker doubled from 15 in 1950 to 30 in 1970. Thanks to mechanization (by 1990 almost 100 per cent of the cotton crop was harvested by machine, as against only 10 per cent in 1949), improved seeds and fertilisers and government subsidies, the United States provided a significant proportion of the world's staple foods, such as wheat, maize and soya beans. The economy at large grew steadily, with the service sector (as in western Europe: page 166) expanding far more rapidly than manufacturing.

But beneath the prosperity lurked tensions. American capitalists tended to spend their profits rather than re-invest them, and industrial workers claimed higher wages and easier conditions of work without regard to the effect such claims (if successful) might have on prices and on the international competitiveness of American industry. The Vietnam War (1965-73: page 162) created high inflation and bitter internal divisions. Explicit discrimination against Blacks and Asians exploded in urban riots during the 1960s and gave rise to a widespread movement for civil rights led by Dr Martin Luther King (map 2). Then came the policies of Presidents Ronald Reagan (1981-9) and George Bush (1989-93), who cut taxes by a third (releasing a flood of spending power on the markets), slashed welfare programmes (turning the inner cities into ghettoes), increased expenditure on armaments (so creating the biggest deficit in history), and failed to remedy the structural defects of American industry (so that the new purchasing power went overwhelmingly into imports, creating an equally unprecedented trade deficit).

Under the presidency of Bill Clinton (1993-2001), Americans rediscovered their national self-confidence. The United States played a decisive role in the conflicts in the Middle East and the Balkans and its economy boomed. America led the world boom in computers and satellite communications. The end of the Cold War left America as the core of the new world order.

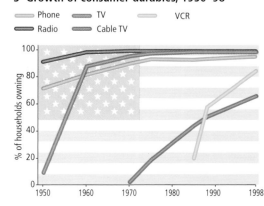

Perhaps against the odds, certainly to the dismay of liberal expectations, one-time Hollywood star Ronald Reagan, seen here *(left)* on the campaign trail with his wife, Nancy, was elected US president in November 1980. Though a noted champion of economic individualism, Reagan proved nothing if not pragmatic in office and presided over a huge increase in government spending. The resulting economic boom, coupled with his genial personality and fierce anti-Soviet rhetoric, ensured him wide popularity and hugely reinforced American economic self-confidence after the uncertainty of the 1970s.

3 Growth of consumer durables, 1950–98

Phone | TV | VCR
Radio | Cable TV

% of households owning (0–100)

1950 1960 1970 1980 1990 1998

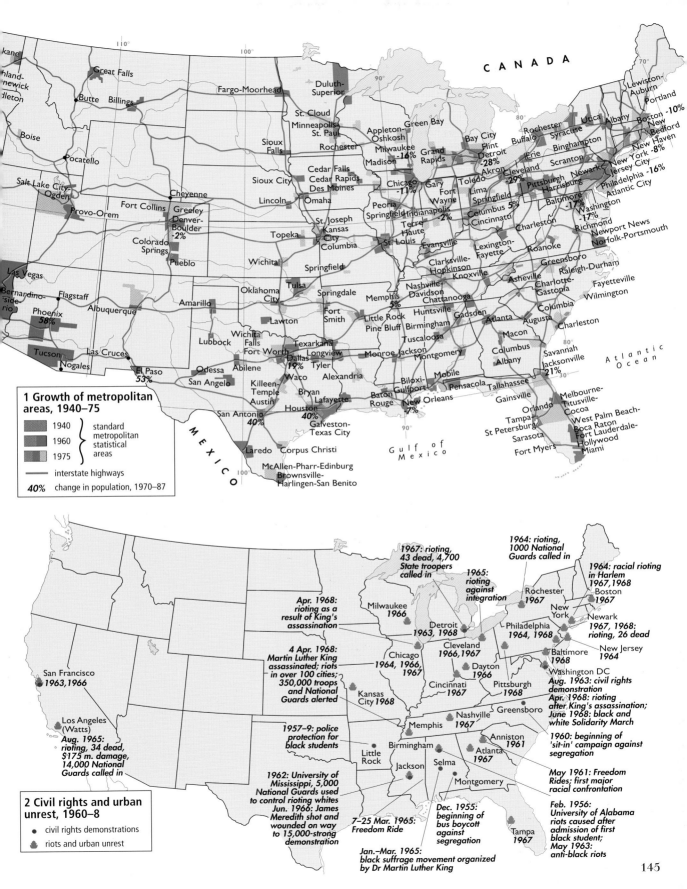

1 Growth of metropolitan areas, 1940–75

	1940
	1960
	1975

standard metropolitan statistical areas

— interstate highways

40% change in population, 1970–87

**Map labels (growth percentages):**

Boston -10%
New Bedford
New Haven -8%
Jersey City
Philadelphia -16%
Atlantic City
Baltimore -17%
Washington -17%
Milwaukee -16%
Detroit -28%
Chicago -11%
Cleveland -29%
Columbus 5%
Indianapolis -2%
Denver-Boulder -2%
Phoenix 58%
El Paso 53%
Tucson
Dallas 19%
Houston 40%
San Antonio 40%
Nashville-Davidson 5%
New Orleans 7%
Jacksonville 21%

CANADA

MEXICO

Gulf of Mexico

Atlantic Ocean

2 Civil rights and urban unrest, 1960–8

● civil rights demonstrations
🔥 riots and urban unrest

Map annotations:

1967: rioting, 43 dead, 4,700 State troopers called in

1964: rioting, 1000 National Guards called in

1964: racial rioting in Harlem 1967,1968

1965: rioting against integration

Apr. 1968: rioting as a result of King's assassination

4 Apr. 1968: Martin Luther King assassinated; riots in over 100 cities; 350,000 troops and National Guards alerted

1957–9: police protection for black students

1962: University of Mississippi, 5,000 National Guards used to control rioting whites
Jun. 1966: James Meredith shot and wounded on way to 15,000-strong demonstration

7–25 Mar. 1965: Freedom Ride

Jan.–Mar. 1965: black suffrage movement organized by Dr Martin Luther King

Dec. 1955: beginning of bus boycott against segregation

Aug. 1963: civil rights demonstration
Apr. 1968: rioting after King's assassination; June 1968: black and white Solidarity March

1960: beginning of 'sit-in' campaign against segregation

May 1961: Freedom Rides; first major racial confrontation

Feb. 1956: University of Alabama riots caused after admission of first black student; May 1963: anti-black riots

1967, 1968: rioting, 26 dead

Aug. 1965: rioting, 34 dead, $175 m. damage, 14,000 National Guards called in

City labels (map 2):

San Francisco 1963,1966
Los Angeles (Watts)
Milwaukee 1966
Detroit 1963, 1968
Chicago 1964, 1966, 1967
Cleveland 1966,1967
Dayton 1966
Cincinnati 1967
Kansas City 1968
Rochester 1967
New York
Boston 1967
Newark
New Jersey 1964
Philadelphia 1964, 1968
Baltimore 1968
Washington DC
Pittsburgh 1968
Nashville 1967
Memphis
Greensboro
Anniston 1961
Atlanta 1967
Birmingham
Little Rock
Jackson
Selma
Montgomery
Tampa 1967

World War II left Europe politically disorganized and economically prostrate, a situation greatly exacerbated by large-scale population movements. The German collapse released millions of incarcerated prisoners-of-war and slave-workers, and a further 5 million Russian prisoners, refugees and servicemen were repatriated. Two more lasting shifts of population also occurred: some 12 million Germans abandoned (voluntarily or forcibly) their pre-war homes in the east, especially in lands annexed by the Nazis after 1938; and over 2 million Russians moved into the territories annexed by the Soviet Union during its westward advance (map 1).

The political frontiers of the new Europe were established at conferences between the victors (USA, USSR, Britain and France) held at Yalta and Potsdam in February and July 1945: the union of Germany and Austria decreed by Hitler in 1938 was dissolved and Germany lost territory to Poland and the Soviet Union; both countries were divided into occupation zones under four power control. In Austria the system worked relatively smoothly, and in 1955 the country achieved independence, albeit as a permanently neutralized state; but co-operation between the USSR and her allies in Germany broke down in 1948. Britain and the United States had already amalgamated their

1 Post-war population movements and territorial change

Territorial change, 1945–9

- cities divided into four occupation zones
- frontiers, 1949
- Germany, 1937
- Allied control zones of Germany and Austria
- annexed by Soviet Union 1940–5
- states which became Communist, 1945–8
- Yugoslav gains from Italy, 1945
- Federal Republic of Germany from 1949
- German Democratic Republic from 1949

Population movements: peoples resettled, evacuated or expelled (with numbers):
- Germans
- Finns driven from area bordering Russia
- Baltic peoples
- Russians
- Russians forcibly repatriated
- Poles
- Czechs
- peoples settled by International Refugee Organisation

zones in 1947 and, in conjunction with France, they now prepared for the formation of a West German government (the Federal Republic: BRD). After an attempt to prevent this by means of a blockade on Berlin, the Soviets prepared their zone for quasi-independence as the German Democratic Republic (DDR): the two states came into existence in 1949 (map 1).

They immediately took their place in the two political blocs into which Europe had become divided. The eastern republics had all come under communist rule by 1948 and economic growth, though continuous, remained slow thanks to Stalinist methods of production. In the western democracies, thanks largely to lavish American aid (the Marshall Plan from 1947; map 3), an economic miracle took place, with smooth and rapid growth year after year. The two blocs had their own military groups – NATO in the west (1949) and the Warsaw Pact in the east (1955) – and their own economic organizations – in the east Comecon (1949) and in the west the European Community (six members 1957; 9 by 1973) and the less successful European Free Trade Association (map 4). However the growth surge suffered a serious check in 1973 when the Arab-led Organization of Petroleum Exporting Countries (OPEC) increased the price of oil by 250 per cent.

On 23 June 1948, the Soviet Union set up a blockade of the Western sectors of Berlin. The Western states mounted an airlift (left) until May 1949, which brought in 2.3 million tons of supplies.

2 Berlin, 1945–90

- American sector
- British sector
- French sector
- Soviet sector
- city borders
- the Berlin Wall, 1961–89

- Autobahn
- international railway
- ⊕ airport
- ■ headquarters
- ▢ allied HQ
- → air corridor

4 European military and economic trading blocs, 1947–73

military partitions

- Nato 1949– (including United States and Canada)
- ★ Warsaw Pact 1948–91

economic blocs

- Benelux customs union, 1947
- joined EEC, 1973
- original European Economic Community (EEC) members, 1957
- founder members of European Free Trade Association (EFTA), 1960
- ▲ subsequent EFTA members
- Council for Mutual Economic Assistance (COMECON) members, 1949
- subsequent COMECON members

3 The Marshall Plan

- applied for and received Marshall aid, with amounts (in US$)
- applied for Marshall aid but withdrew application
- did not apply
- 14.0% Net Marshall aid as percentage of national income 1948–9

ICELAND $24 m 5%

NORWAY $236 m 5.8%

SWEDEN $118 m 0.3%

DENMARK $257 m 3.3%

IRELAND $116 m 7.8%

UNITED KINGDOM $2,825 m 2.4%

NETH. $979 m 10.8%

BELGIUM $546 m 0.6%

WEST GERMANY $1,297 m 2.9%

FRANCE $2,445 m 6.5%

LIECH.
SWITZ. AUSTRIA $560 m 14.0%

SPAIN denied Marshall aid because of Franco's pro-Axis sympathies

PORTUGAL $50 m

applied for Marshall aid but received nothing

ITALY $1,314 m 5.3%

GREECE $515 m

TURKEY $152 m

1945-91
The Soviet Union

1 The USSR and the world, 1945–85

- USSR and client states, 1938
- annexed 1944–5
- territorial ambitions thwarted, 1945–6
- unsuccessful attempt to gain or maintain control by 1949
- control or influence secured by 1954
- Warsaw pact, 1955
- turned antagonistic to USSR from the early 1960s
- acknowledgement demanded from China that 19th-century Russian annexations were by unequal treaties
- ties from USSR loosened from mid 1960s
- brought into or kept in Soviet sphere in 1970s by military intervention
- other allies in 1985
- c,v pro-Soviet regime maintained or installed by Cuban or Vietnamese forces, with date
- Soviet influence aborted or sought unsuccessfully, 1960–85
- Soviet forces in action or deployed in confrontation, with date
- foreign aircraft downed, with detail
- frontiers, 1985

Despite the extensive loss of life and property inflicted on Russia during World War II (page 141 above), remarkable economic recovery began after 1945. The output of heavy industry rose steadily and light industry, neglected under Stalin (who died in 1953), also progressed under his successors. The agricultural problems created by collectivization (page 134) remained – grain production only increased in the late 1950s, and even then the USSR continued to depend on imports – but vast reserves of oil, gas and mineral ores were discovered and exploited in Siberia. Russia's east European satellites were obliged to supply high-quality engineering products and expert personnel (as well as more basic items), which immensely assisted the USSR's economic progress. The development of the atom bomb (1949), of the first satellite (the sputnik: 1957), and of the first manned space flight (1961) all indicated the ability of Russian science to innovate.

After 1945 the Soviet military became a central feature of the state. One-fifth of the budget was devoted to military spending while between 1952 and 1976 101 military leaders became full members of the Central Committee of the Communist Party. The Soviet Union, along with the United States, had become a 'superpower', with a comparable degree of military strength. Although its gross national product fell well short of its rival's, the USSR overtook the USA in the production of iron ore, cement, steel and oil. Nevertheless the Soviet economy entered a period of crisis in the 1970s. Increasingly, the USSR found the arms-race more costly than did the USA (not least because the latter enjoyed far better credit and so could finance much of its expenditure

through loans: page 144), and the position became critical when the USA threatened to extend its defence system into outer space (the 'Strategic Defense Initiative'). In 1985 a new Soviet leader, Mikhail Gorbachev, came to power with a programme of reform designed to achieve a 'revolution within the revolution'.

From 1985 to 1990 Gorbachev successfully improved relations with both China and the west in order to provide peaceful external conditions for reconstruction. He introduced *glasnost* (openness) in the media to encourage criticism of deficiencies in the economy and society; but he could not assure an

A May Day parade in Moscow, 1983 *(left)*. After the war the Communist Party became the dominant presence in Soviet society. Under Stalin, large numbers of workers and peasants entered the party. But by the 1980s it perpetuated an elite and gave few opportunities for social mobility

GREENLAND

✳1 1953
✳2 1956
✳3 1968

Soviet zone of occupation (evacuated, 1955)

FINLAND
EAST GERMANY
POLAND
CZECHOSLOVAKIA
HUNGARY
ROMANIA
YUGO.
ITALY
BULGARIA
Kars and Ardahan
Dodecanese
TUNISIA
TURKEY
SYRIA
IRAQ
Azerbaijan and Kurdistan

UNION OF SOVIET SOCIALIST REPUBLICS
⊕ US spy plane shot down, 1960
1969
Tannu Tuva
Port Arthur (seized 1945, to China 1954)
Sinkiang (East Turkestan) (Soviet influence from 1928)
1969
South Kurile Is, (four is. claimed by Japan)
⊕ *South Korean Jumbo shot down, 1983*

JAPAN

ALGERIA
LIBYA
EGYPT
SAUDI ARABIA
IRAN
AFGHAN-ISTAN
1979
CHINA
INDIA

NORTH VIETNAM
V 1975
V 1978
SOUTH VIETNAM

MALI
C SOUTH YEMEN 1978
C 1980 ETHIOPIA
SOMALIA
UGANDA
CONGO ZAIRE
TANZANIA
C 1975 ANGOLA
MOZAMBIQUE
MADAGASCAR

Pacific Ocean

Indian Ocean

2 State tyranny under Stalin

Deportations
🏃 deported minorities (with numbers and dates of deportation)
→ direction of deportation

The Gulag
• prison camp
■ prison zone
━ maximum German advance, 1942
━ Soviet Union, 1945

Komsomolsk
Amur
S I B E R I A
Lena
Lake Baikal
Novosibirsk
U S S R
Ob'
KAZAKHSTAN
Urals
Barents Sea
Aral Sea
UZBEKISTAN
Archangel
Volga
Gorky (Nizhniy Novgorod)
Moscow
VOLGA GERMAN REPUBLIC
948,829 1941–2
120,192 1945–8
Stalingrad
KALMYK AUTONOMOUS REPUBLIC
91,919 1943–4
Caspian Sea
Leningrad
ESTONIA 10,000 1941
LATVIA 16,000 1941
LITHUANIA 30,000 1941
POLAND c 1,500,000 1939–41
Kiev
CRIMEAN AUTONOMOUS REPUBLIC 1943–4
183,155 1944 (Crimean Tartars)
KARACHAI AUTON. REG. 68,327 1943–4
BALKAR AUTON. REP. 37,406 1944
CHECHEN INGUSH AUTONOMOUS REGION 1943–4
362,282 1943–4
134,178 1943–4
60,640 1943–4
94,955 1944 (Meskhetians, Kurds, Khemshils, Azeris)

3 The Soviet economy, 1950–85				
YEAR	steel (million tons)	coal (million tons)	exports (million roubles)	cars (thousands)	televisions (thousands)
1950	27.3	261	1.6	65	12
1960	65.3	509	5.0	139	1726
1970	116.0	624	11.5	344	6682
1980	148.0	716	49.6	1327	7528
1985	155.0	726	72.7	1332	9371

adequate supply of food, and unrest in the cities grew. In desperation, in 1989 he withdrew Soviet forces from eastern Europe, hoping to reduce costs and thus improve the situation at home; but the resurgence of nationalism in many constituent republics began to threaten the entire union. The Soviet Union comprised many different ethnic, religious, linguistic and cultural groups (map 1). The majority of the population claimed Slavic origin, including the Russians (53 per cent) and Ukrainians (16 per cent) – by far the largest groups. But the minorities, especially those incorporated by force during the 19th century (page 114) and the Baltic states, violently annexed in 1945, eagerly anticipated the chance to assert their independence (page 168).

China since 1949

The establishment of the People's Republic of China in 1949 (page 130) marked a fundamental turning point in the modern history of China. After a century of severe internal conflict and disintegration, usually provoked or exacerbated by external aggressors, China was now reunified and strongly governed by leaders who possessed a decisive vision of the society they wished to create. Whatever the excesses and failures since 1949, not least the systematic repression of much of the population, that remains a fundamental achievement.

For a time, China closely followed the Soviet model of directed economic planning and achieved modest progress in developing heavy industries and raising agricultural production. In 1958, however, the communist leader Mao Zedong became impatient and sought to mobilize the revolutionary energies of China's vast population, launching the 'Great Leap Forward'. Rural China was divided into 26,000 communes, each required to abolish private property and meet huge targets in agricultural and industrial production. Some 600,000 backyard furnaces sprang up across the countryside. The experiment proved an unmitigated disaster: production declined sharply, 20-30 million people died from starvation or malnutrition, and the project was abandoned in 1961.

This failure strengthened the hands of moderate communists who preferred a more centrally-planned, Soviet-style development. Mao responded by forming an alliance with the People's Liberation Army (PLA) and with Chinese youth who, as 'Red Guards', faithfully supported his policies. In 1966 Mao launched the Great Proletarian Cultural Revolution. Red Guards were set loose to prevent the development of 'vested interests' and careerism in party and state by establishing permanent revolution. The guards killed thousands and forcibly resettled millions. Chaos followed throughout China, forcing Mao to call on the PLA to restore order (map 1).

Mao died in 1976 and his widow Jiang Qing with three allies (later denounced as the 'Gang of Four') tried to seize power; but by this time the PLA and the elite had had enough of revolution. The 'Gang of Four' were arrested, tried and expelled from the Communist Party.

In the late 1970s Deng Xiaoping became the dominant figure in China's politics. Following the visit of United States President Nixon in 1972, which began the process of re-opening China to the capitalist West, Deng launched a policy of economic liberalization. He created special economic zones in areas bordering the foreign colonies of Hong Kong and Macao and Taiwan, and in Shanghai, with inducements to encourage foreign investment. By 1992, $36 billion had been invested. Other reforms followed: peasants were permitted to own land and, by 1984, 98 per cent did so. The communes vanished and agricultural output increased by 49 per cent in five years. Private businesses, also now permitted, grew in number from 100,000 in 1978 to 17 million in 1985 (map 2).

Economic reforms led to demands for political liberalization. In December 1986, students demonstrated for democracy in 15 cities. Deng responded

Student demonstrators in Beijing in 1989 (right). Thousands of students occupied Tiananmen square for six weeks in May and June to demonstrate for greater democracy. On 3-4 June the army violently ejected the students. The death toll was later estimated at 400-800.

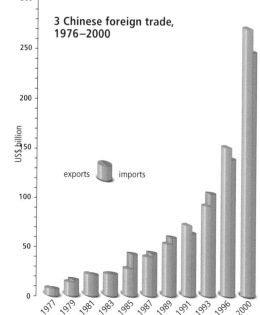

3 Chinese foreign trade, 1976–2000

US$ billion

exports   imports

1977 1979 1981 1983 1985 1987 1989 1991 1993 1996 2000

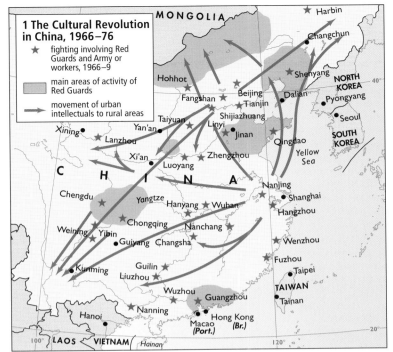

1 The Cultural Revolution in China, 1966–76

★ fighting involving Red Guards and Army or workers, 1966–9

main areas of activity of Red Guards

→ movement of urban intellectuals to rural areas

with repression: he arrested 'troublemakers' and sacked Hu Yaobang, the liberal secretary-general of the Chinese Communist Party. When Hu died in April 1989, students used the occasion to demand democracy, gathering in Beijing's Tiananmen Square, at times numbering over a million, until in June Deng sent in the PLA and the movement was ruthlessly crushed.

After the Tiananmen massacre China swiftly reassured the world that it was a stable economic partner, and most of the world obligingly ignored human rights concerns in return for a share of China's economic boom. Foreign investment soared, and so did China's foreign trade (table 3). Further economic liberalization now took place as most of China operated a 'socialist market economy'. Growth rates, which averaged 10 per cent or more for the 1980s and 1990s, were only slightly affected by the economic turmoil which hit most of the rest of east Asia in 1997–8. In 1997, Britain returned its colony of Hong Kong, which retained a degree of self-government, and two years later Portugal surrendered Macao. With growing freedom in many areas of life, the issue of democracy remained the unfinished business of China's 20th-century achievement.

2 The Chinese economy, 1983–97

672 foreign investment, 1983-97, by province, in million US$

■ Special Economic Zone (SEZ), 1984

GDP per capita <80% of national average, 1997

GDP per capita 80-120% of national average, 1997

GDP per capita >120% of national average, 1997

● open coastal city

● inland city with expanded authority

— "golden triangle" development areas

▲ major oilfields

■ major coalfields

— frontiers, 1992

Japan and Korea

In the wake of the Second World War, United States support for Japan, South Korea and Taiwan, perceived after 1948 as its first line of defence in east Asia, transformed their economies.

Japan, like Germany (page 146), ended the war with its economy in ruins: most towns and industrial plants destroyed; nearly all foreign assets lost; domestic capital run down. Moreover, the victors demanded reparations and occupied the country following its surrender. The Far East Commission, which contained representatives of all the countries that had fought Japan but remained an American enterprise, sought to demilitarize Japan and create a peaceful, democratic state. It reformed the education system (removing from the syllabus all material that had encouraged military and authoritarian values); abolished the divinity of the emperor and made the Diet (parliament) the highest political authority; established an independent judiciary and free labour unions; introduced a programme of land reform; and sought (with little success) to break up the great concentrations of corporate power. With the advance of the Chinese communists after 1948, however, the United States increasingly came to see Japan not only as the key bulwark of Western power in east Asia but also as one whose effectiveness depended on the reconstruction of its economic power. The occupation formally ended in 1951.

Japan's defeat also ended its harsh colonial rule of Korea (since 1910) and led to the peninsula's

EUROPE NETH.
33,500
800
WEST GERMANY
400
8,424 34,710
2,500
UK
1,800 LUX.
FRANCE 330
SOVIET BLOC
860 2,288
U S S R
6,576/11,458
62/482
SOUTH
KOREA
ASIA
404,700
4,868/12,456
JAPAN
MIDDLE EAST
12,000
54
CHINA
1,200
650
15,565 57,239
AFRICA
27,100
SAUDI
ARABIA
THAILAND
250
TAIWAN
370
1,413/2,104
HONG KONG
1,100
LIBERIA 267
4,162 4,244
MALAYSIA
160
272/3,392
SINGAPORE
500
INDONESIA
550
OCEANIA
26,400
2,163 6,300
AUSTRALIA
1,200

Robots on a Toyota assembly plant *(below)*. Car production was an essential component of Japan's post-war economic miracle. The Toyota company produced just 11,000 vehicles in 1950, but by the peak of production (in 1985) this had increased to 5.6 million annually.

5 Japanese exports, 1960–99 (millions US $)

occupation by the victors: Japanese forces north of the 38th parallel surrendered to Soviet Russia, those in the south to the United States. The Soviets supported the establishment of a communist state in the north under Kim Il-Sung, a guerrilla leader who had spent considerable time in the Soviet Union; and the Americans retaliated by sponsoring a representative regime under Syngman Rhee, a strong anti-communist. Both new governments entertained strong ambitions to unite the country under their own rule, and in June 1950 the North attacked, pushing the South Korean and remaining United States troops back toward Pusan (map 1). The US forces counterattacked in September with a daring amphibious landing at Inchon, leading to a further offensive that promised to unify Korea. In November, however, the Chinese committed substantial forces and regained most of the north. A stalemate ensued until an armistice was signed in 1953.

The Korean War boosted the Japanese economy and initiated a period of exceptionally high economic growth – well over 10 per cent a year throughout the 1960s, and over 4 per cent annually between 1974 and 1985, faster than that of any other OECD country. A key feature of Japan's growth was its flexibility in pursuing economic objectives: in the 1950s it emphasized heavy industry, ship-building and iron and steel; in the 1960s it moved into high-technology consumer manufactures largely for export; from the 1970s it concentrated on technological innovation and higher value-added products while transferring the production of lower value-added goods overseas. Industrial production and exports soared (tables 3 and 5) and massive Japanese investment took place in Asia, Europe and North America. In the early 1990s, Japan had the world's strongest economy with the largest per capita GNP and the largest holding of foreign assets and debt (map 4).

Korea epitomized the relative success of the communist and capitalist projects. Until 1970 North Korea had the higher GNP per capita, but by the 1990s GNP was declining at 5 per cent and the state, still communist, came close to economic and humanitarian disaster. From the mid-1960s South Korea embarked on rapid industrialization and by the 1990s boasted the world's 13th largest economy with great strengths in car manufacture, shipbuilding and semi-conductors (table 4). Its regime showed little tolerance of political dissent, however, and crushed open protest.

Although the economic turmoil that hit the east Asian economies in 1997 exposed serious structural weaknesses, particularly in the inefficient and debt-laden finance and banking sectors, the vast underlying strength of the region suggests that the Pacific Rim will remain a lynchpin of the global economic system.

3 Japanese industrial production

index of industrial production (1945=100)

2684.1 — 1980
1736.4 — 1970
487.8 — 1960
112.2 — 1950

2 Japanese investment overseas, 1970–98

trade with region, 1970–4 and 1985–9 (billion Yen)
15,565 / 57,239

value of Japanese direct foreign investment in region, 1987/1999 (US$ million)
6,576 / 3,392

value of Japanese direct foreign investment in country, 1987 (US$ million)
1,200

workers in Japanese-affiliated companies, 1980
404,700

CANADA — 650
NORTH AMERICA — 83,900
USA — 14,700 / 17,170 / 75,190
15,357/21,873
4,814/6,479
BAHAMAS — 730
CAYMAN ISLANDS — 1,200
PANAMA — 2,300
LATIN AMERICA — 128,100 / 2,024 / 2,372
BRAZIL — 230

4 The two Koreas; per capita GNP growth, 1945–99

thousand US$

$13,300 (1999)

— South Korea
— North Korea

1945 1950 1960 1970 1980 1990 1999

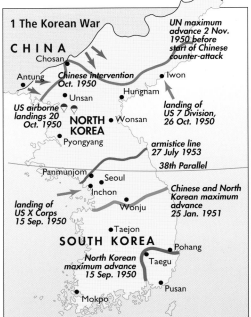

1 The Korean War

UN maximum advance 2 Nov. 1950 before start of Chinese counter-attack

CHINA
Chosan
Antung
Chinese intervention Oct. 1950
Iwon
Unsan
Hungnam
US airborne landings 20 Oct. 1950
landing of US 7 Division, 26 Oct. 1950
NORTH KOREA
Wonsan
Pyongyang
armistice line 27 July 1953
38th Parallel
Panmunjom
Seoul
Chinese and North Korean maximum advance 25 Jan. 1951
Inchon
landing of US X Corps 15 Sep. 1950
Wonju
Taejon
SOUTH KOREA
Pohang
North Korean maximum advance 15 Sep. 1950
Taegu
Pusan
Mokpo

Retreat from empire

The Western empires created in the 19th century (page 118) remained intact in 1939, though most German and Ottoman possessions had passed to Britain, France and Japan as League of Nations mandates. The United States planned to grant independence to the Philippines, acquired in 1898, and did so immediately after World War II; but none of the seven remaining European colonial powers – Britain, France, Spain, Portugal, Belgium, Italy and the Netherlands – surrendered their empires voluntarily. Only Britain even conceived of independence as the ultimate goal, albeit with continued membership of the Commonwealth, a goal already attained in 1939 by Canada, South Africa, Australia and New Zealand. The continental colonial powers thought more in terms of evolution towards a common citizenship, with their colonies as overseas parts of the metropolitan territory. Such plans were complicated, however, by the resistance of European settlers, with consequent inter-racial tensions, and by clashes between the European ideal of evolution along Western lines (in education and economic development) and the powerful Hindu, Muslim, Buddhist and Confucian cultures of the 'subject peoples'.

TIMELINE

1942
Japan overruns Europe's Far Eastern colonies

1947
India partitioned: India and Pakistan independent

1954
Communist Vietnamese defeat French at Dien Bien Phu: start of Algerian War

1957
Suez crisis; abortive French and English invasion of Egypt

1957-68
Independence for British African colonies

1960
Independence for all French sub-Saharan colonies and Belgian Congo

1962
France withdraws from Algeria

1965
Rhodesian white settlers make Unilateral Declaration of Independence resulting in guerrilla war

1975
Portuguese rule in Africa ends

1990
Namibia gains independence from South Africa

1997
Hong Kong returned to China

Azores

Gibraltar
Ceuta   Melilla

MALTA 1964

CYPRUS 1960   SYRIA 1946

LEBANON 1943

TUNISIA 1956

ISRAEL 1948
PALESTINE

IRA

Madeira

MOROCCO 1956

1952-6

Ifni
ceded to Morocco 1969

Canary Is.
Spanish

SPANISH SAHARA
1975
disputed between
Morocco and
Polisario guerrillas

ALGERIA
1962

1954-62

LIBYA
1951

EGYPT 1954

Alexandria   Suez

treaty relations with
Britain 1922-54; British
military presence ends
1956

JORDAN
1946

IRAQ

KUWAIT
1961

QATAR
1971

SAUDI ARAB

Red Sea

1941-52 British
protectorate;
1952-93 federated
with Ethiopia;
1993 independent

YEMEN
ARAB
REP.

REPUBLIC OF
CAPE VERDE
1975

MAURITANIA
1960

MALI 1960

NIGER
1960

CHAD
1960

SUDAN
1956

ERITREA

DJIBOUTI
1977

Aden   1963-

SENEGAL
1960

THE GAMBIA
1965

UPPER VOLTA 1960
(BURKINA 1984)

DAHOMEY 1960
(BENIN 1975)

NIGERIA
1960

1955

ETHIOPIA
1941

GUINEA-BISSAU
1974
1962-74

GUINEA 1958

SIERRA LEONE
1961

IVORY
COAST
1960

LIBERIA

TOGO 1960

CAMEROON
1960-1; joined
Commonwealth
1995

CENTRAL AFRICAN
REP. 1960

UGANDA
1962

KENYA
1963
1952-9

SOMALIA
1960

GHANA 1957
union of
Gold Coast
and British
Togo 1956

Fernando Po
to Equatorial Guinea 1975

EQUATORIAL GUINEA
1968

SAO TOME AND
PRINCIPE 1975

GABON
1960

CONGO
1960

RWANDA
1962

BURUNDI
1962

DEMOCRATIC REP.
OF CONGO
(CONGO 1960
ZAIRE 1971-97)

TANGANYIKA 1961

Zanzibar
1963

TANZANIA
1964

COMOROS
1975

*Atlantic
Ocean*

Ascension

British sponsored Central African Federation of
Northern and Southern Rhodesia and Nyasaland 1953-63

Cabinda
to Angola

ANGOLA
1975
1961-74

MALAWI
1964

Mayotte

MADAGASCAR

*Atlantic
Ocean*
St. Helena

ZAMBIA
1964

MOZAMBIQUE
1975
1964-74
joined
Commonwealth
1995

BAHAMAS 1973

Turks and Caicos Is.

MEXICO   Isla de Pinos
Cayman Is.   CUBA

Sint-Maarten
St. Martin

British Virgin Is.

DOMINICAN
REP.

Anguilla

ANTIGUA-
BARBUDA 1981

SOUTH WEST
AFRICA
(NAMIBIA)
1990

BELIZE 1981
(to Honduras)
Swan Is.

HAITI

Puerto
Rico

American Virgin Is.

St. Barthélemy

Montserrat
Guadeloupe

BOTSWANA
1966

RHODESIA UDI 1965
(ZIMBABWE 1980)

1947-8

JAMAICA 1962
British-sponsored
federation of West
Indies 1958-62

HONDURAS

ST KITTS & NEVIS
1983

ST LUCIA
1979

DOMINICA 1978

Martinique

1971-89
South African
mandate declared
illegal by United
Nations 1971;
from 1989 UN
forces control
move towards
independence

Caribbean Sea

Aruba
Curaçao   Bonaire

ST VINCENT
1979

BARBADOS
1966

GRENADA 1974

SWAZILAND
1968

LESOTHO
1966

NICARAGUA

COSTA RICA

COLOMBIA

VENEZUELA

TRINIDAD &
TOBAGO 1962

GUYANA 1966

SOUTH AFRICA
Republic 1961
Simonstown   left Commonwealth 1961;
evacuated 1957   rejoined 1994

154

France fought stubbornly to maintain its control of Indochina (page 162), and the Netherlands struggled to contain the nationalists of Java, who had proclaimed the Indonesian Republic in 1945. Neither succeeded. Continual unrest forced Britain to grant independence to India and Pakistan (1947), followed in 1948 by Burma and Ceylon (page 162). Nevertheless Britain fought (and won) a long war against communist insurgents in Malaya, and resisted Indonesian attempts to annex Sarawak and Brunei. Only after the evacuation of Aden in 1967 did Britain abandon its presence east of Suez – save only for Hong Kong, retained until 1997, its economic success being of some benefit to Communist China.

In Africa resistance to independence was strongest in colonies with substantial white settler populations. In Algeria, with 1 million whites, a savage war of liberation occurred between 1954 and 1962; but conflict proved bitter, too, in Kenya and Rhodesia. However by 1974 all had achieved independence (page 160). By then, although Britain showed in the Falklands War (1982) its determination to fight on behalf of the few outposts still directly ruled from London, the formal structures of European imperialism had been dismantled and largely replaced by different forms of association such as the British Commonwealth or the French Community.

Mohandas Gandhi (right) became leader of the Indian nationalist movement in 1918, preaching non-violence (satyragha). In 1922 he was imprisoned by the British authorities, but was released in 1924 on becoming president of the Indian National congress. He led a campaign to boycott British cotton imports, and in 1930 encouraged resistance to a proposed salt tax. Although he withdrew from formal politics in 1933 he remained the guiding influence of the nationalist movement, and was a key figure in the eventual negotiations for Indian independence and partition in 1946-8.

1 The post-colonial world in the 1990s

▭	territories independent since 1939, with dates	

colonial possessions in 1998

- ● British
- ● French
- ● Dutch
- ● Portuguese
- ● Spanish
- ● US
- ● Australia
- ● New Zealand
- ● USA Australia New Zealand joint rule

▭ states within British Commonwealth

▭ states that broke away from Commonwealth

▭ states belonging to the ACCT (Francophonie community)

✕ areas of colonial conflict

☐ British stations and bases overseas

━ members of abortive federations

•━•━• border conflict

*Map labels:*

ited Arab Rep.–
leration of Egypt and
ria 1958–61
AFGHANISTAN
Kashmir
TIBET absorbed by China 1965
Sikkim annexed by India 1975
HRAIN
71
Oman
PAKISTAN 1947 left Commonwealth 1972; rejoined 1989
NEPAL
BHUTAN
UAE 1971
INDIA 1947
CHINA
Diu 1961 annexed by India
Daman 1961 to India
EAST PAKISTAN 1947 (BANGLADESH 1971)
BURMA 1948
NORTH VIETNAM 1954
LAOS 1954
Hong Kong to China 1997
Macao to China 1999
1946–54
Goa 1961 annexed by India
PLES DEMOCRATIC UBLIC OF YEMEN 1967 ited with Yemen ab Rep. 1990
Laccadive Is. to India
Pondicherry 1954 to India
Karikal 1954 to India
THAILAND
Andaman Is. to India
SOCIALIST REPUBLIC OF VIETNAM unified 1976
PHILIPPINES 1946
Pacific Ocean
evacuated 1967
CAMBODIA 1953
SOUTH VIETNAM 1954
CEYLON 1948 (SRI LANKA 1972)
MALDIVES 1965 left Commonwealth 1968 rejoined 1982
Malaysian Federation 1963–5
BRUNEI 1984
Sabah
1975
ion of Tanganyika d Zanzibar
MALAYA 1957
1948–66
MALAYSIA 1963
Sarawak
independent republic suppressed by Indonesia 1949–50
1959–65 SINGAPORE
Borneo
Kalimantan
PAPUA NEW GUINEA 1975
ministered France ce 1975, imed by moros
Gan evacuated 1967
Sumatra
Java
South Moluccas
INDONESIA 1949
1945–9
Dutch New Guinea to Indonesia 1963
Christmas I.
East Timor annexed by Indonesia 1976–99; non-self governing territory administered by UN from October 1999

Inset map (Pacific):

New Ireland New Britain 1975 (to Papua New Guinea)
KIRIBATI 1979 (formerly Gilbert Is.)
Pacific Ocean
Fanning I.
NAURU 1968
Ocean I.
Jarvis I.
TUVALU 1978 (formerly Ellice Is.)
SOLOMON IS. 1978
Wallis and Futuna Is.
Tokelau
Marquesas Is.
Rotuma
Manihiki I.
AURITIUS 68
VANUATU 1980 (formerly New Hebrides)
WESTERN SAMOA 1962
American Samoa
Tahiti Is.
Réunion
FIJI 1970
New Caledonia
Niue
Society Is.
Cook Is.
Gambier Is.
AUSTRALIA
Kermadec Is.
TONGA 1970
Pitcairn I.
Lord Howe I.
Norfolk I.
suspended from Commonwealth 1987; rejoined 1997
self-governing territory in free association with New Zealand 1965
NEW ZEALAND

155

The Middle East since 1917

The Middle East has occupied world attention more consistently than any other region since 1945: Israel and its neighbours have engaged in four full-scale wars; Israel has invaded Lebanon twice; two Gulf wars have been fought; military coups have reinforced a regional pattern of internal repression; waves of refugees, from Cyprus to Afghanistan, have been forced to flee.

American support for the state of Israel (founded in 1948), sponsorship of the Baghdad Pact (1955), and intervention in Lebanon (1958) seemed to threaten the USSR's southern frontier, and so it offered assistance to Syria, Egypt and (after 1958) Iraq. The Soviets also championed the Arab states during the Arab-Israeli war of 1967, despite which Israel occupied the west bank of the Jordan, Sinai and the Golan heights, provoking further large-scale Arab emigration (map 1). In 1973 an Egyptian and Syrian attack on Israel met with limited military success, and opened a new phase of negotiation. Egypt and Israel concluded the Camp David Accords (1978) which resulted in the return of Sinai in 1982; but the Israelis refused to return the other territories occupied since 1967, instead installing large numbers of new Jewish settlements. Moreover in 1982, to counter Palestinian guerrilla activity, they invaded and held south Lebanon. Nevertheless, in the wake of a prolonged period of resistance to Israeli rule in the West Bank and Gaza, which excited much outside sympathy, in 1991 the US succeeded in bringing Israel and its Arab neighbours into extended peace talks, which resulted in limited Palestinian self-rule in 1994-5. Israel withdrew from south Lebanon in 2000.

As open conflict between Israel and her neighbours abated, it began around the Persian Gulf. The replacement of the Shah of Iran by Ayatollah Khomeini in 1979 seemed to President Saddam Hussein of Iraq to offer the chance of territorial gain. He attacked in 1980. However, eight years of attritional warfare achieved virtually nothing and in 1990 (map 2), in an attempt to gain new resources with which to liquidate his war debts, Saddam invaded and annexed another neighbour, Kuwait. The United Nations, led by the US, put pressure on Saddam to withdraw and, when he refused, in 1991 used armed force to expel him. These events catastrophically reduced oil production in the Gulf area. Its share of global output fell from 41 per cent in 1979 to 26 per cent in 1991, with production in Iraq and Kuwait reduced almost to zero.

1 Israel and Palestine, 1948–95

Israel after Arab invasion and War of Independence, 1948

Israeli conquests, 1967

Egyptian re-conquests, and Israeli conquests, 1973

Jewish immigration, 1948–64

Arab refugees, 1948

Arab refugees, 1967

Sinai, the Israeli withdrawal:
Egyptian frontline under second Sinai agreement, 1 Sep.1975

○ Israeli settlements given up in 1982

✈ Israeli military and civil airports given up in 1982

⌂ Israeli oil wells given up in 1982

Popular protest played a key role in the fall of the shah of Iran in 1979 and the assumption of power by Ayatollah Khomeini in February that year. The picture was taken in 1987 on the eighth anniversary of the revolution. According to Khomeini, ultimate governmental authority should be vested in a supreme Islamic jurist. Subsequently, a rightly guided Iran should spread the message of true Islam to the rest of the Islamic world. But true Islam had first to be consolidated within Iran: an estimated 10,000 people had been executed by 1985 and 40,000 imprisoned.

Mar. 1994: pro-Islamist Welfare Party scores gains in local elections
Dec. 1995: Welfare Party wins largest percentage of votes in general election; subsequent deal between secular parties keeps it out of power
1998 Welfare Party banned. New Islamist party, Virtue, founded
1999 Virtue Party comes 3rd in general elections

1983: foundation of Hezbollah, radical Islamic movement; becomes principal proxy for Iranian-inspired terrorism in Lebanon

continuing anti-Israeli campaign of suicide bombings

1979: following overthrow of shah, hardline Islamic fundamentalist government, headed by Ayatollah Khomeini, established
late 1980s: Iranian backing for the formation of HAMAS and Islamic Jihad, militant Palestinian Islamic groupings

continuing civil war between Islamic regime and former government forces

Feb. 1982: rioting by Islamic militants in Hama brutally supressed

973: Qadhafi publishes Third Universal Theory, declaring Islam the true path
1977 Libyan "cultural revolution" introduces Islamic socialism

original home of Muslim Brotherhood (founded 1920s), the region's most significant and widespread Islamic organization

autumn 1994: civil disturbances among Shia majority, Iranian instigation alleged

1992: emergence of incipient Islamic political opposition

TURKEY
SYRIA
Hama
Beirut
LEBANON
Damascus
ISRAEL
Jerusalem
Amman
JORDAN
IRAQ
Baghdad
An Najaf
IRAN
Teheran
AFGHAN.
KUWAIT
BAHRAIN
Doha
QATAR
Abu Dhabi
UAE
Muscat
PAK.
USSR
Medina
Riyadh
SAUDI ARABIA
Mecca
LIBYA
Tripoli
EGYPT
Cairo
Nile
SUDAN
Khartoum
Red Sea
ERITREA
ETHIOPIA
OMAN
Arabian Sea
YEMEN
San'a
Aden

June 1989: military coup brings National Islamic Front (NIF) to power, launches violent attempt to Islamicize rebel south Sudan

1998: Islamic army of Aden kidnaps foreign tourists

3 Islamic fundamentalism 1979–99
- countries with radical Islamic governments
- Islamic parties represented in parliament
- ✳ civil war
- ✊ violent anti-government Islamic campaigns
- ▲ countries with significant Shia populations
- ✴ Islamic terrorist attacks

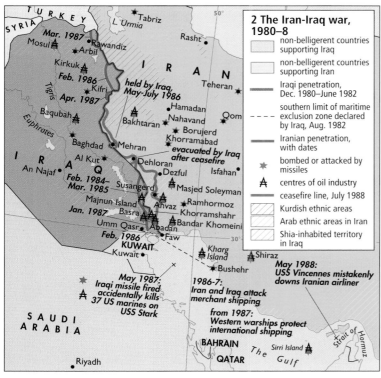

2 The Iran-Iraq war, 1980–8
- non-belligerent countries supporting Iraq
- non-belligerent countries supporting Iran
- Iraqi penetration, Dec. 1980–June 1982
- southern limit of maritime exclusion zone declared by Iraq, Aug. 1982
- Iranian penetration, with dates
- ✳ bombed or attacked by missiles
- ⚒ centres of oil industry
- ceasefire line, July 1988
- ▨ Kurdish ethnic areas
- ▨ Arab ethnic areas in Iran
- ▨ Shia-inhabited territory in Iraq

TURKEY
SYRIA
L. Urmia
Tabriz
Rasht
Mar. 1987
Mosul
Rawandiz
Arbil
Kirkuk
Feb. 1986
Kifri
Apr. 1987
Baqubah
IRAN
Teheran
held by Iraq, May-July 1986
Hamadan
Nahavand
Qom
Bakhtaran
Borujerd
Khorramabad
evacuated by Iraq after ceasefire
Baghdad
Mehran
Al Kut
Dehloran
IRAQ
An Najaf
Feb. 1984–Mar. 1985
Susangerd
Dezful
Isfahan
Masjed Soleyman
Majnun Island
Ahvaz
Ramhormoz
Jan. 1987
Basra
Khorramshahr
Umm Qasr
Abadan
Bandar Khomeini
Faw
Feb. 1986
KUWAIT
Kuwait
Kharg Island
Shiraz
Bushehr
May 1988: USS Vincennes mistakenly downs Iranian airliner

May 1987: Iraqi missile fired accidentally kills 37 US marines on USS Stark

1986-7: Iran and Iraq attack merchant shipping

from 1987: Western warships protect international shipping

SAUDI ARABIA
Riyadh
BAHRAIN
QATAR
Sirri Island
The Gulf
Strait of Hormuz

Tigris
Euphrates

Nevertheless, oil remained the most valuable natural asset of the region. Output and revenue both increased dramatically after the OPEC price-rise in 1973, creating some of the highest per capita incomes in the world in the Arab Gulf states. Their prosperity also attracted massive immigration from Egypt, Jordan, Yemen and the Indian sub-continent, creating a potential problem. The rise of Islamic fundamentalism posed another. After 1979 it became a badge of hostility towards the West in Iran and towards Russia in Afghanistan, and elsewhere toward the regime in power – unless, as in Iran, that regime was an Islamic theocracy. In northern Africa, in the 1990s Islamic fundamentalism stimulated terrorist violence, provoking serious conflict in Algeria and Egypt (map 3).

Although the collapse of the Soviet Union (page 168) ended superpower rivalry in the area, the Western powers continued to exert their influence, both to safeguard the oil supplies on which their economies still depended and to protect blatantly persecuted minorities like the Kurds of northern Iraq. Moreover, the enormous concentrations of conventional weapons – and the interest in developing chemical and biological weapons – in so many antagonistic states ensured that the Middle East continued to occupy world attention.

Latin America since 1930

The Great Depression (page 138) struck Latin America a shattering blow, cutting off supplies of foreign capital and lowering the price of its primary products in the world markets. Chile's exports fell by over 80 per cent between 1929 and 1933; those of Bolivia and Peru by 75 per cent. Only oil-exporting Venezuela more or less weathered the storm. The economic collapse led to widespread disillusion with middle-class liberal or radical parties: in 1930 and 1931, 11 of the 20 republics south of the Rio Grande experienced revolutionary changes in government. Mexico, where Lázaro Cárdenas (1934-40) revived the land distribution policies of 1911 (page 112), experienced a shift to the left; but elsewhere the swing was mainly to the right. The new dictators tended to be populists, appealing directly to the masses and cooperating with organised labour and the trade unions. They also introduced programmes of industrialization – following Soviet or, more often, Fascist models – to reduce dependence on overseas markets and hasten economic development.

Manufacturing industry received a further boost during World War II, which cut off imported consumer goods and stimulated the industrial sector. But industrialization made Latin America dependent upon imported capital goods, raw materials, technology and finance – especially from the United States – creating enormous foreign debts (map 2). Multinational corporations exploited the cheap labour of Latin America without stimulating economic development. Social tensions arose from income concentration, unemployment, lack of opportunities, and from the intrusion of foreign interests. Social revolutions were attempted but frustrated in Guatemala, Bolivia and Chile (map 1), underlining the obstacles to change in economies too narrowly based to sustain welfare programmes, where local elites were prepared to collaborate with the United States.

Cuba after 1959 attempted to achieve social change, economic growth and freedom from the United States simultaneously; but although its revolution led to greater social equality and some improvement in the lot of rural workers, it also brought a repressive regime and dependence on the Soviet Union. Moreover its attempts to spread revolution in Central and South America all failed.

In the face of revolutionary change, with some support from the upper and middle classes, the military seized power in many areas and combined

A government soldier in Peru (below), guards against attacks by the Shining Path guerrillas. The Shining Path (Sendero Luminoso) was founded in 1980 by Abimael Guzmán, a philosophy professor. It adopted a mixture of Maoist political and military tactics and gained control of large areas of the central Andean highlands in the early 1990s. After Guzmán's capture in 1992, the movement fragmented and the level of its attacks diminished sharply.

2 Economic development

direct US investment in Latin America (figures in millions of US dollars)

1929, 1943, 1960, 1979, 1995

chief exports of Latin America, 1955–90

coffee chief exports 1955

coffee chief exports 1990

▲ represents over 50 per cent of total exports

● represents over 25 per cent of total exports

UNITED STATES OF AMERICA

MEXICO
● cotton
coffee
crude petroleum
engines

GUATEMALA
● coffee
EL SALVADOR
▲ coffee
oil
crude petroleum
coffee

HONDURAS
coffee
bananas
NICARAGUA
COSTA RICA
PANAMA
bananas
▲ coffee

BELIZE
▲ sugar
tobacco
sugar
nickel

CUBA

no US investment from 1960
919 526 956
2569 2206 3372
232 373
14,037
23,590
● oil
iron ore
crude petroleum
aluminium
4575

COLOMBIA
VENEZUELA
GUYANA
FRENCH GUIANA
SURINAM
682 286 795
7514

ECUADOR
▲ bananas
coffee
crude petroleum
bananas

PERU
● cotton
sugar
meat/fish meal
zinc
▲ tin
tungsten
● natural gas
zinc

BRAZIL
194 233 953

BOLIVIA
▲ copper
nitrates
● copper
meat/fish meal
5510
423 328 738 291

PARAGUAY
coffee ▲
cocoa
iron ore
coffee

CHILE

URUGUAY
cotton
meat
raw cotton
soya beans
wool ▲
meat
meat
wool

ARGENTINA
wheat ●
meat
vegetable extracts
wheat
7962
2162
332 380 472

political repression with economic liberalization. But by the late 1980s their policies too had largely failed and, in the face of economic recession and popular protest, their power gradually weakened. Instead, democratic government resumed in several states of the subcontinent. In 1992 Mexico signed a free trade agreement (NAFTA) with Canada and the United States, creating the largest integrated trading bloc in the world.

1 Latin America since 1945

political change in Latin America since 1945

Social revolution Fundamental change (attempted or achieved) in economic and social structure by nationalist or Marxist movements

Reformism Moderate socio-economic change or modernization for democratic or other process

Populism Interventionist state based on multi-class alliance for policy of development

Christian Democracy Radical socio-economic change by Christian Democratic parties

Unreformed militarism Military dictatorship of the right without social or modernizing programme

Indigenous guerrilla movements Urban guerrillas from late 1960s following failure of Cuban-inspired rural guerrillas

communism in Latin America, 1974

70,000 communist party membership

M/P loyalty (Moscow/Peking)

communist party status
- in power
- legal opposition
- illegal

Mexican revolution 1910-40
Zapatista revolt, 1994

Guatemalan revolution 1944-54

Military Junta 1979

Sandinista revolution 1979-90; democratization 1990

Figueres 1948

Liberal-Conservative Pact, 1957

Intermittent militarism to 1978
Election of reformist government 1978

Radical militarism 1968
Sendero Luminoso from 1980
Return to civil rule 1980
Fujimori 1990-2000

Bolivian revolution 1952-64
Che Guevara (killed 1967)
Military 1980; democratization 1982

Eduardo Frei 1964-70
Salvador Allende (Popular Unity) 1970-3
Pinochet 1973-88
Democratization 1989

Cuban revolution 1959

Rómulo Betancourt 1945-48, 1959-64; Carlos Andrés Pérez 1974-9
Rafael Caldera 1969-74; Luis Herrera Campins 1979; Jaime Lusinchi 1984
Hugo Chavez 1998-

Getulio Vargas 1930-45; 1950-4 João Goulart 1961-4
Modernizing militarism 1964
Civilian rule 1985; democratization 1986

Military dictatorship Stroessner 1954 Rodriguez 1989

Batllismo 1903-33
Military 1973
Tupamaros
Civilian rule 1985; democratization 1986
Montoneros

Juan Domingo Perón 1943-55, 1973-4
Military 1976-83
Democratization and civilian rule 1983

Falkland Islands (Islas Malvinas) occupied by Argentina 1982: occupation ended by UK Task Force June 1982

UNITED STATES OF AMERICA
US intervention
Dominican Republic 1916-24
Grenada 1983
Haiti 1915-34 1944 1994
Cuba 1921-23 1933 1961
Panama 1903-18 1989
Nicaragua 1912-33
Guatemala 1954
Mexico 1914

MEXICO *5,000*
Mexico City
Puebla
Veracruz
Havana
CUBA *125,000* M
1,400 DOMINICAN REP.
PUERTO RICO (USA)
Cuban-inspired guerrilla movements 1959-68
HAITI *n/a* M

BELIZE
300 M
HONDURAS
GUAT. *750* M
Guatemala City
Tegucigalpa
EL SALVADOR
NICARAGUA *100* M
125 M
Managua
San José
COSTA RICA
1,000 M
PANAMA *500* M
Panama City
Caribbean Sea
GRENADA
Cartagena
Caracas
Port of Spain
VENEZUELA
Georgetown
8,000 M
GUYANA *100* M
Paramaribo
Cayenne
SUR. FR.GUIANA

Bogotá
COLOMBIA *11,000* M/P
Quito
ECUADOR *1,200* M/P
Guayaquil
Piura
3,500 M/P
Trujillo
PERU
Huánuco
Callao
Lima
Cuzco

Macapá
Amazon
Manaus
Belém
Fortaleza
Recife
B R A Z I L *7,000* M/P
Salvador (Bahia)
Brasília
Belo Horizonte
Rio de Janeiro
São Paulo
Santos

La Paz
Sucre
BOLIVIA *3,200* M/P
Arequipa

PARAGUAY
Asunción
Florianópolis
Porto Alegre
Rio Grande
Fray Bentos
URUGUAY *22,000* M
Montevideo

Antofagasta
Copiapó
120,000 M
Tucumán
Córdoba
Santa Fé
Valparaíso
Mendoza
Buenos Aires
Santiago
ARGENTINA *70,000* M
Concepción
Valdivia
Bahía Blanca
Osorno
Rawson
Comodoro Rivadavia
Santa Cruz
Stanley
Tierra del Fuego

Africa since 1945

After World War II, although some French and British liberals sympathetic to African claims for advancement initiated programmes of social improvement and political reform, the need to exploit every asset in order to assist metropolitan recovery led to attempts to reassert colonial control. Nevertheless in the 1950s both Britain and France began to transfer responsibility to elected governments in their West African colonies.

In Muslim North Africa, longer-established nationalist movements received great stimulus from the overthrow of the Egyptian monarchy in 1952 and the rise to power of Gamal Abdel Nasser. In 1956 an Anglo-French-Israeli invasion failed to topple him. Meanwhile France granted independence to Tunisia and Morocco but tried to incorporate Algeria, the colony with the largest white population, into metropolitan France. This sparked a civil war that lasted until France reluctantly granted independence in 1962.

Elsewhere, white settlers strove to maintain their ascendancy. In South Africa, a Nationalist government dedicated to policies of racial separation ('apartheid') came to power; in Kenya, British troops arrived to suppress the Mau-Mau insurrection directed against the settlers; in Central Africa, a federation of Nyasaland and Rhodesia aimed to preserve white dominance. But in 1963 Kenya achieved independence and the Federation collapsed. Southern Rhodesia's white settlers created their own independent state in 1965, but had to accept black majority rule in 1980. Portugal retained its colonies longest, but in all of them guerrilla warfare eventually led to ignominious withdrawal in 1974-5.

Most of the newly independent African states possessed borders drawn by European governments in the 19th century with insufficient attention to ethnic rivalries. Soon after independence, those rivalries began to tear them apart. In 1960, tribal and regional factions in Zaire (formerly the Belgian Congo) led to demands for a federal constitution and, when these were refused, the army mutinied and the mineral rich province of Katanga seceded. United Nations intervention reunited the country in 1963, but two years later the

1976 Western Sahara jointly occupied by Morocco and Mauritania; Polisario guerrilla resistance backed by Algeria
1991 cease-fire between Morocco and Polisario

W. SAHAR

1976-79 war with Polisario
1978 military rule
1991 multi-party elections

MAURITA

1968 civilian government overthrown
1974-85 border conflicts with Burkina

1991 RUF launches civil war
1992 military coup
1996 civilian rule restored under Ahmad Tejan Kabbah
1997 military overthrow Kabbah
1998 Kabbah restored
1999 rebels almost capture Freetown
Nov. 2000 RUF call truce

SENEGAL
GA.
GU.
GUINE
SIERRA LEONE

1989 outbreak of civil war
1993 pan-African peace-keeping force (Ecomog) intervenes in attempt to halt civil war

1957 first Black African country to gain independence
1966 Nkrumah deposed
1967-85 series of military coups

LIB

1967-70 Nigerian civil war
1981 civilian rule restored
1984, 1985, 1993 military coups
1993 elections declared void; riots;interim government ousted by m
1999 civilian ruled restored

1966 military takeover led by Col. Bokassa, crowned emperor 197
1980 republic restored
1981 military coup

army seized power and retained it for 34 years. Similarly, in Nigeria the secession of Biafra in 1967 led to a three-year civil war that restored central control, but likewise delivered power to the army. Elsewhere, ethnic violence caused enormous casualties – in the small state of Rwanda, Hutu-Tutsi violence left over 500,000 dead in 1994 – while repeated droughts (compounded by government inefficiency and corruption) caused famine and massive refugee problems in many areas of East Africa. In Algeria, from 1990 Islamic Fundamentalism challenged government control.

By the 1980s, white supremacy survived only in South Africa where the nationalist regime sought to retain its grip by draconian internal repression, by sending troops against guerrillas in neighbouring states, and by granting spurious independence to some black settlement areas set up under apartheid. Eventually, however, economic crisis and international isolation forced concessions. In 1990, the nationalists released Nelson Mandela, imprisoned leader of the banned African National Congress, and within four years the ANC's victory in the first multi-racial elections in South Africa's history swept away white rule. Despite the problems of healing decades of racial tension, the ANC created a more stable political system than under white rule and preserved the most successful economy on the continent. Mandela retired in 2000. Meanwhile in Zimbabwe (formerly Rhodesia) serious racial conflict broke out.

Nelson Mandela *(right)* joined the African National Congress in 1944 and helped to found its Youth League. In 1961, frustrated at the failure of civil disobedience to undermine apartheid, he adopted the idea of armed struggle. In 1962 he was sentenced to life imprisonment. Released in 1990, aged 72, he became leader of the ANC and, in 1994, South Africa's first president elected by universal franchise. He retired from the presidency in 1999.

1 Africa: post-independence wars and revolutions

- ✴ civil war
- → invasion
- ✊ guerrilla activity
- ✴ border dispute

MOROCCO
1956 independence

TUNISIA
1956 independence
1984 major rioting
1987 Bourguiba ousted

ALGERIA
1962 independence
1960s border conflicts with Morocco
1965 Ben Bella deposed by Col. Boumedienne
1990 election of Islamic fundamentalist-dominated chamber of deputies
1991 election results nullified; anti-government terrorist campaign by Islamic Fundamentalists

LIBYA
1969 King Idris deposed; replaced by military junta under Col. Gadhafi
1986 US bomb Tripoli in retaliation for terrorist attacks

EGYPT

1952 King Farouk deposed by army officers led by Neguib
1954-70 Nasser president
1956 Suez crisis
1967, 1973 wars with Israel
1981 Mubarak president on assassination of Sadat
1991 forces join US-led war against Iraqi occupation of Kuwait

MALI

NIGER

BURKINA FASO

BENIN

IVORY COAST

GHANA

TOGO

NIGERIA

CHAD
1960 civil war; FROLINAT guerrillas supported by Libya
1973, 1981 Libyan invasion and withdrawal
1984 border war with Libya

SUDAN
1963–72 civil war
1969 General Numeiry takes power in military coup, intermittent civil war in South since independence
1984 severe famine
1985 Numeiry overthrown (civil war continues)
1989 military coup; National Islamic Front in effective control
1994–5 ceasefire between feuding southern anti-government forces

ERITREA
1952 federated with Ethiopia
1962 Union
1961-91 armed resistance to Ethiopian rule in both Eritrea and Tigre
1991 Eritrean and Tigrean forces victorious
1993 independence
1998–2000 border war with Ethiopia

DJIBOUTI

ETHIOPIA
1961- war against Eritrea secessionists
1974 Emperor Haile Selassie overthrown by army junta
1984-88 severe famine, aid from West
1991 Mengistu's Communist regime overthrown after civil war

CAMEROON

CENTRAL AFRICAN REPUBLIC

E. GABON

CONGO

DEMOCRATIC REPUBLIC OF CONGO (ZAIRE)

UGANDA

KENYA
1970s border disputes with Uganda and Somalia

SOMALIA
1964, 1970 border disputes with Ethiopia and Kenya
1976-78 occupation of Ogaden and war with Ethiopia
1993 UN military intervention to halt civil war and famine

RWANDA

BURUNDI

1966 Obote expels Kabaka (King) of Buganda
1970 border dispute with Kenya
1971 Obote overthrown by Amin; Asians expelled; large-scale repression
1979 invaded by Tanzania, Amin overthrown; Obote restored (1980), overthrown (Jan 1986)
1986 Yoweri Museveni president

1962 independence
1965 civil war, massacre of Tutsi (in Rwanda and Burundi)
1994 tribal violence/civil war; exodus of refugees to Rwandan borders. Mass killings of Tutsi civilians; large scale UN humanitarian assistance

TANZANIA

Lake Victoria

Lake Tanganyika

1960-69 civil war
1978 invasion of Shaba province by anti-Mobutu dissidents, repelled with French assistance
1997 Mobuto overthrown by rebel movement led by Laurent Kabila
1997–2000 continued civil war
2001 Kabila assassinated

1962 independence followed by civil war/tribal violence, massive refugee movement to neighbouring countries

ANGOLA

ZAMBIA

MALAWI

Lake Nyasa

1975- Marxist MPLA government in conflict with UNITA guerrillas aided by South Africa
1991 peace agreement between MPLA and UNITA breaks down after elections: civil war renewed
1992 renewed fighting
1994 agreement between UNITA and government
1998–9 fighting between UNITA and government restarts

support for black nationalists in Angola, Namibia and Rhodesia
1991 Kaunda defeated in democratic election

NAMIBIA

ZIMBABWE

BOTSWANA

MOZAMBIQUE

Zambezi

MADAGASCAR
1972 military takeover

South African presence resisted by SWAPO to 1990
1991 fully independent from South Africa

1948 implementation of apartheid
1975 invasion of Angola
1976 mounting black urban unrest
1976-81 African homelands (Bantustans) established in Transkei, Bophuthatswana and Ciskei
1984 new constitution, limited representation for Indians and coloureds
1985–87 growing African resistance and civil unrest
1986 commando raids on neighbouring countries
1990 Mandela released President de Klerk starts to dismantle apartheid
1993 multiracial council paves way to free elections
1994 election victory for ANC; Mandela president
1996 National party leaves governing coalition
1999 Mandela steps down as president

SWAZILAND

LESOTHO

REPUBLIC OF SOUTH AFRICA

1975-1993 civil war between Frelimo government and Renamo guerrillas
1980- South African intervention in support of Renamo
1994 multi-party elections following Renamo-Frelimo peace accord

1965-80 independent as Rhodesia under white-minority rule 1980 black majority rule established; increasing steps towards one-party state
2000 resettlement of "war veterans" on white owned land causes serious unrest

Nile

Niger

Congo

Orange

Vaal

South and South East Asia since 1945

The history of southern Asia since independence has been dominated by three factors. First, the seizure of power by military leaders (Pakistan 1958, Indonesia 1967), with the aim – rarely successful – of abolishing corruption and stabilizing the economy; second, the resurgence of long-standing regional, tribal and religious conflicts (Naga and Sikh unrest in India; nationalist uprisings among the Mons, Shans and other 'hill people' in Thailand and Burma); finally, intervention by the Great Powers (Russia in Afghanistan; China and the United States in Vietnam).

Wars between states also characterized certain areas. The partition of the Indian subcontinent in 1947 left numerous points of friction between the new states of India and Pakistan, particularly Punjab, Kashmir and Bengal, and these erupted into war in 1965 and again in 1971 (in connection with the secession of East Pakistan to form the separate state of Bangladesh). Indian forces also expelled the Portuguese from their coastal enclaves (1961), fought China over a frontier dispute (1962), and intervened in Sri Lanka to protect the Hindu Tamil minority (1986-90). Civil wars, however, proved far more common (map 1). Malaya suffered a communist insurrection, led by ethnic Chinese, between 1948 and 1960; the Philippines experienced rebellions by both communists and Muslims from the 1960s; Cambodia was devastated by the civil war between the communist Khmer Rouge and its non-communist opponents.

The most savage conflict, however, occurred in Vietnam (map 2). After the Japanese collapse in 1945 Ho Chi Minh established a communist regime in Hanoi while the French recreated their colonial empire in the south. In 1946 armed conflict began, continuing until a humiliating defeat at Dien Bien Phu in 1954 forced the French to withdraw. Although this left Cambodia and Laos as independent states, it did not create a unified Vietnam: at the Geneva Peace Conference in 1954 Ho accepted a 'temporary' partition of the country at the 17th parallel until nationwide elections, mandated for 1956, took place. However an anti-communist regime in the south, backed by America, refused to hold elections. In 1959 Ho therefore attacked, and the US immediately provided munitions and advisers to the south, with regular troops and air strikes after 1965. Despite saturation bombing and the commitment of 500,000 US ground troops, the communists (supported by both Russia and China) held their own and in 1968 negotiations began between Hanoi and Washington. In 1973 American forces withdrew, although the US continued to supply the south on a massive scale. When the communists launched an orthodox military offensive in 1975, however, the south's army collapsed. Vietnam was now unified, under Hanoi, although its economy was ruined and its invasion of Cambodia in 1978 led to ostracism by the West.

Elsewhere in Asia, however, rapid development occurred. Following the path of Japan (page 152), Taiwan, Malaysia, Singapore, Thailand and eventually Indonesia achieved rapid rates of growth from the late 1960s. Even during the

Indira Gandhi daughter of India's first premier, Nehru, was the country's prime minister from 1972 to 1977 and from 1980 to 1985. She ruled over an India torn by ethnic and religious conflict. Between 1975 and 1977 she imposed a state of emergency following her conviction for electoral malpractice. In 1985 she was assassinated by one of her Sikh bodyguards.

3 Indo-China 1966-8

areas of control, early 1966:

- controlled by the Vietcong
- under Vietcong influence
- controlled by the Government
- under Government influence
- heavily contested area
- 'Tet' offensive, 1968

Vinh
Dong Hoi
NORTH VIETNAM
Vinh Linh
LAOS
Hue
Phu Bai
Da Nang
Ho Chi Minh trail
Chu Lai
Qui Nhon
SOUTH VIETNAM
CAMBODIA
Saigon
Mekong
7th US fleet 1964
South China Sea

1955 supports Baluchistani separatists in Pakistan
Dec. 1979 invaded by USSR; continued resistance by Islamic guerrillas
1988 USSR withdraws
1992 post Soviet-backed regime defeated by Islamic guerrillas
1997 regime overthrown by radical Islamic Taleban movement

AFGHANISTAN

1948 Democratic People's Republic of Korea proclaimed
1950 invasion of South Korea
1994 death of Kim Il Sung. His son, Kim Jong II succeeds

NORTH KOREA

1951 peace treaty with USA and end of occupation
1956 agreement with USSR, ending state of war;
1960 widespread demonstrations against US military bases in Japan and Okinawa
1972 normalization of relations with China
1990 agreements with USSR formally ending 1945 war

JAPAN

1948 Republic of Korea proclaimed
1950-3 Korean War
1961 military coup followed by dictatorship of Park Chung Hee (assassinated 1979);
mounting opposition from 1974
1979 martial law (relaxed 1981)

SOUTH KOREA

1971 secession from Pakistan; civil war followed in 1975 by murder of Sheikh Mujib and military control

CHINA

TIBET

NEPAL

PAKISTAN

INDIA

occupied by US after 1945, Okinawa reverted to Japan 1972

seat of Chinese Nationalist government since 1949
1958 territorial dispute with China over Quemoy and Matsu
1996 China attempts military intimidations as Taiwan holds first free elections

TAIWAN

1954 French withdrawal; civil war
1956-73 US backed South Vietnam and the communist-backed North engaged in escalating conflict
1973 US withdraws all forces
1976 North and South Vietnam reunified under Viet-Minh rule
1978 invasion of Cambodia and border clashes with China
1979 Chinese invasion

spasmodic unrest among Nagas, Sikhs and Tamils
1961 India occupies Portuguese enclaves
1962 Sino-Indian border war
1975-7 state of emergency proclaimed
1984 Sikh separatist uprising suppressed; Indira Gandhi assassinated
1991 Rajiv Gandhi assassinated
1998 nuclear tests conducted

BANGLADESH

BURMA

VIETNAM

LAOS

THAILAND

CAMBODIA

1953-73 civil war
1975 monarchy abolished; Pathet Lao seizes power

Communist and Muslim insurgency since 1968, eruption into civil war 1972-8
1986 Marcos regime ousted following general election. Aquino succeeds
1992 Ramos succeeds as president
2001 President Estrada forced to step down by popular protests

PHILIPPINES

guerrilla activity since independence (1948)
1958, 1962 military coups
1974 Socialist People's Republic inaugurated
May 1990 pro-democracy protests lend to free elections; military refuse to recognise result
1990- opposition leader Aung San Suu Kyi and her pro-democracy movement suppressed by military

58 military coup by Ayub Khan
65 border clashes with India in Rann of Kutch
65 war with India over Kashmir
71 war with India over Bangladesh
72 ceasefire lines established
77 military coup by Zia ul-Haq
88 democratic elections;.
nazir Bhutto prime minister deposed 1990
93 Benazir Bhutto returns as prime minister (deposed 1996)
98 nuclear tests conducted
99 military under General usharraf overthrows government Nawaz Sharif

SRI LANKA

1958, 1961 fighting between Sinhalese and Tamils
1971 government assumes emergency powers after rural guerrilla uprisings; 1983 intercommunal rioting
1986-90 Indian intervention to crush Tamil rebellions
May 1993 President Ranasinghe killed in rebel Tamil attack

Aceh

MALAYSIA

Mindanao

1947 military takeover, guerrilla activity since 1960
1976 border clashes with Cambodia
1978 Cambodian refugee camps in E. Thailand become bases for anti-Vietnamese factions
1987 border clashes with Laos

1970 monarchy abolished
1970-4 civil war; victory of Khmer Rouge who massacre millions of civilians
1978 Vietnamese invasion overthrows Khmer Rouge
1989 Vietnamese forces withdraw
1991 peace agreement leads to May 1993 elections, boycotted by Khmer Rouge which carries on civil war

INDONESIA

Irian Jaya

East Timor

1967 Sukarno ousted by military coup; suppression of Communists
1976- resistance to Indonesian rule in E. Timor
1977-99 secessionist rising in Irian Jaya
1989- GAM independence movement in Aceh fights guerilla campaign against government
1998 President Suharto steps down in face of rising protests
1999-2001 intercommunal violence in the Moluccas
1999 UN peace-keeping force enters East Timor after violence following vote in referendum for independence from Indonesia

1948-60 'The Emergency'- civil war with communist guerrillas
1969 rising by Chinese minority groups
1975-8 Communist guerrilla activity
1978- renewed racial and religious conflict

1 Post-independence wars and revolutions

★ civil war   → invasion   ✊ guerrilla activity   ✹ border dispute

world recession of the 1980s, each experienced an annual growth rate of well over 5 per cent (table 3). Various factors were responsible: all except Singapore possessed large pools of cheap labour; all created a substantial industrial base oriented towards export markets throughout Asia, Europe and North America; all the governments sought to attract substantial foreign investment through tax incentives and infrastructural development. A major part of that investment came from Japan. Finally, political stability – Lee in Singapore; Mahathir in Malaysia; Suharto in Indonesia – underpinned the economic strategy of industrial development and helped to attract foreign investment.

All these economies suffered in the economic turmoil which hit east Asia in 1997, when a currency crisis was transformed into a general crisis of confidence in the Asian economic model. The Thai economy was seriously affected, while Indonesia was badly it by a 75 per cent devaluation of the rupiah, again exacerbated by a major political crisis, as the 35-year old Suharto regime finally collapsed under the weight of nationwide protests. In general the region's economies recovered far faster than expected. Yet Indonesia remained gripped by widespread civil and ethnic unrest (including the withdrawal from East Timor in 1999), which threatened to destabilize the whole country.

3 The economies of South East Asia

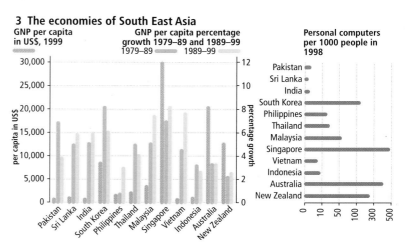

GNP per capita in US$, 1999

GNP per capita percentage growth 1979–89 and 1989–99
1979–89   1989–99

Personal computers per 1000 people in 1998

Pakistan
Sri Lanka
India
South Korea
Philippines
Thailand
Malaysia
Singapore
Vietnam
Indonesia
Australia
New Zealand

1947–89
The Cold War

The defeat of Germany, Italy and Japan and the weakening of Britain and France in World War II left the USA and USSR as the only 'superpowers'. Their ideological and political confrontation expressed itself as the Cold War. Conflict between the two had already appeared before the final victory: The Western Allies had already agreed (reluctantly) at Yalta (February 1945) to allow Soviet control of eastern Europe after the end of the war. By 1949 Stalin had developed an atomic bomb, thus ending the US monopoly of nuclear weapons. In reply, the USA built up the defence of western Europe with the formation of the North Atlantic Treaty Organization (NATO) in 1949 (page 146). In 1952 the US tested a thermo-nuclear (hydrogen) bomb; Russia followed suit in 1953.

Although it started as a conflict over central Europe, the Cold War soon developed into a global confrontation. The US saw the Korean War (1950-3: page 152) as evidence of a world-wide communist conspiracy, and American policy now became the 'containment' of Communism by a series of encircling alliances. NATO was followed by the South-East Asia Treaty Organization (SEATO) in 1954 and the Baghdad Pact (1955); the US maintained over 1400 foreign bases, including 275 bases for nuclear bombers, in 31 countries around the Soviet perimeter (map 1). As long as nuclear devices could only be delivered by aircraft, possession of these bases conferred an enormous advantage on the US. But when in the early 1960s both sides began to deploy ballistic nuclear missiles

US inspectors at a Soviet nuclear weapons site, 20 kilometres from Saratov *(right)*. Under the terms of the disarmament agreement of 1987 both sides agreed to the decommissioning of a large proportion of their nuclear stockpiles and to a system of inspections.

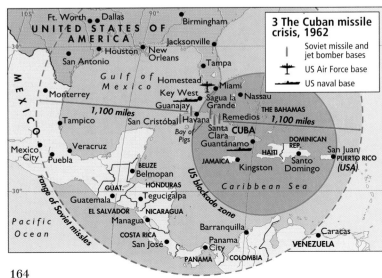

3 The Cuban missile crisis, 1962

| Soviet missile and jet bomber bases
✈ US Air Force base
⚓ US naval base

1 The age of bipolarity

USA and allies, 1958

USSR and allies, 1958

⟵ Soviet ICBM bases (7000 mile range)

⟵ other Soviet missile sites, 1961

▲ principal Soviet military airfields

⟵ US ICBM bases (5000 mile range)

▲ US heavy bomber bases (capable of reaching USSR with airborne refuelling)

■ US nuclear and other major bases (Oct. 1962)

⟶ strategic US fleets

✳ points of conflict in the Cold War

✊ uprisings in the Communist world

Czechoslovakia
✳ 1948
✊ 1968

East Germany
✳ Berlin 1948–9, 1958–62
✊ Berlin 1953

Estonia (E)
✊ 1944–55

Hungary
✊ 1956

Poland
✊ 1945–8, 1956

Lithuania (L)
✊ 1945–7

Ukraine (U)
✊ 1945–50

2 The nuclear balance, 1955–80

USSR intercontinental — bombers, land missiles, sea missiles, warheads
USA intercontinental — bombers, land missiles, sea missiles, warheads
USSR regional — bombers, missiles, warheads
USA regional — bombers, missiles

capable of being launched from land silos and submarines, the odds altered: now, in the event of war, each of the two superpowers could attack the other's cities directly (chart 2).

In October 1962, this scenario was almost put to the test when, following an unsuccessful US attempt to unseat the communist regime, the USSR established nuclear missile sites in Cuba. President Kennedy proclaimed a 'quarantine' of the island and threatened that, if the missiles were fired, the US would immediately retaliate against the USSR. The Russians then agreed to their removal (map 3). In return, Kennedy agreed to remove some of the US missile sites from Turkey.

This crisis, with its real threat of nuclear holocaust, proved a turning point in the Cold War. Already both monolithic blocs had begun to show signs of strain, most seriously on the Soviet side: Hungary and Poland rebelled in 1956, and from 1960 China began to quarrel openly over territory and ideology. In western Europe, France rejected American political leadership after 1958 and left NATO. A desire to limit the spread of nuclear weapons led to the conclusion of a partial test-ban treaty in 1963 and a nuclear non-proliferation treaty in 1968, but not all nuclear or potential nuclear powers signed these agreements (notably France, China and India) while others (such as Iraq) later reneged on their commitment. The Cold War therefore continued and the superpowers created huge nuclear arsenals.

In the event, the economic and political difficulties of the USSR increased to the point where the Soviet leader Mikhail Gorbachev (1985–91) felt that only a dramatic reduction in the crushing burden of military expenditure could bring relief (page 168). First the Soviets withdrew their forces from eastern Europe (1989), then NATO and the Warsaw Pact declared that the other was no longer an enemy (1990), and finally the USSR itself began to disintegrate (1991). Further agreements on the reduction of nuclear and conventional forces soon followed, although the fate of the vast arsenal accumulated by the former USSR gave cause for concern.

Europe since 1973

In 1973 the oil-producing states almost trebled the price of oil in a year, triggering worldwide price inflation. In Europe, the crisis coincided with a general slowdown in productivity and profit growth and mounting unemployment, producing widespread labour unrest. Behind the Iron Curtain, rising oil prices caused economic performance to stagnate or decline.

In western Europe, the crisis encouraged the trend to greater economic integration. By the late 1960s, the original six members of the EEC (European Economic Community) had established themselves as the economic vanguard of the continent. In 1973 Britain, Ireland and Denmark joined, followed in 1981 by Greece, in 1986 by Spain and Portugal, and in 1995 by Austria, Finland and Sweden. In 1985, the EEC agreed to create a single market under which it would became a free-trade zone. The Maastricht Treaty of 1991 then committed members (renamed the EU, European Union, in 1995) to introduce a single currency, the Euro, by 1999 (map 1).

The combined effects of the economic slowdown after 1973 and the realization that clinging to their pre-war authoritarian governments would push them to the margins of Europe helped reintroduce democracy to Portugal (1974) and Spain (1975). Greece also embraced democracy in 1974. But these changes paled in comparison with events in eastern Europe in the late 1980s, where the disintegration of the Soviet Union and the fall of communism in every one of its satellite states produced in its wake no less than 15 new countries (page 168). The nationalist tensions released also led to civil wars in the former Yugoslavia.

Nationalist tensions also continued in western Europe. Many areas achieved a measure of devolution, often on linguistic grounds (as in Belgium) while terrorism sustained Basque separatism in Spain and Irish nationalism in Ulster. Tentative political agreements were reached in both areas in 1998, though tensions survived (map 2). Although much of Europe became freer and more prosperous by the late 1990s, political stability and economic progress could not be guaranteed across the continent.

FAEROE ISLANDS
Faeroe Islanders, 1948

2 Western Europe: separatism and nationalism, 1945–2000

——— territorial autonomy based on ethnic group, with date of autonomy	✓ devolution approved by referendum, with date
——— separate administration/ autonomy for other reasons	linguistic minorities or other communities whose members have used violence in pursuit of greater autonomy or other change of political status, with areas inhabited
✗ devolution rejected by referendum, with date	● ethnic or other communal based party delegated to national parliament in 1985

The success of the EU in modernizing and rationalizing European agriculture produced regular food gluts in the 1970s and 1980s. Here *(right)* Sicilian oranges have been turned, quite literally, into a food mountain. The sheer cost of maintaining farm incomes put a great strain on the European Union's budget, raising periodic calls for reform of the Common Agricultural Policy, especially urgent from the late 1990s, with the prospect of further enlargement to the east.

1 The expansion of the European Union, 1981–2000

- members of the EEC, Jan. 1981
- joined Jan. 1986
- admitted Oct. 1990
- joined Jan. 1995
- applied by June 1996 for EU membership, with date of application
- ★ countries beginning accession negotiations, 1998
- ★ countries beginning accession negotiations, 2000

The European Economic Area (EEA)
- members of the EEA, June 1996

Trondhjem

NORWAY

SWEDEN

FINLAND

Bergen
Oslo
Swedes
Åland Is.
Swedes
Turku
Helsinki
Porkkala
Stockholm

Gothenburg

Århus

DENMARK

Copenhagen
Malmö

Hamburg
NETH.
Bremen
Amsterdam
Hanover
Berlin

GERMANY

POLAND

Leipzig
Dresden
Elbe

Flemings
Bonn
Germans
GIUM
LUX.
Rhine
trasbourg
Stuttgart
strongly autonomous regions
CZECH REPUBLIC

√1974
Munich
LIECH.
Vienna
Danube
Zurich
BOLZANO
strongly autonomous regions
AUSTRIA
HUN.
SWITZ.
Germans
Berne
Turin
Milan
Venice
Verona
FRIULI-VENEZIA GIULIA
Trieste
Friulians, Slovenes, 1963
TRENTINO-ALTO ADIGE
Germans, Ladins, 1948
CROATIA
Genoa
Bologna
ONACO
Florence
SAN MARINO
Perugia
Corsica
Corsicans
(Italians)

ITALY

Rome
Naples
Bari
Taranto

Sardinia
Sards, 1948
Cagliari

Palermo
Messina
Sicily 1946
Catania

Mediterranean
Sea

ICELAND

NORWAY
SWEDEN
FINLAND

ESTONIA *1995*
LATVIA *1995*
LITHUANIA *1995*
RUS. FED.

North Sea

IRELAND
UNITED KINGDOM
DENMARK
NETHER-LANDS
GERMANY
POLAND *1994*
BELGIUM
LUX.
CZECH REP. *1996*
SLOVAKIA *1995*
LIECT.
HUNGARY *1994*
ROMANIA *1995*
FRANCE
SWITZ.
AUSTRIA
SLOVENIA *1996*
CROATIA
BOS. HERZ.
YUGO.
BULGARIA *1995*
Black Sea
MONACO
SAN MARINO
ANDORRA
ITALY
ALBANIA
MAC.
TURKEY *1987*
customs union with EU effective from 1 Jan. 1996
PORTUGAL
SPAIN
Corsica
Sardinia
GREECE
Sicily
Crete
MALTA *1990*
CYPRUS *1990*

MACEDONIA (F.Y.R.O.M.)
BULGARIA
Edirne
Istanbul
ALBANIA
Salonica
Mt. Athos
Ankara

GREECE
Janina
Izmir

TURKEY

Patras
Athens
Adana

Turkish Federated State of Cyprus, estb. 1975; "Turkish Rep. of Northern Cyprus" from 1983
ethnic distribution before 1974
Turks
Cyprus
Nicosia
Greeks

Crete

Sea

167

The collapse of Communism since 1989

The tidal wave that swept away the communist regimes of Eastern Europe arose directly from the changes envisaged Mikhail Gorbachev, leader of the USSR (page 148). Regarding the other communist states as a drain on Soviet resources, he encouraged them to pursue economic and political reform. This policy change came at a difficult time for the Eastern bloc states, whose economic development had been adversely affected by recession in the West and by reductions in trade and aid resulting from renewed Cold War pressures. Economic modernization slowed, and provoked growing popular unrest, particularly in Poland, where a military dictatorship arose in 1981 to suppress the democracy movement. In Romania, the isolated and impoverished regime of Nicolae Ceauçescu became yet more repressive.

Although few showed enthusiasm for the old regimes, popular opposition remained muted until Gorbachev pressured his communist partners to grasp the nettle of reform in 1989. Without Soviet backing, the regimes crumbled one by one: Hungary legalized opposition parties in January; Poland established the first non-communist government since 1948 in August; demonstrations ended communist rule in Czechoslovakia, East Germany and Bulgaria in November. Violence only occurred in Romania, where an army firing squad shot Ceauçescu in December.

Throughout the Eastern bloc, multi-party elections now brought to power coalition governments committed to democratic reform and economic liberalization. In the course of 1990, East Germany voted first for currency union and then for full integration with West Germany; but other former communist countries, exposed to market pressures, soon plunged into economic decline. High unemployment and rural poverty contributed to the revival of deep-rooted ethnic and religious conflicts, conflicts that the communist regimes had only papered over for 40 years. In 1993, tensions between Czechs and Slovaks produced the partition of Czechoslovakia (map 1).

Meanwhile, in the USSR, nationalist unrest grew as the Russian-dominated republics of the USSR sensed an opportunity to emulate the Eastern European states and break free. The president of the Russian Republic, Boris Yeltsin, elected in 1990, urged Gorbachev to give the Soviet republics more independence. In August 1991, a group of hard-line communists attempted a coup and, although Yeltsin suppressed the revolt, the non-Russian republics soon declared their independence. When the Ukraine staged a referendum in December 1991 that resulted in an overwhelming vote for independence, Gorbachev bowed to reality. The USSR was dissolved on 31 December, to be replaced by a Commonwealth of Independent States (the CIS), co-operating on military and economic

issues but no longer controlled from Moscow.

With no country left to rule, Gorbachev slipped into obscurity. Russia embraced a form of presidential democracy, with Yeltsin as its first president. In 1993, hard-line parliamentary delegates hostile to further reform tried to depose Yeltsin, but he crushed them too. Re-elected as president in 1996, Yeltsin finally stepped down in 1999 and power transferred peacefully to Vladimir Putin. Meanwhile some republics – Belarus, Uzbekistan, Kazakhstan, Turkmenistan – maintained reformed communist governments while others adopted some form of democracy. In Russia itself local rulers in the constituent republics seized more power (map 2) and in the case of Chechenia sought to break away from Russia by force (page 170).

Map 2: The Russian Federation, 1991–8

Arctic Ocean

FINLAND
POLAND
BELARUS — St Petersburg
MOLDOVA
UKRAINE
Murmansk
KARELIA 74%
NENETS
Moscow
CHUVASHIA 27%
MARIYEL 47%
KOMI 58%
CHUKCHI AD
KORYAK AD
TAYMYR AD
R U S S I A N
MORDOVIA 61%
Rostov-na-Donu
DYGEYA 68%
Volgograd
TATARSTAN 43%
59
KOMI-PERMYAK
UDMURTIA
KHANTY-MANSI AD
YAMALO-NENETS AD
Yekaterinburg
59%
BASHKORTOSTAN
KALMYKIA 38%
GEORGIA
ARM.
AZER.
DAGESTAN 9%
Caspian Sea
F E D E R A T I O N
EVENKI AD
SAKHA (YAKUTIYA) 50%
Sea of Okhotsk
Omsk
Novosibirsk
KAZAKHSTAN
KHAKASSIA
ALTAY 60%
TYVA 32%
UST-ORDA BURYAT AD
79%
BURYATIA 70%
Chita
AGA BURYAT AD
Irkutsk
JEWISH AO
Khabarovsk
TURKMENISTAN
UZBEKISTAN
IRAN
KYRGYZSTAN
AFGHANISTAN TAJIKISTAN
MONGOLIA
CHINA
Vladivostok

a KARACHAY-CHERKESSIA 42%
b KABARDINO-BALKARIA 39%
c NORTH-OSSETIA 30%
d INGUSHETIA (from June 1992)
e CHECHENIA
} 23% combined

2 The Russian Federation, 1991–8

— the Russian Federation

constituent republics within the Russian Federation, Mar. 1992

independence declared, Nov. 1991; at war with Russia from Dec. 1994 to 1996 and from Aug. 1999

The Commonwealth of Independent States (CIS)

entered close political and economic union with Russia, 2 Apr. 1996

entered close economic union with Russia, 30 Mar. 1996

other members of the CIS

60% percentage of Russians in other members of the Russian Federation

AD autonomous district

AO autonomous oblast

The Polish union leader, Lech Walesa *(above)* addressing a crowd. As leader of the free trade union Solidarity, he led the resistance to communism from 1980 and became Polish president in 1990. He lost office to a former communist minister in elections in 1995.

1 The collapse of communism, 1985–91

— Soviet-dominated eastern Europe to 1989

— Soviet Union to 1991

— Yugoslavia to 1991

united with the Federal Republic of Germany, 1990

achieved independence, 1991

other former communist states, 1991

de facto independent states, late 1991, on former territory of the Soviet Union, internationally unrecognized

overrun by Yugoslav army, July–Dec. 1991

— borders, 1991

Baltic Sea

FINLAND
Tallinn
ESTONIA
Mar. 1990: Congress of Estonia formed, declares Soviet rule illegal
Mar. 1991: referendum endorses independence
Aug. 1991: independence declared
Sep. 1991: independence recognized by USSR

Riga
LATVIA
1989: mass anti-Communist demonstrations
Mar. 1991: referendum endorses independence
Aug. 1991: independence declared
Sep. 1991: independence recognized by USSR

LITHUANIA
Vilnius
RUSSIAN FED.
1989: mass anti-Communist demonstrations
Mar. 1991: independence declared
Apr.–June 1990: economic embargo imposed by USSR
Sep. 1991: independence recognized by USSR

Minsk
BELARUS
June 1989: Popular Front founded
Aug. 1991: independence declared
Dec. 1991: founder member of Commonwealth of Independent States

Moscow
TATARSTAN
RUSSIAN FEDERATION

Mar. 1985: Mikhail Gorbachev becomes leader of Communist Party; initiates perestroika and glasnost, loosens Soviet control of satellite states
June 1991: Boris Yeltsin elected president of Russian Federation
Aug. 1991: hard-line Communist coup against Gorbachev fails
Nov. 1991: Communist Party declared illegal
Dec. 1991: USSR dissolved

Warsaw
from 1988: anti-government demonstrations
Nov. 1989: mass demonstrations end Communist rule
Apr. 1990: new constitution adopted; becomes a federation
June 1990: free elections

from 1987: Communist regime relaxes control
Sep. 1989: allows East Germans to travel to the West
Oct. 1990: Communist rule ends peacefully
Mar.–Apr. 1990: free elections

MOLDOVA
Kiev
UKRAINE
1989: opposition mass-movements emerge
Aug. 1991: independence declared
Dec. 1991: referendum endorses independence; founder member of Commonwealth of Independent States

TRANSNISTRIA
June 1989: Popular Front wins 75% of votes in election
Aug. 1991: independence declared

GAGAUZIA

ROMANIA
Bucharest
Dec. 1989: mass demonstrations lead to armed uprisings and overthrow of Ceauşescu regime
June 1991: free elections
Nov. 1991: new constitution adopted

BULGARIA
Sofia
Nov. 1989: President Zhivkov removed from office
June 1990: free elections
July 1991: fresh elections following adoption of new constitution

Nov. 1988: mass demonstrations against Russification
Mar. 1991: referendum endorses independence
Apr. 1991: independence declared

Sep. 1989: economic embargo imposed by Azerbaijan
Sep. 1991: referendum endorses independence; independence declared

Nov. 1991: independence declared

Jan. 1990: state of emergency declared; Soviet troops intervene
Oct. 1991: independence declared

CHECHENIA
Grozny
GEORGIA
Sep. 1991: independence declared

ARMENIA
AZERBAIJAN
NAGORNO-KARABAKH

Civil wars in the communist successor states

TIMELINE

Jun. 1991
Slovenia and Croatia declare independence

Jun.–Jul. 1991
War in Slovenia. Yugoslav troops withdraw

Jun. 1991
War in Croatia begins

Dec. 1991
Dissolution of Soviet Union

Jan. 1992
Ceasefire in Croatia

Mar.1992
Civil War breaks out in Bosnia

Sep.1992
War breaks out between Armenia and Azerbaijan over Nagorno-Karabakh

Nov. 1995
Dayton Agreement ends war in Bosnia

Jun. 1999
NATO-led force enters Yugoslav province of Kosovo

The greatest casualty of the collapse of the communist bloc was Yugoslavia. Its six republics (Serbia, Croatia, Macedonia, Bosnia-Herzegovina, Slovenia and Montenegro), were held together by an overarching communist apparatus and the personal authority of Tito, the founder of communist Yugoslavia. After his death in 1980, internal divisions began to appear. The trigger for conflict was the rise of aggressive nationalism. In 1987, following the choice of the Slobodan Milosevic as leader of Serbia, tensions between the republics grew stronger. Milosevic suppressed the Albanian minority in Kosovo, and set out to expand Serbia's influence within the federation.

In 1990 multi-party elections brought nationalists to the fore in Slovenia and Croatia and paved the way for their simultaneous declaration of independence in June 1991. It also provoked a vicious seven-month war when Serb forces intervened, allegedly to protect the ethnic Serb minority in Croatia,

Meanwhile another savage civil war broke out in Bosnia-Herzegovina, where Bosnian Muslims (44% of the population) and Croats (17%) pushed for independence in the face of bitter opposition from the Bosnian Serbs (31%). Each ethnic group sought to 'cleanse' the areas under its control of all opponents until by 1993 the Serbs controlled around 70 per cent of Bosnia and besieged the capital, Sarajevo, held by

1 The Yugoslav civil war, 1991–5

- Croatia, June 1991
- Bosnia-Herzegovina Mar. 1992
- secured by Yugoslav army and Bosnian Serb forces by Dec. 1992
- controlled by Bosnian Croat forces, Dec. 1992
- under Bosnian government control , Dec. 1992
- → Croatian advances, Jan. 1993
- → Federation of Bosnia and Herzegovina advances, Oct.–Nov. 1994
- ⇢ Croatian and Federation of Bosnia and Herzegovina advances, spring 1995
- → Bosnian Serb advances, summer 1995
- ⇒ Croatian and Federation of Bosnia and Herzegovina advances, Aug.–Oct. 1995
- overwhelmingly or largely Muslim, 1991; no significant Muslim presence by 1996
- — Autonomous Province of Western Bosnia, Sep. 1993–Aug. 1994
- — remained under Serb control by Dayton Agreement Nov.1995
- returned to Croatian control in Jan. 1998 under Erdut agreement of Nov. 1995
- overrun by Yugoslav army and Croatian Serb forces by Dec. 1991
- UN-designated 'safe areas'

the Muslim-led government. The war caused the death of at least 100,000 and displaced half of the region's 4 million inhabitants. In 1995 a renewed Serb offensive provoked NATO intervention, leading to an uneasy peace (the Dayton Accords) which left Bosnia divided between the three ethnic groups and

3 The Caucasus, 1988–2000

- notional extent of Georgia at independence
- → advance of pro-Gamsa-khurdia forces, Oct. 1993
- → Georgian advance into Abkhazia, Aug. 1992
- — areas of Georgia under Abkhazian control, Oct. 1993
- evacuated by Georgia, Oct. 1994
- notional extent of Azerbaijan at independence
- Armenia at independence
- limit of Armenian control, May 1992
- → Azerbaijani advance into Karabakh, Oct. 1992
- ⇢ secured by Armenia and Karabakh by Nov. 1993
- Chechenia-Ingushetia at independence
- — seceded from Chechenia, joined Rus. Fed., Mar. 1992
- claimed by Ingushetia, 1992
- → Russian advance into Chechenia by May 1995
- ⇒ mass movements of refugees
- autonomous within Russian Federation

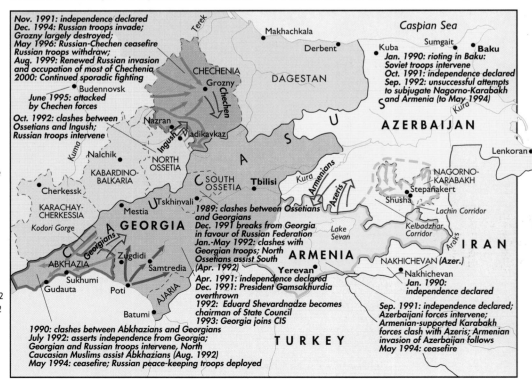

Nov. 1991: independence declared
Dec. 1994: Russian troops invade; Grozny largely destroyed;
May 1996: Russian-Chechen ceasefire Russian troops withdraw;
Aug. 1999: Renewed Russian invasion and occupation of most of Chechenia 2000: Continued sporadic fighting

June 1995: attacked by Chechen forces

Oct. 1992: clashes between Ossetians and Ingush; Russian troops intervene

1989: clashes between Ossetians and Georgians
Dec. 1991 breaks from Georgia in favour of Russian Federation
Jan.-May 1992: clashes with Georgian troops; North Ossetians assist South (Apr. 1992)

Apr. 1991: independence declared
Dec. 1991: President Gamsakhurdia overthrown
1992: Eduard Shevardnadze becomes chairman of State Council
1993: Georgia joins CIS

1990: clashes between Abkhazians and Georgians
July 1992: asserts independence from Georgia; Georgian and Russian troops intervene, North Caucasian Muslims assist Abkhazians (Aug. 1992)
May 1994: ceasefire; Russian peace-keeping troops deployed

Jan. 1990: rioting in Baku: Soviet troops intervene
Oct. 1991: independence declared
Sep. 1992: unsuccessful attempts to subjugate Nagorno-Karabakh and Armenia (to May 1994)

Jan. 1990: independence declared

Sep. 1991: independence declared; Azerbaijani forces intervene; Armenian-supported Karabakh forces clash with Azeris; Armenian invasion of Azerbaijan follows
May 1994: ceasefire

HUNGARY
ROMANIA
CROATIA
Novi Sad
Belgrade
BOSNIA-HERZE-GOVINA
Kragujevac
SERBIA
MONTENEGRO
Podgorica
Niš
KOSOVO
Priština
Skopje
ALBANIA
MACEDONIA

Main Kosovo map labels:
SERBIA
50,000 Serbs
Novi Pazar
Leposavić
refugees 61,700
MONTENEGRO
Kosovska Mitrovica
Podujevo
Istok
patriarchate of Pec
Pec
Dečani
Kosovo Polje 1389
Priština
Gračanica
Vranje
K O S O V O
Gnjilane
Uroševac
ALBANIA
refugees 405,360
Prizren
Blace
Kukës
MACEDONIA (F.Y.R.O.M.)
church of Bogorodica Ljeviska
refugees 197,870
Skopje

2 The crisis in Kosovo, 1999

- flight of Kosovan Albanian refugees, Mar.-May 1999
- towns bombed by NATO forces, Mar.-June 1999
- ⊕ sites of religous significance to Serbs
- NATO zone of occupation with nationality of occupying force

Bosnia map labels:
SLOVENIA
HUNGARY
Drava
Barania
Zagreb
C R O A T I A
Karlovac
Sisak
Osijek
Glina
Okučani
Vukovar
Sava
Bihać
Bosanka Krupa
Prijedor
Banja Luka
Bosna
Oraje
Doboj
Brčko
Sanski Most
B O S N I A -
Drina
Ključ
Maglaj
Tuzla
Vrbas
Mrkonjić-Grad
Žepče
Maslenica
Travnik
Zenica
Jajce
Vitez
D A L M A T I A
Knin
Glamoč
Donji Vakuf
Bugojno
Olovo
Srebrenica
Dinaric Alps
Kupres
Gornji Vakuf
Kiseljak
Sarajevo
Žepa
Šibenik
Livno
Prozor
Pale
Višegrad
Jablanica
H E R Z E G O V I N A
Goražde
Split
Mostar
Brač
Hvar
Korčula
Dubrovnik
Y U G O S L A V I A

utterly devastated by four years of war (map 1).

In 1998, conflict escalated in Serbia's province of Kosovo. Talks brokered by international mediators offered the Kosovo Albanians full autonomy within Serbia, but Milosevic objected. NATO responded with air strikes against Yugoslavia in March 1999 to force Belgrade to sign the peace agreement and to stop the repression of Kosovo Albanians. The Serbian security forces instead accelerated a programme of 'ethnic cleansing' against Kosovo Albanians. After more than two months of NATO bombing, Milosevic agreed in June 1999 to a peace plan that incorporated most of NATO's demands and a NATO-led peace implementation force entered the province (map 2).

Tensions within the Yugoslav Federation continued as the pro-western government of Montenegro sought to assert its independence from Belgrade until Milosevic fell from power in December 2000, after massive popular protests following his false claim of victory in presidential elections. His successor, Vojislav Kostunica, made overtures to the West and promised a return to democratic rule, but the future of the Federation remained uncertain.

The break-up of the Soviet Union, too, saw widespread ethnic and political conflict, particularly in the Caucasus region (map 3). Armenia and Azerbaijan fought over the Christian Armenian enclave of Nagorno-Karabakh; Georgia fought to keep South Ossetia within her boundaries and to prevent the independence of Abkhazia. The worst conflict occurred in Chechenia, which Russian forces invaded in 1994 and 1999 to prevent secession. Russia suffered heavy casualties in both cases and, despite occupying virtually the whole province, could not stifle a vigorous Chechen resistance.

Russia established a fragile democracy in 1992. In October 1993 hard-line parliamentary delegates hostile to further reform tried to depose President Boris Yeltsin. He ordered in tanks and special forces and bombarded the White House, the Russian parliament. On 4 October, the rebels surrendered (left). Yeltsin was re-elected in presidential elections in June 1996, finally stepping down in 1999 as power transferred peacefully to Vladimir Putin.

The World at the Millennium

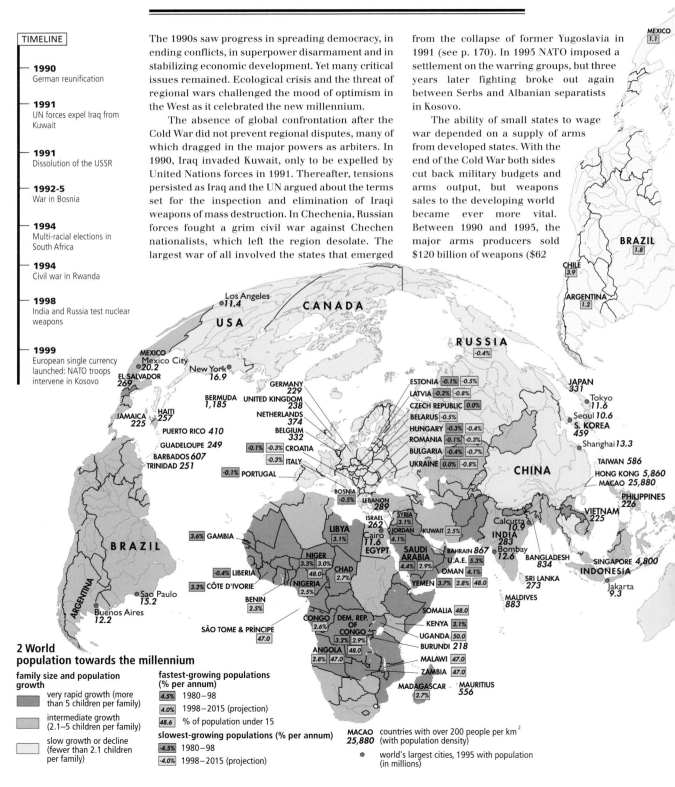

The 1990s saw progress in spreading democracy, in ending conflicts, in superpower disarmament and in stabilizing economic development. Yet many critical issues remained. Ecological crisis and the threat of regional wars challenged the mood of optimism in the West as it celebrated the new millennium.

The absence of global confrontation after the Cold War did not prevent regional disputes, many of which dragged in the major powers as arbiters. In 1990, Iraq invaded Kuwait, only to be expelled by United Nations forces in 1991. Thereafter, tensions persisted as Iraq and the UN argued about the terms set for the inspection and elimination of Iraqi weapons of mass destruction. In Chechenia, Russian forces fought a grim civil war against Chechen nationalists, which left the region desolate. The largest war of all involved the states that emerged from the collapse of former Yugoslavia in 1991 (see p. 170). In 1995 NATO imposed a settlement on the warring groups, but three years later fighting broke out again between Serbs and Albanian separatists in Kosovo.

The ability of small states to wage war depended on a supply of arms from developed states. With the end of the Cold War both sides cut back military budgets and arms output, but weapons sales to the developing world became ever more vital. Between 1990 and 1995, the major arms producers sold $120 billion of weapons ($62

2 World population towards the millennium

family size and population growth

- very rapid growth (more than 5 children per family)
- intermediate growth (2.1–5 children per family)
- slow growth or decline (fewer than 2.1 children per family)

fastest-growing populations (% per annum)
- 4.5% 1980–98
- 4.0% 1998–2015 (projection)
- 48.6 % of population under 15

slowest-growing populations (% per annum)
- -4.5% 1980–98
- -4.0% 1998–2015 (projection)

MACAO 25,880 — countries with over 200 people per km^2 (with population density)

● — world's largest cities, 1995 with population (in millions)

1 The armaments boom

■	countries with nuclear weapons capability
■	countries suspected of nuclear weapons capability
☢	underground nuclear tests conducted, 1945–98
☢	atmospheric nuclear tests conducted, 1945–98
4,900	government military spending on R&D, 1994 (US$ millions)
33.6	military expenditure as % of GNP, 1997
🔫	20 leading arms exporters (with value of exports in US$ millions, 1991–5)
🔫	20 leading arms importers (with value of imports in US$ millions, 1991–5)

CANADA
1.3 876 2,951

USA
39,000 3.3
61,879 2,766

360 2.5 604 SWEDEN

1.2 IRELAND

3,900 2.7 6,611 UK

FINLAND 2,209

76 1.9 2,043 NETHERLANDS

4,900 3.0 5,582 FRANCE

972 SWITZERLAND

6.3 CROATIA

270 1.5 374 2,189 SPAIN

4.3 MOROCCO

ALGERIA 3.9

LIBYA

HUNGARY 1.9

YUGOSLAVIA 560 2.0 564

GREECE 4.6 5,756

TURKEY 4.0 8,096

LEBANON ISRAEL*

JORDAN 9.0

SYRIA 5.6

IRAQ

IRAN 3.0 2,790

EGYPT 2.8 7,138

SAUDI ARABIA 14.5 7,092

KUWAIT 7.5 3,363

RUSSIA
1,200 5.8 15,996

GERMANY 1,200 1.6 10,156 4,045

POLAND 2.3 402

CZECH REPUBLIC 1,240

SLOVAKIA 352

UKRAINE 733

UZBEKISTAN 870

ITALY 1,923

JAPAN
1,200 1.0 6,882

N. KOREA 27.5 743

S. KOREA 360 3.4 3,776

CHINA 2.2 5,158 4,747

TAIWAN 5.2 4,228

PHILIPPINES 1.5

PAKISTAN 5.7 3,212

INDIA 430 2.8 5,158

BURMA 7.6

THAILAND 110 2.3 3,318

MALAYSIA 2.2

SINGAPORE 5.7

INDONESIA 2,120

SRI LANKA 5.1

FIJI 1.6

NEW ZEALAND 1.3

AUSTRALIA 170 2.2

ETHIOPIA 1.9

KENYA 2.1

ISRAEL 9.7 1,159 4,293

ANGOLA 20.5

ZIMBABWE 3.8

MOZAMBIQUE 2.8

SOUTH AFRICA 1.8 65

MARSHALL IS 49.0

TUVALU 400

NEW ZEALAND

AUSTRALIA

A militiaman from Liberia *(right)*. The civil war which began in Liberia in 1989 claimed the lives of up to 150,000 civilians and led to a total breakdown of law and order. Competing militias vied for control of the country. It was only in 1995 that the Abuja Accords began the process that led to the end of the war.

billion by the USA). While defence spending in the USA fell to 4.3 per cent of GDP by the mid-1990s, Middle Eastern states spent up to 8 to 10 per cent. In east and south Asia, where countries confronted the massive military weight of China, defence spending rose steadily in the 1990s, reaching around 3 to 5 per cent of GDP. The trade in arms also led to an illicit trade in technology to support the development of weapons – chemical and biological warfare and nuclear devices – which the West tried to limit. In 1998 India and Pakistan both tested nuclear bombs, while other states (such as Israel) have nuclear expertise and, probably, nuclear weapons (map 1).

Some of the tensions in the Middle East and in south and southeast Asia arose from rapid population growth. In these areas, people under 25 sometimes make up half the total population. Indeed students and schoolchildren played a conspicuous part in protests in India, Indonesia, Burma and in Tiananmen Square in Beijing in 1989. Young South Africans, too, played a central part in achieving democracy in 1990–4. The image of the peasant-soldier typical of the liberation movements of the 1960s gave way to chilling images of pre-teenage boys with modern weapons in their hands.

Population growth has threatened to destabilize the world system for decades. In the late 1990s the growth began to slow, though not fast enough to avert famine and the impoverishment of many developing states (map 2).

The Global economy

By the 1990s electronic communication and worldwide investment and marketing had created a genuinely global economy. Giant transnational companies dominated finance and production. However, world economic development still depended in part on the central management of key economic factors by groups of states, and on collaboration between them. Representatives of the largest industrial economies met regularly as the Group of Seven to co-ordinate financial and trade policies. Additionally, regional agreements sought to expand trade between small groups of states.

MEXICO
USA US$30,600 US$8,350 bn
CANADA
US$590 bn
US$29,280 ICELAND
BERMUDA
US$35,590
see inset map
RUSSIAN FEDERATION
VENEZUELA
GUINEA BISSAU US$160
BRAZIL
ALGERIA
LIBYA
EGYPT SAUDI ARABIA
INDIA
SIERRA LEONE US$130
NIGER
CHAD
ERITREA US$200
US$190
ETHIOPIA
US$220
US$200
DEMO. REP. OF CONGO
BURUNDI
US$100
NEPAL
ARGENTINA
US$740 bn
US$110
US$120
MALAWI
SOUTH AFRICA
US$190

2 The world's top trading nations, 1996

millions US$
600,000
400,000
200,000
0

Exports
% world total

% of world total
12
6
0

United States, Germany, Japan, China, France, UK, Italy, Canada, Netherlands, Belgium

3 Regional distribution of wealth

total world GNP 1995: US$ 27,110,768 million

Europe 32.6%   Asia 30.4%   N. America 29.7%

S. America 4.3%
Africa 1.5%
Oceania 1.5%

1 The world economy and economic groupings

- European Union (EU)
- European Economic Area (EEA)

US$44,640 LUXEMBOURG
US$32,880 NORWAY SWEDEN FINLAND
US$32,030 DENMARK
UK IRELAND
US$1,340 bn NETH.
US$2,080 bn GERMANY
Paris OECD
BEL
Vienna OPEC
FRANCE SWITZ. Basle AUSTRIA
US$1,430 bn
ITALY
US$550 bn SPAIN PORTUGAL
US$38,350 Bank for Int'l Settlements
US$1,135 bn GREECE
US$25,970

JAPAN
US$4,080 bn   US$32,230
N A
US$980 bn
US$29,610 SINGAPORE
INDONESIA
NEW ZEALAND
AUSTRALIA

- North American Free Trade Association (NAFTA)
- Common Market of the Southern Cone (Mercosur)
- Andean Community
- Central American Common Market (CACM)
- Economic Community of West African States (ECOWAS)
- Organization for Economic Co-operation and Development (OECD)
- Organization for Petroleum Exporting Countries (OPEC)
- South African Development Co-ordination Conference (SADCC)
- Association of South East Asian Nations (ASEAN)
- Organization of American States (OAS)
- Organization of African Unity (OAU)
- 10 largest economies by 1999 GNP (in US$ bn)
- 10 largest GNP per capita (1999)
- 10 smallest GNP per capita (1999)

The most successful of these groupings was the European Union, which grew from the original six members of the EEC in 1957 to embrace 15 states by 1996 (page 166). Gradual economic integration culminated on 1 January 1999 in the introduction of a single currency, the euro. Economic groups elsewhere were looser associations aiming to enhance regional economic integration. In 1994, for example, the USA, Canada and Mexico joined in the North American Free Trade Association (NAFTA) (map 1 and inset).

The world's top ten trading nations in 1996 provided 61 per cent of the world's imports and 63 per cent of exports (chart 2). A high proportion of that trade took place between the top traders, rather than trade between the developed and developing world; and an increasing proportion occured within free-trade blocs.

The fruits of the global economic success were spread very unevenly. In 1995, Europe possessed almost 33 per cent of the world's wealth, and North America a further 30 per cent (chart 3). Sustained expansion in Asia, Europe and the United States contrasted with economic decline in Africa, Latin America and the former Soviet bloc. The Russian economy in particular faced serious crisis by 1998 as the rush for capitalism failed to generate the wealth to sustain employment and welfare at the level achieved under communism. Even in east Asia, which grew faster than anywhere else in the world from the 1960s to the mid-1990s, the boom turned sour in 1997. Burdened with debt, high population growth and excessive dependence on a cluster of manufacturing exports, the new Asian economies generated a financial crisis that threatened the health of the whole global economy.

Outside the growth areas, there was persistent reliance on aid and investment from the developed world, much of it supplied by the International Monetary Fund (IMF) or the Organization for Economic Co-operation and Development (OECD). The per capita Gross Domestic Product (GDP) of the poorest states in the late 1990s was less than $300, while per capita GDP in the USA was almost $27,000. For many sub-Saharan African states, aid represented more than half of the value of total GDP. This pattern of aid-dependence altered little over the 1990s, and the gulf between the poverty of the developing world and the vast wealth of the developed industrial core remained one of the unresolved issues of global economics.

A Euro coin (above). Gradual economic integration within the European Union culminated in the introduction of a single currency, the Euro, on 1 January 1999. National currencies were due to be abolished entirely within the Euro-zone by 2002. The Euro was beset by initial controversy, with the United Kingdom refusing to join the currency bloc and an unexpected level of weakness against the dollar.

The Global environment

Until the 20th century, natural changes largely determined the environment. Now, industrialization, modern communications and mass consumption have combined to produce damaging man-made environmental change. Ecological disasters have become urgent global problems.

The onset of large-scale population growth and industrialization in the 19th century (page 100), stimulated a parallel rapid increase in man-made damage to the world's environment. Before 1945, this damage was largely localized, though very visible; the spread of industry worldwide after 1945 produced new threats to the environment which, if less visible, were nonetheless more deadly. Acid rain from waste in the atmosphere destroyed forests and eroded buildings. Pollutants in rivers and seas poisoned wildlife (map 1).

High levels of carbon dioxide released from the burning of fossil fuels raised global temperatures, while other chemicals began to weaken the ozone layer in the earth's atmosphere. Between 1800 and 1900 the level of carbon dioxide in the atmosphere increased by only 4 per cent; in the 20th century it increased by 23 per cent, with most of the change

3 Radioactive fall-out from the Chernobyl accident, 1986

⫶ pattern of fall-out

occurring since the 1950s. This raised world temperatures significantly: the 1990s were the warmest decade of the millennium.

Global warming stemmed in part from a massive increase in energy consumption, most of which consisted of fossil fuels (oil, coal and natural gas). Between 1970 and 1990 energy consumption grew by 60 per cent, despite efforts to find more efficient ways of generating power and to reduce emissions. Fossil fuels released a range of chemicals into the atmosphere which blocked the natural loss of heat and created the so-called 'greenhouse effect', leading to a global rise in temperatures (map 2).

The search for alternative sources of energy produced other types of disaster, however. In 1986, a nuclear reactor at Chernobyl in the Ukraine exploded, spreading a cloud of radioactive waste around the world (map 3). This catastrophe was but the most spectacular of many accidents in the production of nuclear power, eventually causing a reduction in its use.

Environmental issues became a central concern of the 1990s and state action produced some positive results. In Brazil, deforestation fell from a rate of 21,000 square kilometres in 1988 to only 1000 square kilometres by 1993. At Rio de Janeiro in 1992 an assembly of world leaders agreed to reduce harmful pollutants and emissions, a decision reaffirmed at a further meeting in Kyoto in 1997. The richer states also promised to subsidize industrial and agricultural projects in the developing world that respected environmental interests. In European states, political movements developed based entirely on issues of the environment, and in 1998 the environmentalist Green Party won a share of power in Germany. The future of the world ecosystem depended on the willingness of the world's richest states to accept substantial changes in consumption patterns.

1 The crisis of the environment

deforestation: rainforests under threat

- tropical rainforest
- edge of rainforest undergoing the most rapid deforestation
- ★ threatened area with large concentrations of endangered species

ocean and river pollution: oil slicks and tar balls

- high occurrence
- low occurrence

oceanic pollution

- frequent and severe
- partial and intermittent
- 🦅 major oil tanker disaster
- ✳ oil rig blowout
- ⋮ natural seepage

river pollution

- severe
- background

Exxon Valdez 1989

Nakhodka 1997
Yuyo Maru No.10 1974

Braer 1993
Sea Empress 1995
Amoco Cadiz 1978
Aegean Sea 1992
Jakob Maersk 1975
Sea Spirit 1990
Ellen Conway 1976
Khark 5 1989
Haven 1991

Independenta 1979

nearly 50% of rainforest destroyed

complete deforestation

Assimi 1983

Tadotsu 1978

WEST AFRICA
forest almost completely gone

ABT Summer 1991

Castillo de Bellver 1983

Katina P 1992

Wafra 1971

CANADA • UNITED STATES • ICELAND • North Atlantic Ocean • NORWAY • SWEDEN • FINLAND • IRELAND • UK • POLAND • FRANCE • GERMANY • UKRAINE • PORTUGAL • SPAIN • GREECE • TUNISIA • TURKEY • SYRIA • IRAQ • IRAN • RUSSIAN FEDERATION • MONGOLIA • KAZAKHSTAN • Aral Sea • CHINA • NORTH KOREA • SOUTH KOREA • JAPAN • TAIWAN • PHILIPPINES • PAPUA NEW GUINEA • ALGERIA • LIBYA • EGYPT • SAUDI ARABIA • AFGHAN. • PAKISTAN • INDIA • INDIAN SUB-CONTINENT • BURMA • VIETNAM • THAILAND • SOUTH EAST ASIA • PENINSULAR MALAYSIA • MALAYSIA • NORTH WEST BORNEO • INDONESIA • SRI LANKA • MAURITANIA • SENEGAL • MALI • GUINEA • LIBERIA • NIGERIA • CHAD • YEMEN • OMAN • AFRICA • CAMEROON • C.A.R. • SUDAN • ETHIOPIA • SOMALIA • GABON • DEM. REP. CONGO • KENYA • TANZANIA • ANGOLA • MOZAMBIQUE • MADAGASCAR • NAMIBIA • SOUTH AFRICA • QUEENSLAND • AUSTRALIA • NEW ZEALAND • Indian Ocean

2 Global warming

- more humid than before
- drier than before
- principal farming regions
- ● flooding through rise in sea level
- *1°c* increase in surface temperature

melting ice-caps lead to heavy pack ice

sharp fall in grain crop yields

more destructive hurricanes

failure of anchovy fisheries

c 3–4°C

c 1°C

short wet winters, long dry summers

sharp fall in grain crop yields

poor rice crop

c 0.3°C–0.5°C

increase in farming

millions made homeless by flooding

rise in sea level

One of the most dramatic consequences of industrial pollution was acid rain. Damage was particularly great in highly industrialized countries, such as Germany, Britain and the Czech Republic. European forest suffered particularly badly *(left)*. In Britain over 60 per cent of forests were damaged by acid rain.

177

Index

1 HISTORICAL PLACE NAMES

Geographical names vary with time and with language, and there is some difficulty in treating them consistently in an historical atlas, especially for individual maps within whose time span the same place has been known by different names. We have aimed at the simplest possible approach to the names on the maps, using the index to weld together the variations.

On the maps forms of names will be found in the following hierarchy of preference:

a English conventional names or spellings, in the widest sense, for all principal places and features, e.g., Moscow, Vienna, Munich (including those that today might be considered obsolete when these are appropriate to the context, e.g., Leghorn).

b Names that are contemporary in terms of the maps concerned. There are here three broad categories:

i names in the ancient world, where the forms used are classical, e.g., Latin or latinized Greek, but extending also to Persian, Sanskrit, etc.

ii names in the post-medieval modern world, which are given in the form (though not necessarily the spelling) current at the time of the map (e.g., St. Petersburg before 1914, not Leningrad).

iii modern names where the spelling generally follows that of The Times Atlas of the World, though in the interests of simplicity there has been a general omission of diacritics in spellings derived by transliteration from non-roman scripts, e.g., Sana rather than Şan'ā'.

2 THE INDEX

Where a place is referred to by two or more different names in the course of the atlas, there will be a corresponding number of main entries in the index. The variant names in each case are given in brackets at the beginning of the entry, their different forms and origins being distinguished by such words as now, later, formerly and others included in the list of abbreviations (right).

'Bizerta (anc. Hippo Zarytus)' means that the page references to that city on maps dealing with periods when it was known as Bizerta follow that entry, but the page references pertaining to it in ancient times will be found under the entry for Hippo Zarytus.

Places are located generally by reference to the country in which they lie (exceptionally by reference to island groups or sea areas), this being narrowed down where necessary by location as E(ast), C(entral), etc. The reference will normally be to the modern state in which the place now falls unless (a) there is a conventional or historical name which conveniently avoids the inevitably anachronistic ring of some modern names, e.g., Anatolia rather than Turkey, Mesopotamia rather than Iraq, or (b) the modern state is little known or not delineated on the map concerned, e.g., many places on the Africa plates can only be located as W, E, Africa, etc.

Reference is generally to page number/map number (e.g. 118/1) unless the subject is dealt with over the plate as a whole, when the references have been given sub-headings where possible, e.g., Civil War 129/4. Battles are indicted by the symbol ✕.

Though page references are generally kept in numerical order, since this corresponds for the most part with chronological order, they have been rearranged occasionally where the chronological sequence would be obviously wrong, or in the interests of grouping appropriate references under a single sub-heading.

3 ABBREVIATIONS

a/c also called
AD Autonomous District
Alb. Albanian
anc. ancient
AR Autonomous Region
Ar. Arabic
a/s also spelled
ASSR Autonomous Soviet Socialist Republic
Bibl. Biblical
Bulg. Bulgarian
C Century (when preceded by 17, 18, etc.)
C Central
Cat. Catalan
Chin. Chinese
Cz. Czech
Dan. Danish
Dut. Dutch
E East(ern)
Eng. English
Est. Estonian
f/c formerly called
Finn. Finnish

form. former(ly)
Fr. French
f/s formerly spelled
Ger. German
Gr. Greek
Heb. Hebrew
Hung. Hungarian
Indon. Indonesian
Ir. Irish
Is. Island
It. Italian
Jap. Japanese
Kor. Korean
Lat. Latin
Latv. Latvian
Lith. Lithuanian
Mal. Malay
med. medieval
mod. modern
Mong. Mongolian
N North(ern)
n/c now called
Nor. Norwegian
n/s now spelled
NT New Testament

obs. obsolete
OT Old Testament
Pers. Persian
Pol. Polish
Port. Portuguese
Rom. Romanian
Russ. Russian
S South(ern)
s/c sometimes called
Som. Somali
Sp. Spanish
S.Cr. Serbo-Croat
SSR Soviet Socialist Republic
Sw. Swedish
Turk. Turkish
Ukr. Ukrainian
US(A) United States (of America)
var. variant
W West(ern)
Wel. Welsh
WW1 World War 1
WW2 World War 2

Aachen (*Fr.* Aix-la-Chapelle *anc.* Aquisgranum) W Germany Frankish royal residence 53/1; WW1 86/2

Abkhazia autonomous region of Georgia 170/3

Abasgia region of the Caucasus 49/1

Abyssinia (*now* Ethiopia) 111/1

Achaea (*a/s* Achaia) Roman province 37/1

Acragas (*Lat.* Agrigentum *mod.* Agrigento) Sicily Greek colony 32/1

Addis Ababa Ethiopia Italian penetration 111/1

Aden S Arabia early town 81/1; Ottoman Empire 108/1; taken by British 118/1; British base 154/1

Aden Protectorate (*successively renamed* Protectorate of South Arabia, Federation of South Arabia, People's Republic of South Yemen, People's Democratic Republic of Yemen; *now part of* United Yemen)

Admiralty Islands S Pacific Japanese attack 142/1

Adowa N Ethiopia ✕111/1

Adrianople (*anc.* Adrianopolis *mod.* Edirne) W Turkey Byzantine Empire 49/1,2; Ottoman centre 71/1; occupied by Greece 136/1

Aegospotami (*Turk.* Karaova Suyu) NW Turkey ✕33/2

Aegyptus (*mod.* Egypt) Roman province 37/1

Afars and Issas, French Territory of (*form.* French Somaliland *now* Republic of Djibouti)

Afghanistan invaded by USSR 149/1, 163/1; civil war 157/3; Islamic fundamentalism 157/3

Africa early man 12/1, 14/2; cave art 15/1; agricultural origins 17/1; early cultures 27/2; early empires 58/1; slave trade 59/2; early European voyages of discovery 79/1; European expansion and trade 80-81; 18C European trade 103/2; European penetration 111/1; colonial empires 119/2; foreign investment 1914 127/1; Japanese imports 152/2; anti-colonial resistance 154/1; modern political developments 161/1; population growth 172/2; armament imports 173/1; economic groupings 174/2; economy 174/2 environment 177/1,2

Africa (*mod.* Tunisia and Libya) conversion to Christianity 34/1, 44/1; Roman province 36/1; Byzantine province 48/1

Aga Buryat AD S Siberia in Russian Federation 169/2

Aigun NE China treaty port 95/2

Ain Jalut Palestine ✕50/2

Aix (*or* Aix-en-Provence *anc.* Aquae Sextiae) S France archbishopric 53/1; *parlement* 83/2

Ajaria autonomous district of Georgia 170/3

Ajnadain Palestine ✕51/1

Aksum early empire of E Africa 27/2

Åland Islands (*Finn.* Ahvenanmaa) SW Finland neutralized 136/1

Alaska state of USA purchase from Russia 114/1

Albania Black Death 67/1; Ottoman province 108/1; principality 125/2, 137/2; annexed by Italy 145/1; Cold War 165/1; free elections 169/1; Kosovo crisis 171/2; Kosovan refugees 171/2

Albania ancient country of Caucasus 37/1

Albany (*form.* Fort Orange) NE USA seized by English 86/2

Alemannia SW Germany part of Frankish Empire 53/1

Aleppo (*anc.* Beroea *a/c* Yamkhad *Fr.* Alep *Ar.* Halab) Syria Mitannian city 22/3; centre of European trade 103/2

Alessandria N Italy Lombard League 55/2

Aleutian Islands W Alaska to USA 114/1; attacked by Japanese 142/1; retaken by Americans 143/2

Alexandria (*Ar.* Al Iskandariyah) Egypt taken by Alexander 32/3; spread of Christianity 34/1; Roman Empire 37/1; Christian centre 45/1; Arab conquest 51/1; trade 59/2; centre of European trade 103/2

Algeria Ottoman province 70/2; French invasion 111/1; French colonization 118/1; under Vichy control 140/1; independence 154/1; Islamic fundamentalism 157/3; political development 161/1

Algiers (*Fr.* Alger *Sp.* Argel *Ar.* Al Jaza'ir *anc.* Icosium) N Algeria Ottoman rule 70/2; Habsburg Empire 93/1; Allied landing WW2 141/2

Allenstein (*Pol.* Olsztyn) W Poland acquired by Germany after plebiscite 136/1

Almanza Spain ✕83/3

Almohads Muslim dynasty and empire of North Africa 58/1

Almoravids Muslim dynasty of Morocco 58/1

Alpes Cottiae Roman province, France/Italy 36/1

Alpes Maritimae Roman province, France/Italy 36/1

Alpes Poeninae Roman province, France/Italy 36/1

Alsace (*anc.* Alsatia *Ger.* Elsass) in German Empire 55/2; acquired by French 83/2; Habsburg Empire 93/1

Alsace-Lorraine (*Ger.* Elsass-Lothringen) region of E France annexed by German Empire 116/2; ceded to France 136/1

Central African Republic (*form.* Central African Empire *form.* Ubangi-Shari) independence 154/1; political development 161/1

Cephalonia (*mod.* Kefallinia) island of the Ionian Byzantine Empire 49/2

Cerdagne (*Sp.* Cerdaña) region of France and Spain 83/2

Ceuta (*Ar.* Sebta) Spanish enclave in N Morocco Spanish occupation 119/2

Ceylon (*anc.* Taprobane, Sinhala *or* Lanka *a/c* Saylan, Sarandib) 35/1; under British rule 119/2; independence as Republic of Sri Lanka 155/1; political developments 163/1

Chad (*Fr.* Tchad) country of C Africa independence from French 154/1; political development 161/1; economy 174/1

Chagatai Khanate C Asia Mongol state 61/2

Chahar former province of N China 94/1; independent of Nanking 130/1

Chalcedon (*mod.* Kadiköy) NW Anatolia Greek colony 33/1; centre of early Christianity 34/1

Champa Hindu-Buddhist kingdom of Indo-China 47/1, 64/2, 65/1

Chandernagore E India French settlement 97/3

Changchun Manchuria treaty port 95/2; economy 151/2

Changsha C China treaty town 95/2; economy 151/2

Charolais region of E France Habsburg possession 82/1

Chatti Germanic tribe of Roman Empire 36/1

Chauci Germanic tribe of Roman Empire 36/1

Chechenia (*Russ.* Chechnya) automonous region of S Russia 169/1, 170/3

Chechen-Ingush ASSR Caucasus deportations 149/3

Chekiang (*n/s* Zhejiang) province of E China Ming economy 69/1; Manchu expansion 94/1; economy 151/2

Cherbourg N France French naval base 83/2; WW2 141/2

Cherchen Chin. C Asia silk route 39/2

Chernigov Ukraine principality 57/1

Chernobyl N Ukraine radioactive fallout 176/3

Cherusci Germanic tribe of Roman Empire 36/1

Chichén Itzá E Mexico Mayan site 24/2

Chile 18C Atlantic economy 102/1; independence from Spain 113/1; political development 159/1; economy 159/2

China early man 12/1, 15/1; early agriculture 17/1, 19/2; centre of urban civilization 21/1; Sung Empire conquered by Mongols 61/1; Buddhism 35/1; Han expansion 39/1, 41/1; T'ang Empire 47/1; Ming Empire 691; Manchu expansion 94/1; Ch'ing Empire 95/2; European spheres of influence 95/2; 18C European trade 103/2; Japanese occupation 123/2; Communist Party founded 131/1; WW2 142-3; economy 1979-92 151/2; Cultural Revolution 151/1; political development 163/1; Cold War 165/1

Ch'in Empire 39/1

Chukchi AD W Siberia minority district of Russian Federation 169/2

Chungking (*n/s* Chongqing) C China treaty town 95/2; capital during WW2 123/2; industry 151/2

Chuvashi tribe of C Russia conquered 85/1

Chuvashia W Russia republic of Russian Federation 169/2

Cilicia (*Hittite name* Kizzuwadna) region of S Anatolia 33/1; Roman province 37/1; Byzantine Empire 49/1

Cochin region of S India Portuguese rule 81/1; British rule 96/2

Cochin-China region of S Indo-China expansion into Cambodia 89/2; French control 118/1

Cocos Islands (*now* under Australian administration *called* Cocos-Keeling islands) Indian Ocean British control 119/2

Colchis ancient country of the Caucasus Ionian colonization 33/1

Cold War 164-5

Cologne (*anc.* Colonia Agrippina *Ger.* Köln) W Germany archbishopric 53/2; medieval city 55/2; WW2 141/2

Colombia independence from Spain 113/1; political development 159/1; economy 159/2

Colombo Ceylon Portuguese trade 81/1; capital of British colony 97/1; centre of European trade 103/2

Colonia Agrippina (*a/c* Colonia Agrippinesis *mod.* Köln *Eng.* Cologne) NW Germany Roman Empire 36/1

Commagene region of SE Anatolia Roman province 37/1

Commonwealth of Independent States 169/2

Comoro Islands E Africa French colonization 119/2; independence 154/1

Confederate States of America 105/4

Confederation of the Rhine 99/2

Congo (*form.* Middle Congo *or* French Congo) region of Africa independence 154/1; economy 174/1

Congo Free State (*later* Belgian Congo *now* Zaire) 111/1, 119/2

Constance (*anc.* Constantia *Ger.* Konstanz) S Germany Frankish kingdom 55/2

Constantinople (*anc.* Byzantium *mod.* Istanbul) NW Turkey centre of early Christianity 34/1; Avar attack 40/1; patriarchate 45/1; Arab attacks 51/1; Ottoman conquest 71/1

Coral Sea S Pacific ✕142/1

Corcyra (*mod.* Corfu *Gr.* Kerkira) island of NW Greece Greek colony 33/1

Córdoba (*anc.* Corduba) S Spain Muslim conquest 50/1; Umayyad Caliphate and Muslim city 50/2

Corduba (*mod.* Córdoba) S Spain Roman Empire 36/1

Corfu (*anc.* Corcyra *mod. Gr.* Kerkira) island of W Greece Byzantine Empire 49/2; Ottoman siege 70/2; under Venetian rule 71/1

Corinth (*Lat.* Corinthus *Gr.* Korinthos) C Greece parent state 33/1; Byzantine Empire 49/2

Corinthus (*Gr.* Korinthos *Eng.* Corinth) C Greece town of Roman Empire 37/1

Cork S Ireland Viking settlement 54/1

Corregidor C Philippines surrender to Japanese 134/1

Corsica island of W Mediterranean Byzantine Empire 48/1; Muslim conquest 50/1; Saracen attack 54/1; Genoese rule 91/1; annexed by France 117/1

Corunna (*Sp.* La Coruña) NW Spain ✕99/2

Cossacks S Russia 85/1; anti-Bolshevik activity 135/1

Costa Rica country of C America independence 113/1; political development 159/1; economy 159/2

Costoboci early tribe of SE Russia 37/1

Crete (*Lat.* Creta *mod. Gr.* Kriti) Byzantine Empire 49/1; Muslim conquest 50/1; Ottoman province 108/1; cession to Greece 125/2; German capture 141/2

Crimea (*Russ.* Krym) S Russia Mongol Empire 60/1; Ottoman vassal khanate 71/1; acquired by Russia 85/1

Crimean Tartars S USSR deported to central Asia 149/2

Croatia (*S. Cr.* Hrvatska) under Hungarian Kingdom 66/2; Habsburg Empire 93/1; forms part of Yugoslavia 136/1; WW2 140/1; independence and civil war 169/1, 171/2

Croton (*mod.* Crotone) S Italy Greek colony 32/1

Crusades 49/2

Ctesiphon (*a/c* Tayspun) 45/1

Cuba discovered 78/1; Spanish colony 87/1; independence 112/1; US Protectorate 159/1; Cold War crisis 164/3

Cynossema W Anatolia ✕33/2

Cyprus *Gr.* Kypros *Turk.* Kibris *anc.* Alashiya) Greek and Phoenician colonization 33/1; Byzantine Empire 49/1; Muslim expansion 50/1; acquired by Turks 70/2; Venetian possession 71/1; independence 145/1; Turkish Republic of Northern Cyprus 167/2

Cyrenaica region of N Africa Roman province 37/1; Muslim conquest 47/1; Italian conquest 111/1

Cyrene (*It.* Cirene) N Libya Greek colony 32/1; spread of Christianity 34/1; centre of Roman province 37/1

Cythera (*a/c* Cerigo *mod. Gr* Kithira) island S Greece captured by Athens 33/2

Cyzicus NW Anatolia Greek colony 33/1; ✕33/2

Czechoslovakia created 136/1; territory lost to Germany and Hungary 137/2; Comecon and Warsaw Pact 147/4; end of Communist rule 169/1

Czechs post-War migration to West 146/1

Dacia (*mod.* Romania) Roman Empire 37/1; Byzantine Empire 49/1

Dagestan Caucasus 169/2; republic of Russian Federation 170/3

Daghestan region of Caucasus acquired by Russia 85/1

Dahomey (*n/c* Benin) country of W Africa early state 59/2; French colony 111/1, 119/2; independence 154/1

Dairen (*n/s* Dalian *Russ.* Dalny) Manchuria ceded to Russia and Japan 95/2

Dalmatia region of E Adriatic Byzantine Empire 49/2; civil war 171/1

Daman (*Port.* Damão) NW India Portuguese settlement 97/3

Damascus (*Fr.* Damas *Ar.* Ash Sham *or* Dimashq) Syria Levantine city 22/3; Byzantine Empire 49/1; Muslim conquest 51/1; revolt against Ottoman rule 70/2; Ottoman Empire 71/1

Damietta (*Ar.* Dumyat) N Egypt Byzantine Empire 49/1

Da Nang (*Fr.* Tourane) C Indo-China Vietnamese war 162-3

Danzig (*Pol.* Gdańsk) N Poland Free City 136/1

Dardanelles (*Turk.* Çanakkale Boğazi *anc.* Hellespont) straits, NW Turkey demilitarized and remilitarized 136/1

Dar es Salaam E Africa occupied by the Germans 111/1

Darfur region of W Sudan early state 59/2

Dauphiné region of SE France province of France 83/2

Dego N Italy ✕99/2

Deira ancient kingdom of N England 53/1

Delaware state of E USA settled by Swedes 86/2; British colony 1049/1; Depression 139/2

Delhi city and region of N India district of Mughal Empire 63/1; Indian Mutiny 96/2

Delian League Greece 33/2

Delium E Greece ✕33/2

Denain N France ✕85/1

Denmark Reformation 99/1; Industrial Revolution 101/2; war with Prussia and Austria 116/2; WW1 133/1; N Holstein acquired by plebiscite 136/1; WW2 140/1; EEC and NATO 165/1, 167/1

Diu NW India Portuguese settlement 63/1; centre of European trade 103/2

Djerba island Tunisia ✕70/2

Djibouti (*s/c* Jibuti) NE Africa occupied by French 111/1

Dobruja (*a/s* Dobrudja) region of Romania/Bulgaria Ottoman Empire 71/1, 124/1, 136/1

Dodecanese (*Gr.* Dhodhekanisos) islands of SE Aegean occupied by Italy, ceded to Turkey 125/2

Dominica island of West Indies British colony 107/1; independence 145/1 (inset)

Dominican Republic Caribbean independence 112/1; US intervention 159/1

Dorchester-on-Thames S England ✕53/1

Dorestad (*a/c* Duurstede) Netherlands Viking invasion and settlement 54/1

Douala Cameroon W Africa German occupation 111/1

Dresden E Germany ✗99/2; WW2 141/2

Dristov Romania ✗56/2

Dublin (*Ir.* Baile Atha Cliath) Ireland Scandinavian settlement and control 54/1

Dunkirk (*Fr.* Dunkerque) N France fortification 83/2; WW2 140/2

Dura-Europos (*mod.* Salahiyeh) Syria Mithraic site 34/1; Roman Empire 37/1

Durazzo (*anc.* Epidamnus *later* Dyrrhachium *mod.* Durrës) Albania Byzantine Empire 49/2

Dutch East Indies (*now* Indonesia) early Dutch trade 80/2; early Dutch possessions 89/2; occupied by Japanese 142/1; independence 155/1 (inset)

Dutch Guiana (*now* Surinam) S America 87/1, 113/1

Dutch New Guinea (*later* West Irian *n/c* Irian Jaya) East Indies transferred to Indonesia 155/1

Dutch Republic (*or* United Provinces *or* Holland) in War of Spanish Succession 83/3; revolt against Spain 92/2

Dyrrhachium (*earlier* Epidamnus *mod.* Durrës *It.* Durazzo) Albania Roman Empire 37/1; Byzantine Empire 49/1,2

Eastern Rumelia region of Balkans Ottoman province ceded to Bulgaria 125/2

Eastern Turkestan C Asia Chinese protectorate 94/1

East Indies agricultural origins 17/1; early kingdoms 65/1; early trade 80/2; 18C European trade 103/2. See also Dutch East Indies, Indonesia

East Prussia (*Ger.* Ostpreussen) region of E Germany WW2 141/2; divided between Poland and Russia 169/1

East Timor independence from Indonesia 155/1

Eckmühl/Ebersberg S Germany ✗99/2

Ecuador independence 113/1; political development 159/1; economy 159/2

Edessa (*mod.* Urfa) SE Anatolia First Crusade 49/2

Egypt (*officially* Arab Republic of Egypt *form.* United Arab Republic *Lat.* Aegyptus *Ar.* Misr) centre of urban civilization 20/1; Old Kingdom 23/2; early settlement 27/2; campaigns of Alexander 32/3; spread of Christianity and Judaism 34/1; Arab conquest 44/1; Byzantine Empire 51/1; Fatimid Caliphate 50/2; conquered by Turks 70/2; Ottoman province 108/1; expansion into Sudan 111/1; independence 154/1; wars with Israel 156/1; Islamic fundamentalism 157/3; political development 157/3, 161/1

El Agheila Libya WW2 141/2

El Alamein Egypt ✗WW2 141/2

Elam (*a/c* Susiana *modern* Khuzistan) ancient country of Middle East 22/3

England Scandinavian settlement 40/1; expansion of Christianity 44/1; Black Death and religious unrest 67/1; possessions in France 82/1; Reformation 91/1; WW1 133/1. See also Britain, Great Britain, United Kingdom

Ephesus (*Turk.* Efes) W Anatolia Greek colony 33/1; Byzantine Empire 49/1

Epidamnus (*later* Dyrrhachium *It.* Durazzo *mod.* Durrës) Albania Greek colony 33/1

Epirus ancient country of NW Greece 33/1; Roman province 37/1; Byzantine Empire 49/1; to Greece 125/2

Equator, Confederation of the E Brazil 113/1

Equatorial Guinea (*form.* Spanish Guinea *a/c* Rio Muni) country of W Africa independence 154/1

Eritrea region of NE Ethiopia Italian rule 108/1; Italian colony 110/2; political development 161/1

Estonia country of the Baltic acquired by Russia 85/1; Reformation 91/1; independence from Russia 136/1; constituted SSR 140/1; deportations 1941 149/2; independence 169/1

Ethiopia expansion of Christianity 34/1; 16C state 59/1; Italian invasion 111/1, 137/2; independence regained 154/1; economy 174/1

Etruscans ancient people of Italy 33/1

Eupen E Belgium ceded by Germany 136/1

Europe early man 12/1; Iron Age 15/1; agricultural origins 17/1; agricultural settlement 30/1; Hun and Avar invasions 40/1; expansion of Christianity 44/1; Viking, Magyar and Saracen invasions 54/1; Black Death 67/1; revolts and revolutions 98/1; Napoleon's empire 99/2; 19-20C alliances 124/1; foreign investment 1914 127/1; WW1 132-3; post-war territorial changes 146/1; Marshall Plan 147/3; economic blocs (EEC, EFTA, Comecon) 147/4; Japanese imports 152/2; economic blocs from 1957 167/1; collapse of Communist power 169/1; population 172/2; armaments exports 173/1; economic groupings 174/2l foreign direct investment 175/1; environment 177/1,2

European Union 167/1; 175/1 (inset)

Eylau (*a/c* Preussisch-Eylau *now* Bagrationovsk) E Prussia ✗99/2

Faeroe Islands (*a/s* Faroes) Norse settlement 54/1

Falkland Islands (*Span.* Islas Malvinas) islands of S Atlantic 113/1; war 159/1

Fanning Island C Pacific British possession 155/1 (inset)

Faroe Islands (*a/s* Faeroes) Norse settlement 54/1

Fars (*a/c* Persis, Parsa) Persia Muslim conquest 51/1

Fashoda S Sudan British/French confrontation 111/1

Fatimids Muslim dynasty of Egypt 50/2, 58/1

Federated Malay States (*now* Malaysia) independence 155/1

Feodosiya (*a/c* Kefe, Kaffa *anc.* Theodosia) Crimea acquired by Russia 85/1

Ferghana region of C Asia Muslim expansion 51/1

Fernando Po (*Sp.* Fernando Poó *form.* Macias Nguema Biyogo) island of Equatorial Guinea Spanish colony 111/1, 119/2; 145/1

Fez (*Fr.* Fès *Ar.* Al Fas) Morocco early trade 59/2

Fezzan (*anc.* Phazania) region of C Libya occupied by Italians 111/1

Fihl Palestine ✗51/1

Fiji S Pacific Melanesian settlement 27/1; British colony 119/2; independence 155/1 (inset)

Finland acquired by Russia 85/1; Reformation 91/1; WW1 133/1; independence 135/1; EU 167/1

Finns post-war migration from Karelia 146/1

Flanders (*Fr.* Flandre *Dut.* Vlaanderen) region of N Belgium Black Death 67/1; WW1 132/2

Flemings Dutch-speaking inhabitants of Belgium 166/2

Florida British rule 87/1, 104/1; annexed by USA 105/2; Depression 138/2; base for invasion of Cuba 164/3

Foix region of S France acquired by France 82/1

Foochow (*a/s* Fu-Chou *n/s* Fuzhou) SE China treaty port 95/2

Formosa (*n/c* Taiwan) cession to Japan 119/2; air attack by US 143/2; US bases 165/1

Fort Amsterdam (*later* New Amsterdam *now* New York) Dutch post 86/2

Fort Lamy (*now* N'Djamena) C Africa occupied by French 111/1

Fort William (*n/c* Thunder Bay) C Canada growth 120/2

Fouta Djallon (*a/s* Futa Jallon) W Africa early state 111/1

France (*anc.* Gaul *Lat.* Gallia) conversion to Christianity 44/1; Arab invasion 50/1; Viking and Saracen invasions 54/1; Scandinavian settlement 54/1; Black Death 67/1; 15C-16C reunification 82/1; War of Spanish Succession 83/3; administrative system under Louis XIV 83/2; Industrial Revolution 100/2; European alliances 124/1; world trade 1860-1913 127/1; WW1 132-3; EEC, NATO 165/1, 167/1; economy 174/1

Franche-Comté region of E France Habsburg Empire 93/1

Franconia (*Ger.* Franken) state of German Empire 55/2

French Cameroons (*now* part of Cameroon) W Africa independence 154/1

French Congo (*a/c* Middle Congo *now* People's Republic of the Congo) W Africa colony 111/1, 119/2

French Equatorial Africa union of French colonies 110/2

French Guiana S America 113/1

French Guinea (*now* Guinea) W Africa colony 111/1

French Indochina (*now* Cambodia, Laos and Vietnam) colonized 95/2; occupied by Japanese 123/2, 142/1; independence 155/1

French Somaliland (*Fr.* Côte Française des Somalis *later* French Territory of the Afars and Issas *now* Republic of Djibouti) NE Africa 110/2

French Sudan (*now* Mali) W Africa colony 111/1

French Territory of Afars and Issas (Djibouti)

French West Africa former union of French colonies 111/1, 119/2

Friedland (*now* Pravdinsk) E Prussia ✗99/2

Friedlingen W Germany ✗83/3

Fukien (*n/s* Fujian) province of SE China Ming province 69/1; Japanese influence 95/2, 123/2, under Nanking control 130/1; economy 151/2

Gagauzia minority area of S Moldova 169/1

Galatia country of C Anatolia Roman province 37/1

Galicia autonomous region of NW Spain 166/2

Galich (*mod.* Galicia) region of SW Russia Kievan principality 57/1

Gallipoli (*anc.* Callipolis *Turk.* Gelibolu) W Turkey Ottoman centre 71/1; WW1 133/1

Gambia country of W Africa British settlement 59/2; independence 155/1

Gandara (*a/s* Gandhara) region of E Afghanistan Indian kingdom 29/3

Gansu (*f/s* Kansu) province of NW China economy 1979-92 151/2

Gascony (*Fr.* Gascogne) region of SW France part of Frankish 50/2; province of France 83/2

Gaza Palestine Philistine city 33/1; Roman Empire 37/1; Byzantine Empire 49/1

Gaza Strip Palestine autonomy 156/1

Georgia state of S USA colony 104/1; industry 121/1; population 121/3; Depression 138/2

Georgia country of the Caucasus acquired by Russia 85/1; independent after WW1 1236/1; independence 1991 169/1

Germania Inferior province of Roman Empire 36/1

Germania Superior province of Roman Empire 36/1

Germany (*Lat.* Germania *Ger.* Deutschland *now* Federal Republic of Germany and German Democratic Republic) Hun invasion 40/1; Thirty Years' War 93/3; Reformation 91/1; Industrial Revolution 101/2; expansion in Africa 111/1; unification 111/2; colonial empire 116/2; 19C alliances 124/1; world trade 1860-1913 127/1; WW1 132-3; territorial changes after WW1 136/1; expansion 1934-41 137/2; territorial losses to Poland 146/1; Allied control zones 146/1; East and West reunited 168/1

Germany, East (German Democratic Republic *or* DDR) 146/1; Warsaw Pact 147/4

Ivory Coast (*Fr.* Côte d'Ivoire) country of W Africa French colony 112/1, 119/2; independence 154/1

Iwo Jima Japanese island of N Pacific ✗143/2

Jamestown E USA ✗ 104/1

Jammu and Kashmir native state of British India 97/3

Jankau Bohemia ✗93/3

Japan Mongol invasion 61/1; Buddhism and Shintoism 35/1; Chinese cultural influence 47/1; invasion of Korea and China 69/1; 15-16C civil war 68/2; early trade 81/1; modern development 88/1, 122/1; expansion in Asia 123/2; WW2 142-3; industrial products and exports 1945-90 152/5; overseas investment and exports 152-3; US bases 165/1

Jassy (*Rom.* Iaşi *Turk.* Yaş) NE Romania Ottoman empire 71/1; WW2 141/2

Java (*Indon.* Jawa) island of C Indonesia early man 13/1; spread of Buddhism and Hinduism 35/1, 64/2; Mongol expedition 61/1; early trade 89/2; occupied by Japanese 142/1

Java Sea naval battle of WW2 142/1

Jena E Germany ✗99/2

Jericho (*Ar.* Ariha) Palestine site of early village 19/1; autonomy 156/1

Jerusalem (*anc.* Hierosolyma *Roman* Aelia Capitolina *Heb.* Yerushalayim *Ar.* Al Quds) Israel Levantine city 32/1; Roman Empire 37/1; Muslim conquest 51/1; Ottoman Empire 70/2; in Arab-Israeli conflict 156/1

Jiangsu (*f/s* Kiangsu) province of E China economy 1979-92 151/2

Jiangxi (*f/s* Kiangsi) province of SE China economy 1979-92 151/2

Jilin (*f/s* Kirin) province of NE China economy 1979-92 151/2

Joppa (*mod.* Jaffa *Ar.* Yafa *Heb.* Yafo) Palestine Philistine city 33/1

Jordan independence 154/1; conflicts 156/1. See also Transjordan

Juan-juan (*a/c* Avars) tribe of N China 41/1

Judaea Palestine Roman province 37/1

Jutland Denmark ✗133/1

Kabardino-Balkaria Caucasus republic of Russian Federation 169/2, 170/3

Kabul Afghanistan Muslim conquest 53/1; district of Mughal Empire 63/1

Kaffa (*It.* Caffa *Turk.* Kefe *anc.* Theodosia *mod.* Feodosiya) Crimea Ottoman conquest 71/1

K'ai-feng N China Mongol attack 61/1; Ming provincial capital 69/1; industry 151/2

Kalmykia Caucasus republic of Russian Federation 169/2

Kalmyks people of Caucasus deportations 1943-4 149/4

Kamchatka territory of E Russia 84/2

Kanem-Borno early empire of NC Africa 58/1

Kano Nigeria Hausa city-state 58/1, 59/2; taken by British 111/1

Kansu (*n/s* Gansu) province of NW China 47/1; Manchu expansion 94/1; economy 151/2

Karachay-Cherkessia Caucasus republic of Russian Federation 169/2, 170/3

Karafuto *southern part of Sakhalin* island of Pacific Russia acquired by Japan 123/2; reoccupied by Russia 143/2

Karagwe early state of Uganda 59/2

Karakhanids (*a/s* Qarakhanids) Muslim dynasty of C Asia 51/2

Kara-Khitai Mongol empire of C Asia 61/1

Karakorum Mongolia Mongol capital 61/1

Karakoyunlu district of E Anatolia 71/1

Karaman (*anc.* Laranda) S Anatolia Turkoman principality 71/1

Karelia region of Finland and N Russia to Russia 57/1; Republic of Russian Federation 169/2

Kars E Anatolia conquered by Ottomans 70/2

Kashgar Sinkiang Mongol attack 61/1; Han expansion 38/1; Muslim risings against Chinese 94/1

Katsina Hausa city-state of N Nigeria 58/1, 59/2

Katyn Poland 140/1

Kaunas (*form. Russ.* Kovno) Lithuanian SSR WW2 141/2

Kazakhs Turkic people of C Asia, conquered by Russians 114/1; 140/1

Kazakhstan C Asia horse-based pastoralism 20/1; gulag 149/2

Kazan C Russia 1905 Revolution 115/3; Bolshevik seizure 135/1

Kazan Mongol khanate of C Russia conquered by Russia 85/1

Kenya (*form.* British East Africa) British colony 111/1; independence 154/1; political development 161/1

Kerbela (*Ar.* Karbala) Mesopotamia ✗51/1

Khakassia C Asia republic of Russian Federation 169/2

Khalkha Mongol tribe 69/1

Khanbalik (*mod.* Peking) N China Mongol attack 61/1

Khanty-Mansi AR W Siberia 169/2

Kharkov Ukraine founded 85/1; 1905 Revolution 115/3; Bolshevik seizure 135/1

Khartoum British occupation 111/1

Khazar Empire S Russia 51/1

Khiva (*a/c* Khwarizm *anc.* Chorasmia) region of C Asia independent khanate 114/1

Khmer (*mod.* Cambodia) SE Asia kingdom under Hindu influence 47/1; temple kingdom 65/1

Khoisan people of S Africa 58/1

Khurasan (*a/s* Khorasan) region of C Persia Muslim conquest 51/1; under Abbasid sovereignty 51/2

Khwarizm (*a/c* Khiva *anc.* Chorasmia) region of C Asia under Abbasid sovereignty 51/2

Kiangsi (*n/s* Jiangxi) province of SE China under the Ming 69/1; Manchu expansion 94/1; Nationalist control 130/1; Soviet under Mao Tse-tung 131/2; economy 151/2

Kiangsu (*n/s* Jiangsu) province of E China Manchu expansion 94/1; economy 151/2

Kiev (*Russ.* Kiyev *Ukr.* Kyyiv) Ukraine Mongol attack 60/1; bishopric 45/2; Viking trade 54/1; principality 57/1; 1905 Revolution 115/3

Kievan Russia 56-7

Kirghiz Turkic people of C Asia, destroy Uighur Empire 47/1; conquered by Russians 114/1

Kiribati (*f/c* Gilbert Is) Pacific 155/1 (inset)

Kirkuk N Iraq oilfield 157/2

Kirman (*a/s* Kerman *anc.* Carmana) region of S Persia Muslim conquest 51/1

Kiska island of Aleutians, Alaska captured by Japanese 142/1; retaken by Americans 143/2

Kiukiang C China treaty town 95/2

Kiungchow S China treaty port 95/2

Knossos (*Lat.* Cnossus) Crete 31/2

Kokand (*a/s* Khokand) C Asia Muslim khanate conquered by Russia 114/1

Komi W Siberia republic of Russian Federation 140/1

Komi-Permyak AR W Siberia 169/2

Kongo early kingdom of W Africa 59/1

Königsberg (*since 1946* Kaliningrad) W Russia Reformation 91/1; WW2 140-1

Konya (*anc.* Iconium) S Anatolia revolt against Ottoman rule 70/2

Korea (*anc.* Koryo *or* Silla *Jap.* Chosen) spread of Buddhism 35/1; conquered by Chinese 39/1; invaded by Japan 69/1; invaded by Manchus 95/1; end of Chinese tributary status 95/2; acquired by Japan 119/2, 123/2; WW2 143/2; 1950-53 war 153/1

Korea, North militarization 165/1

Korea, South militarization and US bases 165/1

Koryak AD E USSR 169/2

Kosovo SW Yugoslavia ethnic cleansing and NATO occupation 171/2

Kosovo Polje SW Yugoslavia ✗171/2

Kowloon S China acquired by Britain 95/2

Krasnoi W Russia ✗99/1

Krasnovodsk Russ. C Asia on railway 114/1

Krasnoyarsk S Siberia founded 84/2; railway 114/1

Krivoy Rog S Ukraine WW2 141/2

Kronstadt (*Russ.* Kronshtadt) NW Russia 1905 Revolution 115/3

Kumasi Gold Coast, W Africa 111/1

Kumbi Saleh W Africa possible site of capital of Ghana Empire 58/1

Kunming W China French sphere of influence 95/2; economy 151/2

Kuomintang China 130/1

Kurds people of N Iraq, uprisings 157/2

Kurile Islands (*Russ.* Kurilskiye Ostrova *Jap.* Chishima-retto) acquired by Japan 142/1; reoccupied by USSR 143/2; disputed with USSR 149/2, 163/1

Kursk W Russia 1905 Revolution 115/3; WW2 141/2

Kush early kingdom of Sudan 27/2

Kutch (*f/s* Cutch) region of W India border dispute with Pakistan 163/1

Kuwait country of Persian Gulf British protectorate 108/1; independence 155/1

Kwajalein Marshall Islands, C Pacific occupied by US 143/2; US base 165/1 (inset)

Kwangchowan S China acquired by France 95/2

Kwangsi (*n/s* Guangxi) province of SW China under Ming 69/1; Manchu expansion 94/1; economy 151/2

Kwangtung (*n/s* Guangdong) province of S China under Ming 69/1; Manchu expansion 94/1; Kuomintang 130/1; economy 151/2

Kwararafa W Africa early state 58/1

Kweichow (*n/s* Guizhou) province of SW China under Ming 69/1; Manchu expansion 94/1; Kuomintang 130/1; economy 151/2

Kyakhta S Siberia Russian trade with China 94/1

Labrador region of NE Canada rediscovered 78/1; to Newfoundland 120/2

Labuan N Borneo British colony 118/1

La Fère Champenoise NE France ✗99/2

Lagos Nigeria taken by British 111/1; British colony 118/2

Lahore NW India district of Mughal Empire 63/1; industry in British India 97/3

Languedoc region of S France French Royal domain 82/1; province of France 83/2

L'Anse aux Meadows Newfoundland Norse colony 25/1

Laodicea (*mod.* Denizli) W Anatolia Christian community 45/1

Laodicea (*mod.* Latakia *Fr.* Lattaquié) Syria Christian community 45/1

Laon N France ✗99/2

Laos country of SE Asia 65/1; kingdom of Luang Prabang 89/2; end of Chinese tributary status 95/2; French protectorate 119/2; independence 155/1; Pathet Lao 163/1

Lapita early people of Melanesia 27/1

Larisa (*a/s* Larissa *Turk.* Yenişehir) C Greece Byzantine Empire 49/1

Las Navas de Tolosa S Spain ✗50/2

Latin Empire 49/2

Latvia country of the Baltic independence from Russia 136/1; SSR 140/1; deportations 1941 149/2; independence 169/1

Lausanne Switzerland 1924 Conference 136/1

Lazica early country of the Caucasus 49/1

Lebanon independence 155/1; Middle East conflict 156/1

Lechfeld S Germany ✗54/1

Leipzig (Battle of the Nations) E Germany ✗99/2

Middle East (a/c Near East) Cold War 165/1

Midway island of C Pacific US base 165/1 (inset)

Milan (It. Milano anc. Mediolanum) N Italy Lombard League 55/2

Miletus W Anatolia Mycenaean city 31/2; Greek colony 33/1; Byzantine Empire 49/1

Mindanao island of S Philippines Japanese occupation 142/1; retaken by US 143/2

Ming Empire China 69/1

Min-yüeh region of S China 39/1

Mixtec States S Mexico 24/2

Mitanni ancient kingdom of Middle East 22/3

Mocha (Ar. Al Mukhā) S Yemen centre of European trade 103/2

Modena (anc. Mutina) N Italy Lombard League 55/2; unification of Italy 117/1

Moesia region of Balkans district of Byzantine Empire 49/1

Moesiae late Roman province of Greece 37/2

Moesia Inferior Roman province of the Balkans 37/1

Moesia Superior Roman province of the Balkans 37/1

Mogadishu (n/s Muqdisho It. Mogadiscio) Somalia Muslim colony 59/1; Italian occupation 110/1

Mohács Hungary ✗70/2

Moldavia (Turk. Boğdan Rom. Moldova) region of Romania/Russia Moldavian 66/2; under Ottoman control 71/1; part of Romania 125/2; independence (Moldova) 169/1

Moluccas (Indon. Maluku Dut. Molukken form. Spice Islands) islands of E Indies Muslim expansion 64/2; early Portuguese trade 81/1; Dutch control 89/2

Mondovi NW Italy ✗99/2

Monemvasia (It. Malvasia) S Greece Byzantine Empire 49/2; Ottoman conquest 70/2

Mongol Empire 60-61

Mongolia (form. Outer Mongolia) nomadic pastoralism 21/1; Mongol Empire 60-61; under Han Empire 41/1; Chinese incursions under Ming 69/1; Chinese protectorate 94/1; autonomy 95/2; Russian sphere of influence 119/2; limit of Japanese expansion 123/2

Montenegro (S. Cr. Crna Gora) region of S Yugoslavia under Ottoman rule 108/1; 19C alliances 124/1; independent state 125/2; WW1 133/1; forms part of Yugoslavia 136/1; WW2 141/2; Kosovo crisis 171/2

Montenotte N Italy ✗99/2

Montereau N France ✗99/2

Montmirail N France ✗99/2

Montreux Switzerland 1936 conference 136/1

Montserrat island West Indies British colony 155/1 (inset)

Moravia (Czech. Morava Ger. Mähren) region of C Czechoslovakia medieval German Empire 55/2; acquired by Bohemia 66/2; Hussite influence 67/1; Reformation 91/1; Habsburg Empire 93/1; forms part of Czechoslovakia 136/1

Mordovia W Russia republic of the Russian Federation 169/2

Morea (a/c Peloponnese) region of S Greece Byzantine Empire 49/2; conquered by Ottomans 71/1

Morocco (Fr. Maroc Sp. Marruecos) under Almohads 50/2; Sharifian dynasties 59/2; Spanish conquest 110/2; French and Spanish protectorates 111/1, 119/2; independence 154/1; conflict with Algeria 161/1; US bases 165/1

Morotai island N Moluccas, E Indies captured by Allies 143/2

Moscow (Russ. Moskva) W Russia early bishopric 45/2; city of Vladimir-Suzdal 57/1; captured by Napoleon 99/2; Industrial Revolution 101/2; industrial development 134/2; Bolshevik seizure of power 135/1

Mossi early states of W Africa 59/2

Mostar Herzegovina, Yugoslavia civil war 171/2

Mosul (Ar. Al Mawsil) Iraq Muslim conquest 51/1; Ottoman Empire 70/2; oilfield 157/2

Mozambique (form. Portuguese East Africa Port. Moçambique) early trade 81/1; Portuguese settlement 81/1; centre of European trade 103/2; Portuguese colony 119/2; independence 154/1; political development 161/1

Mughal Empire India 63/1

Mukden Manchuria capital of Manchuria 94/1; treaty town 95/2; Japanese occupation 123/2

Muscat and Oman (now Oman) SE Arabia British protectorate 119/2

Muscovy early principality of W Russia 85/1

Muslims minority in Bosnia and Serbia 171/2

Mwenemutapa early state of SE Africa 59/2

Mysia ancient country of W Anatolia 33/1

Muslims minority in Bosnia and Serbia 171/2

Mysore (now Karnataka) region of S India district of Mughal Empire 59/1; native state 96-97

Mytilene (a/s Mitylene) island of Aegean ceded to Greece 125/2

Nagasaki W Japan early European trade 81/1; Dutch trade 103/2; bombed by US 143/2

Nagorno-Karabakh Caucasus 169/1, 170/3

Nakhichevan region of SW Azerbaijan 170/3

Namibia (form. South West Africa earlier German South West Africa) German colony 111/1, 119/2; independence from South Africa 154/1, 161/1

Nanking (n/s Nanjing) N China Ming provincial capital 65/1; treaty port 89/2; occupied by Japan 117/2; economy 143/2

Nan-yüeh early kingdom of SW China 39/1

Nan-chao tribal kingdom of SW China 47/1

Nanning S China treaty port 95/2

Nantes NW France Scandinavian settlement 54/1

Naples, Kingdom of Black Death 67/1; to Austria 83/3; Habsburg Empire 93/1; satellite of France 99/2; unification of Italy 117/1

Narbonensis (a/c Gallia Narbonensis) Roman province of S France 36/1

Narbonne (anc. Narbo) S France Muslim conquest 50/1

Nations, Battle of the (Leipzig) E Germany ✗99/2

Naucratis Egypt Greek colony 33/1

Nauru island W Pacific independence 155/1 (inset)

Navarre (Sp. Navarra) region of N Spain/SW France acquired by France 83/2; Habsburg Empire 93/1

Navas de Tolosa S Spain ✗50/2

Neapolis (mod. Napoli Eng. Naples) S Italy Greek colony 33/1; Roman Empire 37/1

Nepal tributary state of Chinese Empire 94/1; 95/2

Nerchinsk, Treaty of 94/1

Netherlands (a/c Holland form. Dutch Republic United Provinces) Habsburg Empire 93/1; Industrial Revolution 100/2; trade with Africa and Asia 103/2; colonial power 119/2; NATO 147/4; EU 167/1. See also Belgium, Flanders, Holland

Netherlands, Austrian (mod. Belgium) revolt against Emperor 98/1

Netherlands East Indies (now Indonesia) occupied by Japanese 142/1. See also East Indies, Borneo, Java, Moluccas, Sumatra

Netherlands, Spanish (later Holland or United Provinces; and Belgium) Reformation 91/1; Dutch revolt 92/2

Neustria the Frankish lands of N France 52/1

Nevis island W Indies British colony 112/1; self-government with St. Christopher 155/1 (inset)

New Amsterdam (earlier Fort Amsterdam now New York city) colonized by Dutch 86/2

New Britain island Papua New Guinea early Melanesian settlement 27/1; retaken from Japanese 143/2; to New Guinea 155/1 (inset)

New Brunswick province of E Canada joins Confederation 1120/2

New Caledonia islands S Pacific early Melanesian settlement 26/1; French colony 119/2, 155/1; US base 142/1

Newchwang Manchuria treaty port 95/2

New England NE USA British settlement 86/2

Newfoundland province of E Canada rediscovered 78/1; British colony 86/2; British settlement 87/1; joins Dominion 120/2

New France French possessions in Canada 86/2

New Granada (mod. Colombia) Spanish colony 87/1; vice-royalty in rebellion against Spain 99/1; 18C Atlantic economy 102/1

New Guinea (now part of Papua New Guinea) early settlement 27/1; Dutch/German/British control 119/2; attacked by Japanese 142/1; retaken by Allies 143/2. See also West Irian

New Hampshire state of NE USA colony 104/1; population 121/1, Depression 138/2

New Hebrides (Fr. Nouvelles Hébrides now Vanuatu) islands S Pacific early Melanesian settlement 27/1; British/French condominium 119/2; US base 142/1; independence 155/1 (inset)

New Ireland island Papua New Guinea early Melanesian settlement 26/1; occupied by Japanese 142/1

New Jersey state of E USA colony 86/2, 104/1; population 115/3; Depression 131/2

New Mexico state of SW USA ceded by Mexico 107/1; population 121/1; Depression 138/2

New Orleans S USA French/Spanish occupation 87/1

New Sarai S Russia Mongol city 60/1

New South Wales state of SE Australia settlement and development 106/1; statehood 118/1

New Spain (mod. Mexico, C America and Caribbean) Spanish vice-royalty 78/1; early voyages of discovery 87/1; rebellion against Spain 99/1

New Territories S China acquired by Britain 95/2

New York City (1653-64 called New Amsterdam earlier Fort Amsterdam) 86/2; industry 121/1; population 121/3; economic growth 145/1

New Zealand early Polynesian settlement 27/1; settlement and development 107/2,3

Nicaea (mod. Iznik) W Anatolia Mithraic site 34/1; Byzantine Empire 49/2

Nicaragua country of C America early exploration 78/1; independence 112/1; Sandinista revolution 159/1

Nicobar Islands Indian Ocean territory of British India 119/2

Nicomedia mod. Izmit) W Anatolia Christian centre 45/1; Byzantine Empire 49/1

Nicopolis W Greece Byzantine Empire 49/2

Niger country of W Africa French colony 111/1; independence 154/1; economy 174/1

Nigeria country of W Africa British colony 111/1, 119/2; independence 154/1; political development 161/1; economy 174/1

Nihavand (anc. Laodicea in Media) W Persia ✗51/1

Nineveh Mesopotamia early farming village 19/1; Assyrian Empire 22/3; Mitannian city 23/1

Ningpo (n/s Ningbo) E China treaty port 95/2

Ningxia (*f/s* Ningxia) province of N China economy 1979-92 151/2

Nippur C Mesopotamia Sumerian city 23/1

Nish (*S. Cr.* Niš *anc.* Naissus) E Yugoslavia Ottoman Empire 71/1

Nishapur (*Pers.* Neyshabur) W Persia Mongol conquest 61/1; Safavid conquest 63/1

Nisibis (*mod.* Nusaybin) E Anatolia Roman Empire 37/1

Nizhniy Novgorod (*since 1932* Gorkiy) C Russia town of Vladimir-Suzdal 57/1; 1905 Revolution 115/3; Bolshevik seizure 135/1

Nomonhan (*a/c* Khalkin Gol) E Mongolia Russo-Japanese conflict 123/2

Nördlingen S Germany ✕93/3

Noricum Roman province of C Europe 37/1

Normandy region of N France Scandinavian settlement 54/1; French Royal domain 82/1; province of France 83/2

North Carolina state of E USA colony 86/2, 104/1; population 121/3; Depression 138/2

Northern Cook Islands (Manihiki Islands)

Northern Ireland religious divide 166/2

Northern Rhodesia (*now* Zambia) British colony 111/1, 119/2

North Ossetia Caucasus republic of the Russian Federation 169/2, 170/3

Northumbria early kingdom of N England 53/2

North Vietnam independence 155/1. See also Vietnam, Indo-China

North West Frontier Province N Pakistan in Indian Empire 96/2, 97/3

Norway conversion to Christianity 45/2; Black Death 67/1; Reformation 91/1; WW2 140/1, 141/2; NATO and EFTA 147/4; economy 175/1

Notium W Anatolia ✕33/2

Nova Scotia (*form.* Acadia) province of E Canada ceded by France 87/1; British possession 86/3, 104/1; joins Confederation 120/2; economy 120/2

Novgorod (*Norse* Holmegaard) NW Russia bishopric 45/2; Viking trade 57/1; WW2 141/2

Novgorod Empire NW Russia 53/2; conquered by Muscovy 851

Novgorod-Seversk early principality of W Russia 57/1

Novibazar, Sanjak of Ottoman province of Yugoslavia 124/1

Nubia region of NE Africa early settlement 27/2

Numidia Roman province of N Africa 36/1

Nupe Nigeria early Hausa state 58/1, 59/2

Nyasaland (*now* Malawi) British protectorate 111/1, 119/2

Oaxaca early civilization of Mexico 24/2 (inset)

Odessa S Ukraine founded 85/1; 1905 Revolution 115/3; Bolshevik seizure 135/1; WW2 141/2

Odessus (*mod.* Varna) Bulgaria Greek colony 33/1; Roman Empire 37/1

Offa's Dyke 53/1

Okinawa island SW Japan captured by US 143/2; reversion to Japan 163/1; US base 165/1

Olbia S Russia Greek colony 33/1

Old Calabar Nigeria 59/2

Oldenburg country of N Germany 116/2

Old Sarai S Russia Mongol city 60/1

Olmec States C Mexico 24/2

Oman region of E Arabia Muslim expansion 51/1; under Abbasid sovereignty 51/2; British sphere of influence 154/1

Ontario province of E Canada joins Confederation 120/2

Oran (*Ar.* Wahran) N Algeria Habsburg Empire 93/1; WW2 140/1

Orange principality of S France 83/2

Oregon state of NW USA acquired by USA 105/2; population 121/1; Depression 138/2

Orenburg (*1938-57 called* Chkalov) C Russia founded 85/1; Bolshevik seizure 135/1

Orissa (*form.* Jajnagar) region of E India district of Mughal Empire 63/1; state of modern India 97/3

Orkney islands of NE Scotland Norwegian Viking settlement 54/1

Orléanais region of C France 82/1; 83/2

Ormuz (*a/s* Hormuz *anc.* Harmozia) S Persia Portuguese control 63/1; Portuguese base 81/1

Oslo (*until 1924* Kristiania *a/s* Christiania) Norway WW2 140/1

Otford S England ✕53/1

Ottoman Empire Mongol invasion 60/2; expansion into Europe 70-1; decline 108/1, 125/2; WW1 133/1

Oudenaarde (*Fr.* Audenarde) Belgium ✕83/3

Outer Mongolia (*now* Mongolia) Chinese protectorate 94/1; independence 131/2

Pacific Ocean early Polynesian settlement 27/1; WW2 142-43; sovereignty of islands 155/1 (inset)

Paeckche Korea early state destroyed by T'ang 47/1

Pagan C Burma Mongol attack 61/1; Buddhist site 35/1; early empire 65/1

Pakhoi S China treaty port 95/2

Pakistan independence 154/1; secession of Bangladesh 163/1; boundary dispute with India 163/1; Baghdad Pact and US alliance 165/1

Palatinate (*Ger.* Pfalz) historical region of W Germany Reformation 91/1; German unification 116/2

Palau (*f/s* Pelew) SW Caroline Islands, W Pacific occupied by US 143/2

Pale Bosnia-Herzegovina Bosnian Serb capital 171/2

Palestine (*Lat.* Palaestina *now* Israel and Jordan) Levantine cities and ports 22/1; Byzantine Empire 49/1; Ottoman province 108/1; WW2 140/1; partition between Israel and Jordan 156/1

Pamphylia ancient country of southern Anatolia 33/1, 37/1, 49/1

Panama independence 113/1; US intervention 1989 159/1; US base 165/1

Panama Canal opening 118/2

Panipat N India ✕63/1

Panmunjom Korea 1953 armistice 153/1

Pannonia C Europe Avar Kingdom 53/2

Pannonia Inferior Roman province of C Europe 37/1

Pannonia Superior Roman province of C Europe 37/1

Panticapaeum (*mod.* Kerch) Crimea Greek colony 33/1; Roman Empire 37/1

Papal States C Italy Black Death 67/1; Reformation 91/1; unification of Italy 117/1

Paphlagonia ancient country of N Anatolia 33/1; 49/1

Papua New Guinea SW Pacific independence 155/1. See also New Guinea

Parhae (*Chin.* Pohai) early Korean state 47/1

Paris N France *parlement* 83/2; ✕99/2; Industrial Revolution 100/2

Parma N Italy Roman Lombard League 55/2; unification of Italy 117/1

Passchendaele NW Belgium WW1✕ 132/2

Pearl Harbor Hawaii bombed by Japanese 142/1

Pechenegs tribe of Ukraine, 48/2, 56/2, 57/1

Pecsaete tribe of early England 53/1

Pegu early state of S Burma, Buddhist site 35/1; early trade 89/2

Peking (*form. Mong.* Khanbalik, *Chin.* Beijing) N China Ming capital 69/1; Japanese occupation 123/2; economy 151/2

Peloponnesian War 33/2

Peninsular War 98/2

Pennsylvania state of E USA colony 86/2, 104/1; population 121/1; Depression 138/2

Pereyaslav early principality of Ukraine 57/1

Pergamum (*Gr.* Pergamon *Turk.* Bergama) W Anatolia Roman Empire 37/1

Périgord region of C France annexed to France 82/1

Perm (*1940-57 called* Molotov) C Russia founded 85/1; Bolshevik seizure 135/1

Persepolis Persia taken by Alexander 32/3; Muslim conquest 51/1

Persia (*now* Iran) Mongol invasion 61/1; campaigns of Alexander 32/3; Zoroastrianism 34/1; attacked by White Huns 40/1; under Abbasid sovereignty 51/2; Safavid Empire 63/1; Islamic state 157/3

Persian Gulf (*a/c* Arabian Gulf *or* The Gulf) Iran-Iraq War 157/2

Peru Spanish colonization 87/1; 18C Atlantic economy 102/2; independence 113/1

Petrograd (*before 1914* St. Petersburg *since 1924* Leningrad) WW1 133/1; Russian Revolution 135/1

Petsamo (*Russ.* Pechenga) NW Russia Russian conquest from Finland 141/2

Phazania (*mod.* Fezzan) region of S Libya 37/1

Philadelphia E USA founded 86/2

Philippines early trade 81/1; Spanish conquest 89/2; occupied by Japanese 123/2, 142/1; retaken by Americans 143/2; independence 155/1; political development 163/1; US bases 165/1

Philippine Sea ✕143/2

Philippopolis (*mod.* Plovdiv *Turk.* Filibe) Bulgaria Byzantine Empire 49/1; Ottoman Empire 71/1

Philomelium (*mod.* Akşehir) C Anatolia Byzantine Empire 49/2

Phnom Penh Cambodia 65/1, 89/2; Vietnam war 162/3

Phocaea W Anatolia Greek colony 33/1

Phoenicia at time of Greeks 33/1

Phoenicians move into Africa 27/2

Phrygia ancient country of W Anatolia 33/1; Byzantine Empire 49/1

Picts early tribe of Scotland 40/1

Piedmont (*It.* Piemonte) region of N Italy 117/1

Pigs, Bay of Cuba CIA invasion 164/3

Pisidia ancient country of C Anatolia 49/1

Podolia region of S Ukraine acquired by Lithuania 66/2

Pohai (*Kor.* Parhae *mod.* Manchuria) NE China early state 47/1

Poitiers (*anc.* Limonum) C France 17C seat of intendant 77/2

Poitou region of W France province of France 83/2

Pola (*mod.* Pula) N Yugoslavia Roman Empire 37/1

Poland conversion to Christianity 45/2; union with Lithuania 66/2; Black Death 67/1; acquired by Russia 85/1; Reformation 91/1; revolt against Russia 98/1; WW1 133/1; WW2 140-41; territorial changes 146/1; Warsaw Pact and Comecon 138/3, 165/1; end of Communist rule 169/1

Polish Corridor 136/1

Polynesia islands of C Pacific early settlement 27/1

Pomerania (*Ger.* Pommern *Pol.* Pomorze) region of N Europe medieval German Empire 55/2; Reformation 91/1; unification of Germany 116/2

Pomerelia (*Ger.* Pommerellen) region of N Europe occupied by Teutonic Knights 66/2

Pondicherry (*Fr.* Pondichéry) SE India French enclave 97/3

Pontus district of N Anatolia 33/1; Roman province 37/1,2; Byzantine Empire 49/1

Port Arthur (*Chin.* Lushun *Jap.* Ryojun) Manchuria ceded to Russia and Japan 95/2, 119/2

Port Arthur (*now* Thunder Bay) C Canada growth 120/2

Port Moresby SE New Guinea Allied base WW2 142/1

Port Said N Egypt Egyptian-Israeli war 156/1

Portugal (*anc.* Lusitania) Muslim conquest 50/1; 18C Atlantic economy 102/1; trade with Africa and Asia 80-81, 103/2; colonial empire 119/2; WW1 130/1; NATO 147/4; US bases 165/1; EU 167/1

Portuguese East Africa (*now* Mozambique) 119/2

Portuguese Guinea (*now* Guinea-Bissau) W Africa Portuguese colony 119/2; independence 154/1

Portuguese Timor E Indies annexed by Indonesia 155/1

Posen (*Pol.* Poznań) W Poland unification of Germany 116/2; ceded by Germany 136/1

Posidonia (*later* Paestum *mod.* Pesto) S Italy Greek colony 32/1

Potidaea N Greece Greek colony 33/1

Prague (*Cz.* Praha) Czechoslovakia bishopric 45/2; Communist coup 169/1

Pressburg (*Cz.* Bratislava) C Czechoslovakia ✕54/1

Preveza C Greece ✕70/2

Prince Edward Island (*form.* St Jean) island of E Canada joins Dominion 120/2

Priština SW Yugoslavia Kosovo crisis 171/2

Prizren SW Yugoslavia Kosovo crisis 171/2

Provence region of S France Frankish Empire 53/2; medieval German Empire 55/2; province of France 83/2

Providence NE USA founded 86/2

Prusa (*mod.* Bursa) W Anatolia Byzantine Empire 49/2

Prussia (*Ger.* Preussen) region of E Germany Reformation 91/1; unification of Germany 116/2

Puerto Rico W Indies conquered by US 112/1

Pugachev uprising Russia 98/1

Punjab region of NW India Muslim expansion 51/1; state of British India 96/2, 97/1

Pusan (*Jap.* Fusan) S Korea 1950-3 war 153/1

Pylos (*a/s* Pilos *It.* Navarino) SW Greece Mycenaean palace site 31/2

Pyongyang (*Jap.* Heijo) N Korea 1950-53 war 153/1

Qadisiyal (*a/s* Al Qadisiyya) S Mesopotamia ✕51/1

Qarabagh region of Caucasus conquered by Ottomans 70/2

Qatar sheikhdom of Persian Gulf Gulf War 147/3; independence 154/1; Islamic fundamentalism 157/3

Qinghai (*f/s* Tsinghai) province of N China economy 1979-92 151/2

Quadi Germanic tribe 37/1

Quebec city, E Canada capital of New France 86/2; population 120/2

Quebec province, E Canada joins Confederation 120/2; economic development 120/2

Quelimane Mozambique Portuguese settlement 111/1

Quemoy island SE China Nationalist outpost 165/1

Quentovic (*a/s* Quentowic) N France Vikings 54/1

Qui Nhon S Vietnam war 162/3

Rabaul Papua New Guinea Japanese base in WW2 142/1

Ragusa (*now* Dubrovnik) W Yugoslavia Byzantine Empire 49/1; Ottoman vassal republic 70/2; Reformation 91/1

Rai (*anc.* Rhagae *Bibl.* Rages *Gr.* Europus) N Persia Mongol attack 61/1; Muslim conquest 51/1

Rajputana NW India region of native states 96/2, 97/3

Ramillies Belgium ✕88/3

Ramla Palestine ✕51/1

Rangoon (*anc.* Dagon) Burma early trade centre 89/2; occupied by Japanese 142/1; retaken by British 143/2

Rann of Kutch region of W India boundary disputes with Pakistan 163/1

Rapallo N Italy 1922 Conference 136/

Ratisbon (*Ger.* Regensburg) S Germany ✕99/2

Reformation 91/1

Regensburg (*anc.* Castra Regina *obs. Eng.* Ratisbon) S Germany bishopric 45/2; Frankish royal residence 53/2

Reggio (*a/c* Reggio di Calabria *anc.* Rhegium) S Italy Ottoman siege 70/2

Réunion (*form.* Bourbon) island Indian Ocean French colony 119/2

Rhaetia (*mod.* Switzerland) Roman province 37/1

Rhegium (*mod.* Reggio di Calabria) N Italy Greek colony 32/1, 33/2

Rheims (*Fr.* Reims *anc.* Durocortorun *later* Remi) N France archbishopric 52/2; ✕99/2

Rhine, Confederation of the Napoleonic creation 99/2

Rhineland (*Ger.* Rheinland) region of W Germany remilitarized 136/1, 137/2

Rhode Island state of NE USA colony 86/2; population 121/1; Depression 138/2

Rhodes (*mod. Gr.* Rodhos *Lat.* Rhodus *It.* Rodi) *island* SE Aegean Greek state 33/1; ✕51/1; Ottoman conquest 70/2. See also Dodecanese

Rhodesia (*form.* Southern Rhodesia *now* Zimbabwe) British colony 119/2; independence (UDI) 154/1

Rhodus (*mod. Gr.* Rodhos *Eng.* Rhodes) island SE Aegean Roman Empire 37/1

Riga Latvia, NW USSR WW2 141/2

Rio Barbate Spain ✕50/1

Rio Muni (*a/c* Spanish Guinea *now* Equatorial Guinea) W Africa Spanish colony 111/1

Rivoli N Italy ✕99/2

Riyadh (*Ar.* Ar Riyāḍ) C Saudi Arabia 157/3

Rocroi NE France ✕93/3

Romagna region of N Italy unification of Italy 117/1

Roman Empire 36-7

Romania Industrial Revolution 100/2; independence 108/1; inter-war alliances 124/1; on break-up of Ottoman Empire 125/2; WW1 133/1; acquisition of Transylvania 136/1; Warsaw Pact and Comecon 146/1; end of Communist rule 169/1. See also Moldavia, Wallachia

Rome (*anc.* Roma *It.* Roma) C Italy arrival of Christianity 34/1, 44/1; Roman Empire 36-7; sacked by Visigoths 40/1; Magyar raid 54/1; papal patrimony 55/2; under French rule 99/2; annexed by Italy 117/1; WW2 141/1

Roncesvalles N Spain ✕52/2

Rouen (*anc.* Rotomagus) N France archbishopric 52/2; Scandinavian settlement 54/1; urban revolt 67/1; *parlement* 83/2

Royale, Ile (*now* Cape Breton Island) E Canada French settlement 86/2

Ruhr region of NW Germany Industrial Revolution 95/2; occupied by French 128/1

Rum early sultanate of E Anatolia 50/2

Rupert's Land region of N Canada Hudson's Bay Company 86/2; British possession 87/1

Russia (in Europe) conversion to Christianity 45/2; Kievan Russia 56/1; Viking trade 56/1; Black Death 67/1; expansion 85/1; opposition to Napoleon 99/2; Industrial Revolution 100/2; serfdom 115/2; 1905 Revolution 115/3; 19C European alliances 124/1; world trade 1860-1913 127/1; foreign investment 1914 127/1; WW1 133/1; development 1926-40 134/2; Revolution 135/1; Allied intervention 135/1. See also USSR and Russian Federation

Russia (in Asia) expansion 84/2; acquisition of Maritime Province from China 95/2; 19C spheres of influence 1192

Russian Federation free elections 169/1; constituent republics 169/2

Ruthenia region of SW Ukraine acquired by Poland-Lithuania 66/2; incorporated into Czechoslovakia 136/1 occupied by Hungary 137/2

Rwanda (*form.* Ruanda) early state of C Africa 59/2; independence 154/1; political development 161/1

Ryazan C Russia town of Murom-Ryazan 57/1; acquired by Muscovy 85/1

Ryukyu Islands (*f/c* Loochoo Islands) E China Sea acquired by Japan 95/1

Saar (*Ger.* Saarland *Fr.* Sarre) district of W Germany League of Nations mandate and plebiscite 136/1

Sabrata (*a/c* Abrotonum) Libya Roman Empire 37/1

Sadowa (*a/c* Königgrätz) Bohemia ✕116/2

Safavid Empire Persia 63/1

Sahara region of N Africa trade routes 59/1

Sahel region of W Africa early settlement 27/2

Saigon (*n/c* Ho Chi Minh) S Vietnam early trade centre 89/2; Japanese base WW2 142/1; war 162/3

St. Christopher and Nevis W Indies British colony 112/1; 155/1 (inset)

Saint-Domingue (*now* Haiti) French colony 87/1

St. Petersburg (*1914-24* Petrograd *1925-91* Leningrad) W Russia founded 85/1; acquired by Muscovy 85/1; Industrial Revolution 101/2

Saipan island Marianas. C Pacific Japanese base in WW2 142-43

Sakhalin (*Jap.* Karafuto) island Russ. Far East north acquired by Russia 114/1; south acquired by Japan 123/2; south reoccupied by Russia 143/2; claimed by Japan 163/1

Sakha-Yakutiya (*form.* Yakut ASSR) Siberia republic of Russian Federation 169/2

Salamanca N Spain ✕98/2

Salamantica (*a/c* Helmantica *mod.* Salamanca) N Spain Roman Empire 37/1

Salamis (*later* Constantia) Cyprus Roman Empire 37/1

Salisbury (*n/c* Harare) S Rhodesia 111/1

Salonae (*a/s* Salona) Albania Roman Empire 37/1; Byzantine Empire 49/1

Salonika (*a/s* Salonica *a/c* Thessalonica *Gr.* Thessaloniki *Turk.* Selanik) N Greece bishopric 45/1; occupied by Ottomans 71/1; WW1 133/1

Samara (*1935-91* Kuybyshev) C Russia founded 85/1; on railway to east 114/1; Bolshevik seizure 135/1

Samarkand (*anc.* Maracanda) C Asia Mongol attack 61/1; Muslim conquest 51/1; Tamerlane's Empire 60/2

Samoa islands S Pacific early settlement 27/1; German colony 119/2 . See also Western Samoa

Samogitia (*Lith.* Žemaitija) region of NW Russia occupied by Lithuania 66/2

San Agostín (*now* St. Augustine) SE USA Spanish fort 86/2

Sandinista revolt Nicaragua 159/1

San Francisco (*form.* San Francisco de Asís) W USA Spanish settlement 87/1; economic growth 145/1

Santa Cruz (*n/c* Ndeni) Solomon Islands WW2 ✕143/2

Santa Fé de Bogotá (*n/c* Bogotá) Colombia Spanish capital of New Granada 87/1

Santo Domingo (*now* Dominican Republic) W Indies Spanish colony 87/1

Santuao E China treaty port 95/2

São Tomé and Príncipe islands W Africa united as independent republic 154/1

Saracens invasion of S Europe 54/1

Saragossa (*anc.* Caesaraugusta *mod.* Zaragoza) N Spain bishopric 44/1; ✗98/1; captured by French 98/1

Sarajevo C Yugoslavia captured by Ottomans 71/1; WW1 133/1; WW2 140/1; civil war 171/2

Saratoga NE USA ✗104/1

Sardinia (*It.* Sardegna) island W Mediterranean Roman empire 36/1; Byzantine Empire 48/1; Muslim conquest 50/1; Saracen attacks 54/1; Habsburg Empire 93/1; Kingdom 99/2, 117/2

Sardis (*a/s* Sardes) W Anatolia Roman Empire 37/1; Byzantine Empire 49/2

Sarkel S Russia ✗56/2

Sarmatians (*Lat.* Sarmatae) tribe of Caucasus and S Russia 33/1, 37/1

Sarmizegetusa Romania Roman Empire 37/1

Sasanian Empire Western Asia 41/1

Saudi Arabia Gulf War 157/3

Savoy (*Fr.* Savoie *It.* Savoia) region of France/Italy medieval state 55/2; Calvinism 91/1; Habsburg Empire 93/1; ceded to France 117/1

Saxon March 53/2

Saxony region of N Germany Frankish Empire 53/2; Black Death 67/1; Reformation 91/1

Scandinavia (*anc.* Scandia) Viking invasions of Europe 54/1. See also Denmark, Sweden, Norway

Scapa Flow N Scotland WW1 133/1

Schleswig-Holstein region of N Germany unification of Germany 116/2

Scotland (*anc.* Caledonia) Scandinavian settlement 54/1; Black Death 67/1; Reformation 91/1; Devolution 166/2

Scupi (*mod.* Skoplje *Mac.* Skopje *Turk.* Üsküb) Byzantine Empire 49/1

Scythians ancient tribe of S Russia 33/1

Sebastopol (*Russ.* Sevastopol) Crimea. S Russia 1905 Revolution 115/3; WW1 133/1

Sedan N France ✗116/2; WW2 140/1

Selinus (*mod.* Selinunte) Sicily Greek colony 32/1, 33/2

Seljuks Turkish Muslim dynasty of Middle East 49/2, 51/2

Senegal W Africa French colony independence 154/1

Senegambia region of W Africa source of slaves 59/2; slave trade 102/1

Seoul (*Jap.* Keijo) S Korea Korean war 153/1

Septimania ancient region of S France, part of Frankish Empire 52/2

Serbia (*now part of* Yugoslavia) country of SE Europe conversion to Christianity 45/2; Byzantine Empire 49/2; empire under Stephen Dushan 66/2; Black Death 67/1; Ottoman province 71/1; Industrial Revolution 101/2; independence 108/1; WW1 133/1; forms part of Yugoslavia 136/1; WW2 141/2; Kosovo crisis 171/2

Serdica (*a/s* Sardica *mod.* Sofia) Bulgaria Roman Empire 37/1; Byzantine Empire 49/1

Seringapatam S India ✗97/1

Sevastopol (*Eng.* Sebastopol *med. Turk.* Akhtiar) Crimea acquired by Muscovy 85/1

Seville (*Sp.* Sevilla *anc.* Hispalis) S Spain Emirate of Cordoba 50/1

Shaanxi (*f/s* Shensi) province of N China economy 1979-92 151/2

Shakas early dynasty of N India 29/4

Shanghai E China treaty port 95/2; occupied by Japanese 123/2; Nationalist control 130/1; industry 131/2; economy 151/2

Shansi (*n/s* Shanxi) province of N China Ming province 69/1; Manchu expansion 94/1; economy 151/2

Shan State(s) Burma part of India 97/3

Shandong (*f/s* Shantung) province of E China economy 1979-92 151/2

Shantou (*f/s* Swatow) S China special economic zone 151/2

Shantung (*n/s* Shandong) province of E China under Ming 69/1; Manchu expansion 94/1; Japanese influence 130/1; economy 151/2

Shanxi (*f/s* Shansi) province of N China economy 1979-92 151/2

Shensi (*n/s* Shaanxi) province of N China under Ming 69/1; Manchu expansion 94/1; economy 151/2

Shenzhen S China special economic zone 151/2

Shetland (*form.* Hjaltland) NE Scotland Norwegian settlement 54/1

Shias Muslim minority of S Iraq 147/3

Siam (*now* Thailand) spread of Buddhism 64/2; conquests 89/2; under Japanese influence 123/2; occupied by Japanese 142/1

Sian (*n/s* Xi'an) China Ming provincial capital 69/1

Siberia cave art 15/1; Russian expansion 79/2

Sichuan (*f/s* Szechwan) province of W China economy 1979-92 151/2

Sicily (*Lat. and It.* Sicilia) island C Mediterranean Greek colonization 32/1; Byzantine Empire 49/1; Saracen raids 54/1; German attacks 55/2; to Savoy 83/3; Habsburg Empire 93/1; Kingdom of the Two Sicilies annexed to Piedmont/Sardinia 117/1; WW2 141/2

Sidon (*mod.* Saïda *Ar.* Sayda) Lebanon Phoenician city 33/1; taken by Alexander 32/3

Sierra Leone country of W Africa slave trade 102/1; British settlement 111/1; British colony 119/2; independence 154/1

Sikkim country of Himalayas British protectorate 95/2 dependency of India 96/3; annexed to India 155/1

Silesia (*Ger.* Schlesien *Pol.* Śląsk) region of Germany/Poland medieval German Empire 55/2; Habsburg Empire 93/1; unification of Germany 116/2; divided between Germany and Poland 136/1

Silla (*Eng.* Korea *Kor.* Koryo) occupied by T'ang 47/1

Singapore (*earlier* Tumasik) S Malaya early trade 89/2; occupied by Japanese 142/1; independence 155/1; economy 175/1

Sinkiang (*n/s* Xinjiang) province of NW China part of Han Empire 95/2; cession of territory to Russia 95/2; economy 151/2

Sinope (*mod.* Sinop) N Anatolia Greek colony 33/1; Roman Empire 37/1; Byzantine Empire 49/1

Slovakia forms part of Czechoslovakia 136/1; occupied by Hungary in WW2 141/2

Slovenia in Yugoslavia 128/1; independence 169/1

Smolensk W Russia bishopric 45/2; principality 57/1; acquired by Lithuania 66/2; captured by Napoleon 99/2; Bolshevik seizure 135/1

Smyrna (*mod.* Izmir) W Anatolia Roman Empire 37/1; Byzantine Empire 49/1,2; Ottoman Empire 71/1; centre of European trade 103/2

Socotra island Arabian Sea acquired by Britain 119/2

Sofala Mozambique Portuguese settlement 59/2; early trade 81/1

Sofia (*anc.* Serdica *a/s* Sardica *med.* Sredets) Bulgaria Ottoman control 71/1; WW2 141/2

Sogdiana (*a/c* Sogdia, Suguda) ancient region of C Asia Chinese protectorate 46/1

Solferino N Italy ✗117/1

Solomon Islands SW Pacific British protectorate 119/2; occupied by Japanese 142/1; retaken by Allies 143/2; independence 155/1 (inset)

Somalia (*form.* British and Italian Somaliland) independence 154/1; political development 161/1

Somaliland divided between British, Italians and French 119/2

Somme river NE France WW1 offensive 124/2

Songhay (*a/s* Songhai) early empire of W Africa 58/1

Soochow E China treaty port 95/2; industry 131/2

Sopron (*Ger.* Ödenburg) Hungary to Hungary after plebiscite 136/1

Sorbs Slavic tribe of C Europe 53/2

South Africa Union 119/2; Republic 154/1; political development 161/1

South Carolina state of SE USA colony 86/2, 104/1; population 121/1; Depression 138/2

South-East Asia early civilizations 29/1; Mongol attacks 61/1; post 1945 conflicts 163/1

Southern Rhodesia (*now* Zimbabwe *f/c* Rhodesia) British colony 111/1, 119/2

South Ossetian Caucasus 170/3

South Tyrol (*Ger.* Südtirol *It.* Alto Adige) region of Austro-Hungarian Empire acquired by Italy 136/1

South Vietnam independence 155/1; war 162/3. See also Vietnam, Indo-China

South Yemen (*also called* People's Democratic Republic of Yemen *form.* Federation of South Arabia *earlier* Protectorate of South Arabia *earlier* Aden Protectorate) independence 154/1; union with north Yemen 154/1

Spa Belgium 1920 Conference 136/1

Spain (*anc.* Hispania) early invasions 40/1; conversion to Christianity 44/1; Muslim conquest 50/2; Umayyad caliphate 50/2; Reformation 91/1; War of the Spanish Succession 83/3; colonial empire 119/2; opposition to Napoleon 98/1; Industrial Revolution 100/2; 18C Atlantic economy 103/2; 19C alliances 124/1; US bases 165/1

Spanish Guinea (*now* Equatorial Guinea) W Africa colony 118/1

Spanish March 52/2

Spanish Sahara (*a/c* Western Sahara *includes* Rio de Oro) NW Africa 103/2; Spanish colony 111/1; partition between Morocco and Mauritania 154/1, 161/1

Spanish Succession, War of the 83/3

Sparta (*a/c* Lacedaemon) S Greece Peloponnesian War 33/2; Roman Empire 37/1

Spartalos N Greece ✗33/2

Sphacteria S Greece ✗33/2

Srebrenica NE Herzegovina UN safe area 171/2

Srinagar N India capital of Kashmir 97/3

Srivijaya E Indies early empire 65/1

Stalingrad (*until 1925* Tsaritsyn *since 1961* Volgograd) S Russia WW2 141/2

Stresa N Italy 1935 Conference 136/1

Styria (*Ger.* Steiermark) province of SE Austria acquired by Habsburgs 66/2; Habsburg Empire 93/1

Sudan (*form.* Anglo-Egyptian Sudan) Mahdist state 111/1; Anglo-Egyptian condominium 111/1, 119/2; independence 154/1, 161/1; Islamic fundamentalism 157/3

Sudetenland C Europe German annexation 137/2

Suez Canal N Egypt Egyptian-Israeli war 156/1

Suifen NE China treaty port 95/2

Sukhothai C Thailand Buddhist site 35/1; major political centre 65/1

Sumatra (*Indon.* Sumatera) E Indies spread of Buddhism 35/1; Dutch possession 119/2; occupied by Japanese 142/1

Sumerians ancient people of Mesopotamia 23/1

Sung Empire China Mongol conquest 61/1

Süntel N Germany ✗53/2

Surabaya (*Dut.* Soerabaja) Java trading centre 89/2; occupied by Japanese 142/1

Swabia (*Ger.* Schwaben) province of medieval German kingdom 55/2

Swakopmund SW Africa German settlement 111/1

Swatow (*n/s* Shantou) S China treaty port 95/2; Japanese occupation 123/2; 151/2

Picture credits